Health and social change

ISSUES IN SOCIETY
Series Editor: Tim May

Current and forthcoming titles

Health and social change

A critical theory

GRAHAM SCAMBLER

OPEN UNIVERSITY PRESS
Buckingham • Philadelphia

Open University Press
Celtic Court
22 Ballmoor
Buckingham
MK18 1XW

email: enquiries@openup.co.uk
world wide web: www.openup.co.uk

and
325 Chestnut Street
Philadelphia, PA 19106, USA

First Published 2002

A catalogue record of this book is available from the British Library

ISBN 0 335 20479 1 (pb)   0 335 20480 5 (hb)

Library of Congress Cataloging-in-Publication Data
Scambler, Graham.
    Health and social change : a critical theory / Graham Scambler.
      p. cm. – (Issues in society)
    Includes bibliographical references and index.
    ISBN 0-335-20480-5 – ISBN 0-335-20479-1 (pbk.)
      1. Health – Social aspects.   2. Social change.   3. Social medicine.
    I. Title.   II. Series.

RA418.S295   2002
306.4′61–dc21   2001036207

Typeset by Graphicraft Limited, Hong Kong
Printed in Great Britain by St Edmundsbury Press, Bury St Edmunds, Suffolk

Contents

Series editor's foreword

Collectively, the social sciences contribute to a greater understanding of the dynamics of social life, as well as explanations for the workings of societies in general. Yet they are often not given due credit for this role and much writing has been devoted to why this should be the case. At the same time, we are living in an age in which the role of science in society is being re-evaluated. This has led to both a defence of science as the disinterested pursuit of knowledge and an attack on science as nothing more than an institutionalized assertion of faith, with no greater claim to validity than mythology and folklore. These debates tend to generate more heat than light.

In the meantime, the social sciences, in order to remain vibrant and relevant, will reflect the changing nature of these public debates. In so doing, they provide mirrors upon which we can gaze in order to understand not only what we have been and what we are now, but to inform possibilities about what we might become. This is not simply about understanding the reasons people give for their actions in terms of the contexts in which they act, and analyzing the relations of cause and effect in the social, political and economic spheres, but also concerns the hopes, wishes and aspirations that people, in their different cultural ways, hold.

In any society that claims to have democratic aspirations, these hopes and wishes are not for the social scientist to prescribe. For this to happen it would mean that the social sciences were able to predict human behaviour with certainty. One theory and one method, applicable to all times and places, would be required for this purpose. The physical sciences do not live up to such stringent criteria, while the conditions in societies which provided for this outcome, were it even possible, would be intolerable. Why? Because a necessary condition of human freedom is the ability to have acted otherwise and thus to imagine and practise different ways of organizing societies and living together.

It does not follow from the above that social scientists do not have a valued role to play, as is often assumed in ideological attacks upon their place and function within society. After all, in focusing upon what we have been and what we are now, what we might become is inevitably illuminated: the retrospective and prospective become fused. Therefore, whilst it may not be the province of the social scientist to predict our futures, they are, given not only their understandings and explanations, but equal positions as citizens, entitled to engage in public debates concerning future prospects.

This new international series was devised with this general ethos in mind. It seeks to offer students of the sciences, at all levels, a forum in which ideas and topics of interest are interrogated in terms of their importance for understanding key social issues. This is achieved through a connection between style, structure and content that aims to be both illuminating and challenging in terms of its evaluation of those issues, as well as representing an original contribution to the subject under discussion.

Given this underlying philosophy, the series contains books on topics that are driven by substantive interests. This is not simply a reactive endeavour in terms of reflecting dominant social and political preoccupations, it is also proactive in terms of an examination of issues that relate to and inform the dynamics of social life and the structures of society that are often not part of public discourse. Thus, what is distinctive about this series is an interrogation of the assumed characteristics of our current epoch in relation to its consequences for the organization of society and social life, as well as its appropriate mode of study.

Each contribution contains, for the purposes of general orientation, as opposed to rigid structure, three parts. First, an interrogation of the topic which is conducted in a manner that renders explicit core assumptions surrounding the issues and/or an examination of the consequences of historical trends for contemporary social practices. Second, a section which aims to 'bring alive' ideas and practices by considering the ways in which they directly inform the dynamics of social relations. A third section then moves on to make an original contribution to the topic. This encompasses possible future forms and content, likely directions for the study of the phenomena in question, or an original analysis of the topic itself. Of course, it might be a combination of all three.

Linking an individual to the social conditions of which they are a part is not a denial of their uniqueness. On the contrary, it is a celebration of that uniqueness in terms of their place within a configuration of social, economic and political relations. Individualism, expressed as the abstraction of the individual from their social context, is a false view of social reality. To extract people from the social dynamics in which they act renders explanation so limited as to be of little use for understanding. That noted, it often functions to relieve people of the need to think more broadly and furnishes them with a convenient target constituted by the personal failings and attributes of an individual.

One means through which social problems are translated into individual solutions is via the application of a body of knowledge that brackets people from their environments. There is a tendency for this to occur when it comes to the health of a population. In some instances genetic predisposition may well be of relevance, but so too are precipitory factors and the former can be targeted without due consideration being given to the latter. Indeed, when such factors are considered they may be dismissed on the basis of the assumed moral laxity of particular sections of the population who, regardless of the situations in which they may find themselves, are held responsible for any outcomes. Whenever such thinking proves seductive, what is needed is a form of analysis that links experiential elements of health to those of the systems in and through which health services are delivered.

A critical approach to the sociology of health is extremely well equipped to fulfil this role and Graham Scambler is one of its leading exponents. His approach is critical in the sense that it is based on a normative, realist ontology which is not content to submit to an epistemological relativism, but instead sits within a line of thought that takes capitalism and its effects on life chances as core to explanation. Therefore, following a survey of various sociological approaches, each of which has made its own lasting contribution to our understandings of society and health, he moves on to examine social change. In the process he is not content to let elite power, class relations and social change be separated from other transformations and their role in understanding health.

It is against this backdrop that he moves on to evaluate health care reforms. With a breakdown in the consensus that surrounded the formation of welfare states accompanied by a fiscal crisis of the state, particular agendas were brought to the fore of public debate and policy making. Here we witnessed the success of the New Right and their belief that rising expectations brought about by liberal democracy were in tension with the needs of the market economy. To express this tension in Isiah Berlin's terms, one represents the source of control that informs someone's actions, whereas the other is regarded as freedom from interference. However, individual freedom (as he noted in 'Four Essays on Liberty') cannot be the only criterion by which social action is judged. Yet when we turn to the 'power to determine' it is often the state that is the object of our critical faculties. Why should this not also be attributed to the power of market forces that seek to seduce consumers in the name of profit and glide over democratic aspirations?

With these issues in mind there is no doubt that in the UK and US contexts, the power to shape health care reforms rested within an agenda represented by neo-liberalism in the shape of Thatcher and Reagan. More recently this has been manifest in the so-called 'Third Way'. Yet what have been the effects in terms of income distribution, employment and relative deprivation on the population, all of which are central factors in informing issues relating to class and health, but have been relatively silent in recent studies? Studies have tended to be conducted on poor workers rather than rich capitalists. In concentrating upon the latter in terms of the adaptive behaviour of a loosely globalized elite, Graham Scambler turns his attention to an analysis of GBH ('greedy bastards hypothesis').

Arguing for a strong link between class inequalities and health leads him on the relationship between lifeworld narratives and expert culture. Here we find that assumptions regarding increasing fluidity within society are not evident for some groups. The intersection between the experiential elements of (ill) health and how they are viewed and processed are informed by the systems of health care in which these interactions take place. Lifeworlds are infused with issues of class and command and these are met, within expert cultures, by bureaucracy and money. How people are then positioned is open to analysis and informed not only by what Foucault called 'technologies of the self', but the logic of capital accumulation and regimes of expertise that 'fix' the individual according to various attributes. What we discover is a heady brew of preventative medicine mixing with 'community empower-ment' whereby, once again, individuals are presumed to make rational choices, but those abstracted from the social relations of which they are a part.

As Graham Scambler argues, relations between individualistic technicism and socio-economic problems inform the health of a population. In the light of this a question may be posed: what is to be done? This is where he turns to a critical sociology in which no single programme is assumed to have a monopoly of wisdom, and also to an interesting discussion of civil society and the role of social movements, including those concerned with health. The basis is then provided to inform five theses for a critical, medical sociology.

Calling for social scientists to recover their political 'nerve' when confronted with social problems, he notes that too many prefer cosy enclaves in which critical insights are diminished and with that the challenges they raise for actions. An individualistic technicism can then raise its head in triumph. Nevertheless, it will solve nothing, but spend enormous amounts of energy on seeking to silence and marginalize its effects. The consequences in the sphere of health are apparent in this book and for this reason it deserves to be read by all those in this broad field who seek to learn from the past in order to shape a better future.

Tim May

Acknowledgements

Even single-authored books are the result of teamwork. I owe thanks to my family for tolerating so much out-of-hours work; to Annette and Sasha Scambler for good-humoured encouragement and debate; to Paul Higgs for his voracious reading and willingness to challenge every orthodoxy; to Liz Wake and Eileen Horton for help with the manuscript; to our MSc and PhD students at UCL for keeping me reading; and to colleagues in medical sociology for their 'exemplars'. Special thanks go also to Tim May, editor of the 'Issues in Society' series, for his patience and insightful comments on the first draft of the manuscript. The book is dedicated to yet another group, those medical students who elected to take a year away from their studies to do a BSc in Sociology as Applied to Medicine in the University of London and who were such a pleasure to teach for twenty years. I alone am culpable for the end-product.

Introduction

This book touches on a wide range of issues, and does so in ways which may not be familiar either to medical sociologists or to colleagues closer to mainstream sociology and social theory. This is another way of saying that too often sociology comprises discrete specialized discourses which become and remain transparent only to those who regularly engage with them. More specifically, and notwithstanding the existence of excellent books featuring both 'health' and 'social change' in their titles (for example, Bury 1997), works of 'synthesis' which necessarily span different discourses within (and even beyond) sociology are, as it were, 'unexpected', and may strike specialist colleagues as odd. This book is written out of the conviction that works of synthesis are as important in sociology as they are rare in relation to investigations of health, illness, disease and health care. It is not that there is no theory in contemporary medical sociology, far from it, but rather that the theory is generally confined in ambition to that of Merton's (1963) 'middle-range'; there have been remarkably few attempts to address matters of health against the background of the broad sweep of social, cultural, political and economic change.

Time and place are a function of social formations. And social formations evolve and develop and are displaced in unpredictable as well as more predictable ways. Indeed, if health, illness and disease often seem awkward, contestible concepts for medical sociologists, politicians, policy-makers and health professionals, those of social formations and social change might be judged problematic almost beyond redemption. While it may be true, as Haferkamp and Smelser (1992: 10) venture, that 'social change is such an evident feature of social reality that any social-scientific theory, whatever its conceptual starting point, must sooner or later address it', it is no less true that in what many now regard as the 'postmodernized' specialist or expert as well as public cultures of 'developed' societies there is more confusion than ever, and some *angst*, over 'conceptual starting points'. Certainly what Sztompka (1993) identifies as the 'three grand visions of human history' – evolutionism, cyclical theories and historical materialism – have lost the bulk of their adherents inside and outside sociology.

Yet surely Giddens (1991: xv) seems justified in asserting that

> we live today in an era of stunning social change, marked by transformations radically discrepant from those of previous periods. The collapse of Soviet-style socialism, the waning of the bi-polar global distribution of power, the formation of intensified global communication systems, the apparent world-wide triumph of capitalism at a time at which global divisions are becoming acute and economic problems looming more and more large – all these and other issues confront social science and have to be confronted by social science.

Moreover, as we shall see, many components of this 'stunning social change' have direct or indirect ramifications for health, illness and disease and for health care systems.

It would be reckless in a volume this size, the more so given my own suspicions of the kind of 'grand visions' or overarching theories of historical and social change favoured by a shrinking minority of disciples of an (unreconstructed, late eighteenth-century European) Enlightenment project, to seek to link health and social change from a pre-Neolithic era characterized by nomadic 'hunter-gatherers', through phases of varied simple-to-complex agricultural settlements, to an industrial or post-industrial era marking out the 'developed' West and stretching through to the millennium. Instead I have elected to focus on the latter; that is, on occidental societies and from the 1960s and 1970s to the present, a period, as Giddens claims, of considerable discontinuity.

And I shall restrict too the health foci: I shall concentrate on core themes familiar to medical sociologists and their students and of abiding, even sharpening, interest in high/late modernity/postmodernity. There are seven of these: the social determination and patterning of health, illness and disease; health and illness behaviour; the social organization of paid and unpaid health-work; paid health worker–patient encounters, interactions and communications; the health worker-mediated experience of, and coping strategies for, illness and disease; health inequalities; and health policy formation and implementation and the organization, auditing and funding of systems for delivering treatment and care. Although the emphasis will be on health and social change in Britain, attention will also be paid, for comparative purposes, to recent events in the USA and elsewhere. Occasionally, necessarily and mercifully, I shall stray historically and from the seven themes listed.

The volume is divided, in line with others in the 'Issues in Society' series, into three parts. Part one, termed 'Health and medicine in society', provides brief critical expositions of paradigms or research programmes that have underwritten and continue to inform bodies of substantive work in medical sociology. The object here is neither to chart an 'intellectual and political history' after the manner of Gerhardt (1989), nor (in this part at any rate) to arrive at a theoretical synthesis. It is instead, on the one hand, to expose the limitations of these paradigms/research programmes and, on the other, to signal possible ways of preserving, reframing and ultimately retheorizing their more credible 'findings'. In Chapter 1, consideration is given first to positivism and its astonishingly healthy offspring the 'neo-positivisms', then, following Gerhardt's sequence if not her intent or conclusions, to structural-functionalism, interactionism, phenomenology and conflict theory.

Chapter 2 outlines a number of select theses pertaining to the 'postmodern turn'. Provisional explications of general concepts like 'postmodern culture' and 'postmodernity', as well as more specific and applied concepts like 'embodiment', are given and the potential for a new postmodern paradigm/research programme for medical sociology is provisionally discussed. A focused discussion of topical and diverse social constructivist perspectives again suggests a need for a reframing and retheorization of their contributions to our grasp of health and social change. Chapter 3 side-steps the orthodox literature on the sociology of social change (for which see, for example, Spybey 1992; Sztompka 1993) in favour of positing a framework within which linkages between health and social change might be plausibly retheorized. The discussion concentrates on the period of 'disorganized capitalism' discernible since the 1970s and owes much to the critical theory of Habermas and the critical realism of Bhaskar.

Part two, entitled 'Structured divisions in health and health care', attempts the process of theoretical synthesis in relation to health and social change that is promoted and partially anticipated in Part one. To this extent it draws in different measure from structural-functionalism, interactionism, phenomenology, conflict theory and postmodernism. It is a process facilitated by the late Frankfurt writings of Habermas which, despite their silences on certain pivotal social issues, not least around health, display remarkable and enduring qualities of theoretical synthesis. Chapter 4 seeks to anchor, give substance and apply to the health arena the processes of social change retheorized in the previous chapter. It addresses the notion of crisis in welfare statism current since the early 1970s, the barely related historical ebbs and flows of health and health care, and focuses in some detail on the issue of health care reform in Britain and the USA.

Chapter 5 reflects on health inequalities in disorganized capitalism. The (neo-)positivist literature is summarized and shown to be of limited value to sociology. After some discussion of the contributions of commentators like Wilkinson and Coburn, it is argued that class relations, robustly theorized, remain crucial if we are to appreciate the enduring nature of health inequalities in Britain and elsewhere. Chapter 6 discusses the construction of narratives of health and illness in the lifeworld and the interrelation between these and the narratives of disease deployed by doctors in doctor–patient encounters. It also distinguishes between different subtypes of relations of healing, identifying in the process relations of 'caring', 'fixing' and 'restoring' in the 'popular', 'professional' and 'folk' sectors of Kleinman's (1985) local health care systems respectively.

In Chapter 7, which comprises Part three of the book, entitled 'The need for a critical sociology', the threads of the previous chapters are pulled together under the volume's central rubric of *health and social change*. A theoretical and research agenda for the future is constructed. This both represents an application and extension of the critical theory of Habermas and points out the lacunae and internal problems yet to receive adequate attention. It is argued that 'critical sociologists' working within the health domain (as in other spheres) face rational and moral imperatives to engage with contentious political issues, and that their responsibilities – towards lifeworld decolonization – embrace the 'political healthiness' of the 'protest sector' of civil society and of the public sphere (see Scambler 1996, 1998b, 2001). As this implies, the volume as a whole is underscored by a strong sense of what sociology is and should be.

The purpose of this short book will have been fulfilled if it encourages the ideas that the sociology of health, illness and disease, like other branches of the discipline, is unambiguously a theoretical enterprise, and that there is a logical, moral and vital case for investing in a critical sociological approach. It is not a conventional textbook. This is partly because excellent textbooks already exist (for example, Nettleton 1995; Annandale 1998), and partly because, this being the case, there would be something depressingly tedious and unadventurous in merely settling into the grooves of colleagues' work. While it will become apparent how much I am indebted to colleagues inside and outside of medical sociology, I try to lay down a number of challenges, constituting an agenda of sorts, which I believe we should not allow ourselves collectively to (continue to) shirk.

PART ONE

Health, medicine and society

1

Paradigms and presuppositions

Mainstream sociology and its subdiscipline of medical sociology have been informed, sustained, inspired and occasionally put off, even corrupted, by a plethora of paradigms in their short histories. In this opening chapter sufficient critical attention is paid to (neo-)positivism to remind readers of its interminably documented deficits and to hint at a plausible alternative – critical realist – explanatory model appropriate to a critical sociology. Even more concise, given their originality, vitality and depth of influence, are the discussions, inspired in part by the pioneering historical research of Gerhardt (1987), of the paradigms of structural-functionalism, interactionism, phenomenology and conflict theory, of their relevance to our grasp of health and healing and of their future potential. If each of these discussions is critical, it is stressed too that each paradigm has made a lasting contribution.

The backdrop of (neo-)positivism

It is apt and reasonable to portray the academic discipline of sociology as a fairly recent product of modernity, but it did not of course emerge in either a social or a philosophical vacuum. Among its more influential philosophical antecedents, especially in its British and American forms, was a longstanding, wavering, stop–start tradition of empiricism, hinted at initially in the writings of the pre-Socratic Greeks but only consolidated many centuries later in the foundationalist epistemologies of Locke, Berkeley and Hume. Of this triad of 'British Empiricists' Hume is the pivotal figure, and most pertinent for us is Hume's – understandably for a young innovator and sceptic – tentative and unsettled account of causality and constant conjunctions in his *Treatise of Human Nature*, published in 1739 and 1740. It seems to the phenomenalist Hume that if we are asked for our evidence that A is the cause of B, the only possible answer is that A and B have been constantly conjoined in the past. This does not *prove* that they are invariably associated. The only recourse then left to us is to admit the *psychological* origins of our inferences: 'all our reasonings concerning causes and effects are derived from nothing but custom' (Hume 1896: 183). So the connection between A and B 'consists in the fact that we cannot help – the necessity being psychological, not logical – under certain circumstances having certain expectations. If we are asked to justify causal inferences, all we can do is to describe how men actually think' (Passmore 1968: 41). This analysis, countless times since revisited, reinterpreted and revised, has proved seminal.

As far as sociology is concerned, Hume's analysis of causation and constant conjunctions haunts as well as informs contemporary positivist research. Historically, Comte's promotion of a positive science of society in his *Cours de philosophie positive*, issued in six volumes between 1830 and 1842 (see Comte 1853), proved a vital catalyst. John Stuart Mill (1965), less interested in Comte's sociological analysis than in his pursuit of a proper methodology for social science, added a refinement of sorts which is of particular pertinence here. He elaborated on Hume's analysis. For Mill, the cause of any event is a set of conditions or factors which, taken together, constitute a sufficient condition for it; his 'sets of conditions' replace Hume's single events. Developing an inductive model of social science from a perspective of uncompromising methodological individualism (leading him to a psychological reductionism quite inimical to Comte), he spelled out a series of 'canons' or procedures – of 'agreement', 'difference', 'residues' and 'concomitant variation' – for testing hypotheses or causal relationships. These will strike an immediate chord with advocates of variable analysis in social research.

Two principles lie at the core of what Trusted (1979) terms Mill's 'eliminative induction': that nothing which was absent when an event occurred could be its cause, and that nothing which was present when an event failed to occur could be its cause. Mill did not himself distinguish between necessary and sufficient conditions (in fact, by 'cause' he understood 'sufficient condition' not 'necessary condition'); but his canons are perhaps best explicated using this dichotomy.

His method of 'agreement' states that 'if two or more instances of the phenomenon under investigation have only one circumstance in common, the circumstance in which alone all the instances agree is the cause (or effect) of the given phenomenon'. It is a method, in other words, intended for determining possible necessary conditions by elimination. His method of 'difference' states that 'if an instance in which the phenomenon under investigation occurs, and an instance in which it does not occur, have every circumstance in common save one, that one occurring only in the former, the circumstance in which alone the two instances differ is the effect or the cause, or an indispensable part of the cause, of the phenomenon.' Translated once more, it is a method intended for determining possible sufficient conditions by elimination. Mill also allows for the deployment of a 'joint method of agreement and difference'.

Mill's other two proposed methods are those of 'residues' and 'concomitant variation'. The former states that if known causes cannot account for a phenomenon, then it is necessary to seek a cause elsewhere; there must be some residual factor which is not known and/or has not been taken into account. It is a method which relies on deduction rather than induction. The method of 'concomitant variation' states that 'whatever phenomenon varies in any manner whenever another phenomenon varies in some particular manner is either a cause or an effect of that phenomenon, or is connected with it through some fact of causation.' It is a method to be used when a given factor cannot be removed, rendering the method of difference inapplicable (see Trusted 1979: 115–25).

Mill's account may well be vulnerable to critical interrogation, philosophical and practical, beyond high modernity's surviving (neo-)positivisms. But the point to be made is that he laid the foundations for those (neo-)positivisms (Willer and Willer 1973). Indeed, it is arguable that his account, refined many times over by social statisticians, is more congruent with present (neo-)positivist social research practice than the philosophically more sophisticated standpoints or models routinely cited, namely:

1 The 'deductive-nomological' model associated with Hempel, in which the premisses, statements of general laws and statements of antecedent conditions (the *explanans*) permit the deduction of a conclusion, a statement describing the event to be explained (the *explanandum*).
2 The 'inductive-statistical' model, in which the statements of general laws in the deductive-nomological model give way to probablistic, or statistical, generalizations, and the relationship between premises and conclusion is one of inductive probability not deductive necessity.
3 The 'hypothetico-deductive' model devised by Popper, and here defined as a variant of (neo-)positivism, in which the emphasis is placed not on (indecisively) confirming a conjecture or theory but on (decisively) falsifying it by a counter-observation (see Keat and Urry 1975; Benton 1977).

All this, it is worth reiterating, harks obstinately back to Hume's regularity theory of causation. But what forms has (neo-)positivist research taken in the study of health and health care? It may be helpful to distinguish between three types of (neo-)positivist investigations designed and/or conducted and/or used by medical sociologists: *accounting*, *explaining/predicting* and *advising*.

Accounting

'Accounting' refers to the collection and/or collation of data to identify (often changing) social patterns of behaviour and circumstance. Many of the publications from bodies like Britain's Office for National Statistics (ONS) fall into this category. Statistics on rates of mortality, of illness and disease and of people's use per annum of 'popular', 'folk' and 'professional' sectors of 'local health care systems' (Kleinman 1985), all represent forms of accounting in this sense. Among the classic examples of accounting are the national cross-sectional surveys of aspects of health and health care carried out from London by Cartwright and her colleagues from the 1950s onwards.

Explaining/predicting

Investigations oriented to 'explaining/predicting' occur at another level (if only just). The object of these studies is not merely to identify social patterns of behaviour and circumstance but to explain them, and for (neo-)positivists explaining and predicting must be seen as two sides of the same coin. Much historical and recent research into the social determinants of health inequalities has been conducted in this vein (as is explored in detail in Chapter 5). The spirit of Mill lives on in such studies, which tend to follow the inductive-statistical model (Hempel's deductive-nomological model having been largely abandoned and Popper's hypothetico-deductive model largely untried). Critiques of (neo-)positivist forms of variable analysis for explaining/ predicting have become routine since the 1960s and do not need to be re-hearsed again here (see, for example, Willer and Willer 1973; Pawson 1989). It will be sufficient to make a few general points which both echo past criticisms and anticipate an alternative approach to be developed in Chapter 3.

Returning to (neo-)positivism's Humean origins, Lawson (1997: 19) writes: 'if particular knowledge is restricted to atomistic events given in experience, the only possibility for general, including scientific, knowledge is the elaboration of patterns of association of these events. It is thus such constant event patterns, or regularities of the form "whenever event x then event y", that constitute the Humean or positivist account of causal laws.' But as critical realists like Lawson (who owes much to Bhaskar) rightly argue, the world is not composed, as the (neo-)positivists would have it, merely of events (the *actual*) and experiences (the *empirical*), but also of underlying mechanisms (the *real*) that exist whether or not detected and govern or facilitate events (see Archer *et al.* 1998). This is so for the social as well as the natural sciences. Moreover, events are typically (a) 'unsynchronized with the mechanisms that govern them', and (b) 'conjointly determined by various, perhaps countervailing influences so that the governing causes, though necessarily "appearing" through, or in, events can rarely be read straight off' (Lawson 1997: 22). In other words, the true theoretical ('beneath-the-surface') objects of sociological enquiry – that is, mechanisms like relations of class, gender, ethnicity and age – only manifest themselves in 'open systems' where ('surface') 'constant event patterns' or 'regularities' of the kind pursued through variable analysis (which exaggerates the potential for experimental 'closures') rarely, if ever, obtain.

A second and related point is that the modes of inference suggested by critical realism and arguably optimal for a critical sociology include neither induction nor deduction. They are, rather, *retroduction* and *abduction*. Lawson (1997: 24) refers to retroduction in terms of '*as if* reasoning': 'it consists in the movement, on the basis of analogy and metaphor amongst other things, from a conception of some phenomenon of interest to a conception of some totally different type of thing, mechanism, structure or condition that, at least in part, is responsible for the given phenomenon.' A retroductive mode of inference in critical sociology, then, involves a move from a knowledge of events to a knowledge of mechanisms, 'at a deeper level or stratum of reality', which contributed to the generation of those events. Abduction is similarly geared to the identification of mechanisms, but, arising out of interactionist and phenomenological approaches, involves a process of inference from lay (or first-order) accounts of the social world to sociological (or second-order) accounts of the social world (for a discussion, see Blaikie 1993).

A final point is that although 'constant' event patterns or 'invariant' regularities may not obtain in open systems, 'partial' regularities do. Lawson (1997: 204) labels these *demi-regularities* or 'demi-regs'. A demi-reg, to adopt his shorthand, is 'a partial event regularity which *prima facie* indicates the occasional, but less than universal, actualization of a mechanism or tendency, over a definite region of time-space. The patterning observed will not be strict if countervailing factors sometimes dominate or frequently co-determine the outcomes in a variable manner. But where demi-regs are observed there is evidence of relatively enduring and identifiable tendencies in play.'

Lawson attaches special significance to *contrastive* demi-regs, which he argues are pervasive in the social sphere. Examples of contrastive demi-regs on offer from medical sociology include: 'women show higher rates of self-reported morbidity than men'; 'working-class people have poorer health/ shorter lifespans than middle-class people'; 'the provision of health care is inversely related to the need for it' (widely known as Tudor Hart's (1971) 'inverse care law'); 'the introduction of the "internal market" into the British National Health Service in 1991 has been associated with higher administrative costs'; and 'the general health of populations in affluent societies is enhanced when there is great income equality' (a proposition linked in Britain with the work of Wilkinson: see especially 1996). Lawson (1997: 207) contends that such contrastive demi-regs can commend and 'direct' social scientific research by 'providing evidence that, and where, certain relatively enduring and potentially identifiable mechanisms have been in play'.

Advising

'Advising' refers here to the prediction of social patterns and circumstance with the express purpose of supporting the formation and/or implementation of policy. Much research commissioned in the 1980s and 1990s by British government departments falls into this category, including, for example, audits of clinical or health care interventions utilizing measures of health-related quality of life, studies to discriminate between rival schemes of health service delivery or health promotion in the community and socio-epidemiological projects on 'health variations'. It is an instrumental form of (neo-)positivist endeavour, pragmatically defined by the system-driven needs it purports to meet. That, according to the logic of (neo-)positivism, to predict is to explain, is secondary and incidental.

This brief critical comment on (neo-)positivism, a continuing paradigmatic presence in medical sociology despite countless damning interrogations of its empiricist presuppositions since the 1960s, is compatible with at least three provisional conclusions. First, there remain serious philosophical problems with empiricism and (neo-)positivism (for at least some of which critical realism promises resolutions). Second, if accounting and advising are worthy pursuits for sociologists, neither qualifies as a core activity of a critical sociology: the former is too unambitious and the latter too system-driven. And third, although explaining/predicting may yield revealing (contrastive) demi-regularities, these gains are largely fortuitous: (neo-)positivist investigations oriented to explaining/predicting are misconceived and unhelpful to the critical sociologist.

Structural-functionalism

There has been little mention of theory so far. This is because (neo-)positivism is (erroneously) held to be free of theoretical baggage. In this respect, American structural-functionalism is its obverse: its main protagonist, Parsons, is infamous for his analytic and systematic theorizing. From the outset Parsons (1937) opposed positivist social science because it failed to recognize the purposeful nature of human action. He sought an approach which recognized that people are both goal-oriented and constrained. The notion of 'social system' became central to his thought: a social system refers to a durable organization of interaction between 'actors' and 'contexts', and embraces both micro-level systems and macro-level systems like the nation-state and global society. Some of the key features of Parsons's framework for analysing social systems will be outlined briefly, then some illustrations given of attempts to apply it.

Social systems, Parsons (1951b) maintains, are structured by value patterns, without which actors' behaviour would be directionless. Value patterns, in turn, are structured by 'pattern variables': these refer to universal dichotomies which represent basic choices underlying social interaction. These dichotomies are as follows:

1 *Universalism versus particularism*: actors relate to others on the basis of general criteria or criteria unique to the individual concerned.
2 *Performance versus quality*: actors relate to others on the basis of criteria of performance or 'achievement' or criteria of some form of endowment or 'ascription'.
3 *Specificity versus diffuseness*: actors relate to others for a specific, restricted purpose or in a general or holistic way.
4 *Affective neutrality versus affectivity*: actors relate to others in a detached, instrumental manner or with the engagement of feelings and emotions.

Parsons, as we shall see, argued that modernity has witnessed a general shift in the direction of universalism, performance, specificity and affective neutrality.

Social systems are characterized too by needs or 'functional prerequisites'. If the notion of pattern variables accents the voluntaristic dimension to Parsons's perspective, that of functional prerequisites, by contrast, refers to the extent to which people's relations to others are embedded in and constrained by social subsystems. Social systems can only exist, in fact, if four functional prerequisites are met. These are *adaptation* (A) (that is, to the external or natural environment), *goal-attainment* (G) (or the mobilization of resources to meet relevant ends), *integration* (I) (or the achievement of regulation and coordination for coherence and stability) and *latency* or *pattern-maintenance* (L) (or the provision of means to sustain the motivational energy of actors) (Baert 1998). Parsons refers to this as the *AGIL*-scheme. Social systems which develop institutions capable of more efficiently performing all four AGIL functions enjoy an evolutionary advantage over their rivals.

Parsons argues that in modernity the macro-level social system of the nation-state can be divided into four sub-systems. The *economic* subsystem is concerned with adaptation; the subsystem of the *polity* is concerned with goal-attainment; the subsystem of *social community* is concerned with integration; and the *cultural* subsystem is concerned with latency or pattern-maintenance. The AGIL-scheme and the pattern variables are interrelated here. For example, subsystems like the economy, where adaptation is the functional prerequisite, are characterized by universalism, performance, specificity and affective neutrality, while subsystems like social community, where integration is the functional prerequisite, are characterized by particularism, quality, diffuseness and affectivity.

Returning to the issue of evolutionary change and modernity, and remaining with the macro-level social system (and subsystem) of the nation-state, Parsons introduced a number of additional concepts: *differentiation, adaptive upgrading, inclusion* and *value generalization*. Baert's (1998: 62) explication of these usefully binds together material in the preceding paragraphs:

> First, with time, a process of 'differentiation' occurs in that different functions are fulfilled by subsystems within the social system . . . Second, with differentiation goes the notion of 'adaptive upgrading'. This means that each differentiated subsystem has more adaptive capacity compared to the non-differentiated system out of which it emerged. Third, modern societies tend to rely upon a new system of integration. Process differentiation implies a more urgent need for special skills. This can only be accommodated by moving from a status based on 'ascription' to a status on the basis of 'achievement'. This implies the 'inclusion' of previously excluded groups. Fourth, a differentiated society needs to deploy a value system that incorporates and regulates the different subsystems. This is made possible through 'value generalization': the values are pitched at a higher level in order to direct activities and functions in various subsystems.

Parsons (1939, 1951a) regarded the evolution of the professions as a significant moment in modernity (his pattern variables actually emerged from his study of the professions). He did not regard the professions primarily as self-interested economic actors, but as regulated by a normative code of conduct towards clients. 'Markets dominated by individual self-interest could not explain the stable rule-bound patterns of social interaction that we see when we look at the operation of professional-client relations' (Holton 1998: 102). The role of the American doctor, for example, epitomizes modernity's trend towards universalism, performance, specificity and affective neutrality commented on earlier (Parsons 1951b). And this is functional for the doctor–patient relationship, the more so since both doctor and patient 'are committed to breaking their relationship rather than forming a social connection as a stable and permanent system of interaction' (Turner 1995: 39).

Contiguous with Parsons's delineation of the physician's role is his analysis of what Turner (1995: 38) has called the 'sick-role mechanism', one of medical sociology's more celebrated items. It is worth a little more attention than typically afforded in textbooks. 'The problem of health', Parsons (1951b: 430) writes, 'is intimately involved in the functional prerequisites of the social system . . . Certainly by almost any definition health is included in the functional needs of the individual member of the society . . . from the point of view of the functioning of the social system, too low a general level of health, too high an incidence of illness, is dysfunctional: this is in the first instance because illness incapacitates the effective performance of social roles.'

Parsons (1975) claims that there is typically a 'psychic' dimension or a 'motivatedness' to illness, an insight which encouraged him to define illness as a form of *deviance*. Even accidents and infections may have a motivational aspect in that the individuals involved might, consciously or otherwise, have exposed themselves to risk (Gerhardt 1987, 1989). Gerhardt (1989) argues at this point that most commentators neglect what she calls the 'crucial two-model structure' of Parsonian thought. 'In most writings on Parsons', she maintains, 'illness is noted for its character of deviance while its care and cure are perceived in terms of the sick role as a device of social control aiming at redressing the balance towards health or normality' (Gerhardt 1989: 14). Such writings naturally but mistakenly go on to criticize Parsons's idea of the sick role; for example, as inadequate for theorizing chronic illness. But, according to Gerhardt, Parsons (1975) later insisted that for him deviance and the sick role are two *different* aspects of the problem. He related the sick role to the concept of 'capacity', and deviance to the concept of the 'motivatedness' of illness.

In Gerhardt's suggested reading, the focus of the *incapacity* model is on the 'negative-achievement' aspect of illness. It embodies a view on the causation of illness which stresses the 'erosion of a person's role capacity' and accounts for this breakdown in terms of a failure to keep well. Since it is in role capacity that the person fails, it is through a role – that is, the sick role – that she or he recovers: the sick role is seen as a 'niche in the social system' where incapacitated individuals may 'withdraw while attempting to mend their fences, with the help of the medical profession'. The *deviancy* model focuses on the 'positive-achievement' aspects of illness, or the motivational forces at play.

Psychoanalysis influences Parsons here. 'If only slightly altered to serve a *tabula rasa* rather than an instinct-drive image of the (un)socialized person, psychodynamic views are behind the concept of the unconsciously motivated aetiology of illness. They also inspire the idea of "unconscious psychotherapy" incorporated in medical treatment' (Gerhardt 1989: 15).

Certainly Gerhardt's interpretation is a challenge to take Parsonian structural-functionalism more seriously on issues of health and healing than has become customary. Nor did Parsons just contribute the sick-role mechanism to medical sociology. Turner (1995) draws attention to his work on the ethical or non-profit orientations of the professions, referred to earlier; on the effects of social structure and culture on health; and on the relationship between death, religion and the 'gift of life', which he saw as allied to wider issues of meaning. Each of these contributions has triggered discrete literatures. But rather than delve further it may be more productive to consider three general but persuasive criticisms of the structural-functionalist paradigm Parsons promoted (see Baert 1998). There is arguably more to learn from these than from more provincial two-a-penny critiques of mere characterizations of the sick-role.

First, quite independently of how all-consuming and analytically tight Parsons's structural-functionalism may be, it remains unclear just how much explanatory power his theory possesses. It is difficult, for example, to fathom how Lawson's demi-regularities might add to or subtract from their plausibility. And theories which are untestable, even in principle, must be deemed, as Popper would say, pseudo-scientific. A second and standard criticism of the structural-functionalist paradigm is that it fails to address (even the possibility of) conflict or disequilibrium. Thus Baert (1998: 53) writes of Parsons:

> in his earlier work he developed a theoretical argument aimed at understanding how social order is brought about. Likewise, his system analysis was primarily aimed at explaining how the stability of a system is achieved – how it manages its boundary maintenance and its internal integration. Parson's frame of reference not only fails to account sufficiently for widespread dissensus and major political or industrial conflicts, but also occasionally to exclude the very possibility of their existence.

Third, it is far from self-evident *how* Parsons's four functional prerequisites to any social system – namely, adaptation, goal-attainment, integration and latency/pattern-maintenance – actually secure the maintenance and survival of the system; and nor is it plain *how much of each* is indicated.

(Neo-)positivist sociology is not of course atheoretical, it merely presents as such. The theories articulated thick-and-fast through Parsonian structural-functionalism on the other hand are pitched at such a level of generality that they seem to defy test or revision by empirical investigation. The route from (neo-)positivism to structural-functionalism is one from 'systematic' or 'abstracted empiricism' to 'grand theory', from one of C. Wright Mills's (1963) twin evils to the other. What then might provisionally be said of structural-functionalism? Apart from the issue of its lack of testability, two further observations suggest themselves. The first concerns agency. Despite both Parsons's early objections to positivism's silence on purposive action and his resultant pursuit of his pattern variables, it must be acknowledged that his own agents quickly became 'oversocialized' (Wrong 1961). In this respect his work was to be readily distinguished from that of the interactionists (Dawe 1970). For a combination of reasons, agency goes missing in Parsonian structural-functionalism (which is not to say it is irrecoverable). The second observation is more positive. If Parsons has relatively little of lasting value to contribute to our understanding of the lifeworld, the relevance of his studies for comprehending the system may be more compelling. It will be argued in later chapters that medical sociologists have tended not to allow fully for the significance of the system (active via (excessive) system rationalization and lifeworld colonization), not least because it 'functions' largely 'beneath the surface' and 'behind people's backs'. It is possible to take this much on board without being seduced and compromised by 'systems analysis' of the type espoused by the American neo-functionalists and, especially, Luhmann.

Interactionism

When the term 'variable analysis' was used in the account of (neo-)positivism, the criticisms were directed chiefly towards the 'analysis'; but as Pawson notes, Blumer's (1956) classic critique of variable analysis had a different aim. Blumer's objection was to the 'variable' in variable analysis: 'the interpretative critique objects to the very notion that the social world can be broken down into a set of stable, identifiable elements' (Pawson 1989: 35). In comparison to structural-functionalism, interactionism was agent- rather than system-oriented. We shall concentrate for the most part on Mead and on Blumer's espousal of 'symbolic interactionism', although mention will also be made of Goffman.

Mead's social psychology, informed by the American philosophy of pragmatism, was a prime source for symbolic interactionism, although the actual phrase was first used in 1937 by one of his students, Blumer, and the movement probably peaked in the 1960s. Mead taught with Dewey in Chicago and, in an audit-free zone, published his first paper at the age of 40; his influential *Mind, Self and Society* (1934) was based on lecture notes. Eschewing Cartesianism, he argued that the self must be a *social* self, bound up as it is with social interaction and language. Baert (1998) distinguishes between 'interactionist' and 'symbolic' dimensions to this social self. The former refers to people's capacity to adopt the attitude of other individuals and of the 'generalized other', and the latter refers to the dependency of the social self on the sharing of symbols (including non-verbal gestures and communication). A further distinction, that between the 'I' and the 'me', is less apparent in Mead's text than in commentaries. In general terms, the 'I' stands for the acting, innovating aspect of the self, while the 'me' represents the 'I's' object: the 'I' can only be observed or recalled as the 'me'.

Blumer drew heavily on Mead's conceptual tools. He moved from Chicago to Columbia, where it fell to him to develop Mead's ideas to counter the local functionalism of Merton and positivism of Lazarsfeld. Arguably, there are four main ideas underlying Blumer's symbolic interactionism (Baert 1998). First, he follows Mead in emphasizing that individuals have social selves and hence a capacity for 'self-interaction'. Second, this time departing from Mead, he echoes Parsons in alluding to the problem of social order. Social order, he argues (anticipating Garfinkel's paradigm of ethnomethodology), is contingent upon people's recurrent use of identical schemes of interpretation. Third, he claims that individuals act towards an object in their environment on the basis of the meaning they attribute to it. Meaning is not intrinsic to an object; rather, the meaning of an object can and does vary in line with individuals' projects. 'The actor selects, checks, suspends, regroups, and transforms the meanings in the light of the situation in which he is placed and the direction of his action' (Blumer 1969: 5). This attribution of meaning to an object is, in turn, 'constituted, maintained and modified by the ways in which others refer to that object or act towards it' (Baert 1998: 73). And, fourth, Blumer uses the term 'joint action' to refer to a 'societal organization of conduct of different acts of diverse participants' (Blumer 1969: 17). Examples of joint actions, which always grow out of previous joint actions, would be marriage, a doctor–patient encounter or an academic seminar. However stable, joint actions are made up of the component acts, and hence are dependent on the attribution of meaning; but at the same time they are different from each component act and from the aggregate of those acts.

The impact of the studies of Mead and Blumer on medical sociology, although indirect, has been considerable. Gerhardt (1989) distinguishes between two models of illness found within the interactionist paradigm, the *crisis* and *negotiation* models. The former she associates with the 'labelling' perspective on deviance of theorists like Lemert and Becker, as well as with the 'antipsychiatry movement'; societal reaction is viewed as 'public crisis' and the changes it induces as 'the irreversible consequences of a once-and-for-all impact'. The 'ceremonial' application of a diagnostic label of mental illness, for example, 'ascribes' (d'Arcy 1976) a new 'master status' (Hughes 1945) which (a) 'validates identity' (Schur 1971), but also (b) leads to 'retrospective interpretation' ('I always thought he was odd, do you remember . . .') (Kitsuse 1964) and (c) sticks, often for life (Freidson 1970). Scheff's (1966) *Being Mentally Ill* is in many respects an exemplar. Medicine is here viewed as the 'application of diverse therapeutic strategies under the auspices of "professional dominance"' (Gerhardt 1989: 89–90).

The negotiation model envisages a more open exchange between patient and health worker in medical settings which may or may not be dominated by the latter's authority. Taking her cue from the work of Strauss *et al.* (1963), Annandale (1998: 25) puts it clearly:

negotiation connotes meaning which develops in the course of interaction; it is through meaning-making that individuals know the world and are able to act effectively in it. Consequently, action in the health-care context involves a process of definition of others, and, thereby, negotiating a consensus (which may be fleeting enough to allow one to 'get by' in a particular task, or sufficiently long-term to anticipate a changed self or new social policy).

Glaser and Strauss's (1965) study of 'awareness contexts' in relation to dying patients, and Roth's (1963) study of the construction of 'timetables' in the illness careers of patients with tuberculosis exemplify this approach.

This is perhaps the most appropriate juncture at which to mention the 'dramaturgical analysis' of Goffman, a figure as important for medical sociology as he is difficult to categorize (see Strong 1979a, b). If he cannot be subsumed under the rubric of symbolic interactionism, for all that he was a graduate student of Blumer, several of his contributions to understanding health and healing show a marked affinity with Gerhardt's negotiation model. Like Blumer, Goffman avoided explaining human conduct in terms of system imperatives but, unlike Blumer, he fought shy of producing a consistent theoretical frame of reference. His sociology is one of 'co-presence' (Gouldner 1970: 379). His main interest is in rule-governed, but not wholly scripted, 'performances' in face-to-face encounters. He analyses *impression management* in 'front regions' (in respect of the 'personal' as well as of 'settings'), and pays attention too to the significance – for example, as emotional outlets – of 'back regions' (Goffman 1969).

Goffman (1968a) most conspicuously influenced medical sociologists through his analysis of *asylums*, which charted the 'moral career of the mental patient' as part of a wider appreciation of 'total institutions', and in his analysis of *stigma* (Goffman 1968b). In the latter he distinguishes between 'virtual social identity', or the stereotypical notions of the 'other' which we make in routine social interaction, and which become transformed into 'normative expectations' about how the individual other *ought* to be; and 'actual social identity', or the attributes the individual other actually possesses. Thus a stigma 'is really a special kind of relationship between attribute and stereotype' (Goffman 1968b: 14). It is an account, or 'sensitization', of stigma which has proved compelling (see Williams 1987); my own distinction between 'felt' and 'enacted stigma' is indebted to Goffman's conceptual and theoretical spadework (Scambler and Hopkins 1986).

What general criticisms might be proffered of Mead, Blumer and the interactionists, and of Goffman too? First, it is commonly asserted that they are necessarily silent on social structure. This may in fact be truer of Blumer than of Mead, especially if structure is conceptualized, as is frequently the case in modern social theory, in terms of rules and resources. After all, Mead's notions of the self and of the generalized other imply a concept of structure of sorts: 'to adopt the arguments of others implies the internalisation of the community's implicit shared rules' (Baert 1998: 74); but it is a limited – enabling rather than constraining – appreciation of structure.

Second, interactionism in this guise seems also to neglect the unintended consequences of purposeful action. Neither Mead nor Blumer, nor even

Goffman, distinguishes adequately between people's capacity to reflect on their actions ('first-order reflexivity'), which is inherent in interactionism, and their capacity to reflect on the underlying structural conditions of these actions ('second-order reflexivity'). Baert (1998) rightly points out that second-order reflexivity, thus defined, has become a key characteristic of high modernity (see Beck *et al.* 1994).

It might be said of interactionism, then, in its symbolic and other forms, that it more naturally accommodates agency than structure, and the day-to-day activities of the lifeworld than the – often covert and conflictual – media of money and power associated with the system. But this may in fact be more true of the interactionist paradigm at its American (1960s) and British (1970s) peaks than of its current output (see Annandale 1998). It is a question we shall return to.

Phenomenology

When Husserl set out to repair what for him were the damaged goods of Hume's empiricism (which underwrote the (neo-)positivisms) on the one hand, and Descartes's rationalism (epitomized in the Cartesian 'method of doubt') on the other, it was in the name of founding an indisputable, objective and rigorous 'new' science. He claims that we are born into the (pre-scientific) *Lebenswelt* or lifeworld, which he then distinguishes from the objective-scientific world. These are 'two different things': 'the knowledge of the objective-scientific world is 'grounded' in the self-evidence of the lifeworld. The latter is pre-given to the scientific worker, or the working community, as ground; 'yet, as they build upon this, what is built is something different' (Husserl 1970: 130–1). If we are to understand the structures of *both* the lifeworld *and* the world of objective science, together with how these worlds are interrelated, then we must do so on the basis of a transcendental phenomenology grounded in transcendental subjectivity (Bernstein 1976: 131). But how might this be accomplished?

Husserl picks up on Brentano's assertion that consciousness is always in the accusative: consciousness is always 'consciousness of . . .'. What is required to render the lifeworld and the world of objective science 'transcendentally understandable' is a move from the 'natural attitude', according to which neither the reality of these worlds nor our knowledge of them is ever questioned, to the philosophical attitude. This is done via the phenomenological reduction or *epoche*, which involves 'bracketing' or suspending all presuppositions about the objects of consciousness: the residue is an individual consciousness or empirical ego. A further transcendental reduction takes us to pure consciousness or the transcendental ego.

Husserl's project is a radicalization of Descartes's method of doubt. He asks what, stripped of all appearances, *there must be*. The phenomenon given in pure consciousness, he argues, is the essence of the object experienced empirically in the natural attitude. The essence or 'eidos' of a phenomenon is that which is present in pure consciousness, and hence that which 'makes the object knowable, experiencable by consciousness'. The method for isolating or intuiting essences is the 'eidetic reduction': by an imaginative exercise termed 'free variation', the object's location in consciousness is set aside and its unchanging or universal characteristics are exposed. The ontology of essences arrived at in this way provides the ground upon which the lifeworld and the world of objective science are constructed. Ultimately on offer, then, is a new 'first philosophy' or 'eidetic science'.

Schutz was among those with deep reservations about aspects of Husserl's transcendental phenomenology; but he nevertheless took a lead from Husserl in striving to develop a phenomenological understanding of the lifeworld. In *The Phenomenology of the Social World* (Schutz 1970), first published in 1932, he claims to have found in Husserl's work solutions to problems left unresolved by Weber. For Schutz, the primary goal of the social sciences is to reach an understanding of the constitution and maintenance of 'social reality'. And he defines social reality as

> the sum total of objects and occurrences within the social cultural world as experienced by the commonsense thinking of men living their daily lives . . . It is the world of cultural objects and social institutions into which we are all born, within which we have to find our bearings, and with which we have to come to terms. From the outset we, the actors on the social scene, experience the world we live in as a world both of nature and of culture, not as a private but an intersubjective one, that is, as a world common to all of us, either actually given or potentially accessible to everyone; and this involves intercommunication and language.
>
> (Schutz 1962: 53)

What Weber had failed to do was to elucidate precisely *how* the social scientist might study the lifeworld. Schutz argues that social reality is intersubjective and that we therefore share schemes of meaning. The interpretations which we jointly make in everyday life are based on the common *stock of knowledge* which we all share. This is in part personal and idiosyncratic, but it is also inherited rather than invented anew by each generation. Furthermore, 'our involvement in the flow of action and our use of the stock of knowledge is, in the natural attitude, one predominantly directed towards practical ends' (Anderson *et al.* 1986: 91). An individual's stock of knowledge consists of 'typifications' which are taken-for-granted unless/until revealed as such by phenomenological reductions of the kind prescribed by Husserl. These typifications are organized according to a dynamic/system of *relevances* determined by an individual's (ever-changing) interests.

The lifeworld can be stratified into different social dimensions, each with its distinctive spatio-temporal structures. Primary among these is the social dimension of face-to-face relations and interactions (the 'pure' We-relation). Here individuals 'participate' in each other's conscious life and there is a 'synchronization of two interior streams of consciousness' (Schutz 1964: 26). The world of contemporaries has different properties; it involves persons 'whom

I informally encounter face-to-face'; persons 'whom I have never met but may soon meet'; persons 'of whose existence I am aware as reference points for typical social functions (e.g. the post office employees processing my mail)'; as well as 'a variety of collective social realities (e.g. Governmental agencies) which exist and affect my life, but with whom I may have no direct contact' (Bernstein 1976: 149). Whereas a face-to-face interaction is constituted mainly by a 'Thou-orientation', a relation in the 'non-concrete' social dimension of contemporaries is constituted mainly by a 'They-orientation'. But both social dimensions share a time zone in which others are either directly encountered or can be encountered. This is not true of two other social dimensions about which Schutz has less to say – those of 'predecessors' and 'successors'.

Overlapping with this concept of social dimensions is that of 'multiple realities'. By this Schutz means that within clearly demarcated forms of social life (e.g. daily life, but also fiction, science, social science and so on), that is, within ' "finite" provinces of meaning', 'the systems of relevancies invoked and the stocks of knowledge available enable us to bestow the character of "factuality" in different ways' (Anderson *et al.* 1986: 93). Social scientists have not realized, Schutz contended, that the subjectivity found in the lifeworld needs to be made available under the 'theoretical attitude'. Sociologists are *not* concerned with the experiences and meanings of actual individuals, but rather with 'typical actors' with 'typical motives' who pursue 'typical goals' via 'typical courses of action'; that is, with 'second-order typifications' (or typifications of typifications). Schutz arrives at three postulates for social scientists. The first is that of logical consistency. The second is that of subjective interpretation: action must be taken as meaningful for social actors. The third is that of explanatory adequacy: social scientists cannot attribute to 'actors in the theory' anything other than common-sense theories (Anderson *et al.* 1986).

Garfinkel's (1952: 114) debt to Schutz is apparent from his PhD thesis: the question he sets himself is 'how men, isolated yet simultaneously in an odd communion, go about the business of constructing, testing, maintaining, altering, validating, questioning, defining an order *together*' (see Heritage 1984). Mead and the symbolic interactionists were influences too, as was Parsons, who supervised Garfinkel's doctorate and bequeathed to him the Hobbesian problem of social order. But Garfinkel's ethnomethodology was also distinctive. Its focus was on the study of the routines of everyday life. He used the term *reflectivity of accounts* to refer to the fact that people constantly make sense of their surroundings and that 'these sense-making practices are constitutive of that which they are describing' (Baert 1998: 85). He argues, in a manner evocative of Wittgenstein's *Philosophical Investigations* (1958), that people know the 'rules' only in that they are skilful in acting in accordance with them. Our knowledge in everyday life – which is tacit and practical rather than discursive or theoretical – is 'seen-but-unnoticed'. A related theme is that of *indexicality*, which is that the meaning of objects and social practices depends on the context in which they arise.

In his empirical studies, Garfinkel (1967) was fond of 'breaching experiments' which disrupted the routines of everyday life. He emphasizes that people develop emotional attachments to rules and that, if these are broken, rather than adjusting their interpretive procedures they tend to heap moral condemnation on the 'deviant'. The phrase 'documentary method of interpretation' in Garfinkel's work alludes to a 'recursive mechanism in which people draw upon interpretive procedures to construct "documentary evidences", which are, in their turn, employed to infer the interpretive procedures' (Baert 1998: 87). In this way interpretive procedures are durable through and beyond circumstances which threaten them.

For Gerhardt (1989: 196), the phenomenological paradigm gives rise to a single model of illness, as *trouble*. Focusing mainly on (diverse) work in ethnomethodology, she claims that illness as trouble elicits one of two responses: 'either the sick person's environment is shown to use neutralization practices to reduce potential blunders, together with discriminatory practices to reduce participation. Or the trouble is diagnosed and dealt with by an expert (in the case of illness usually, but not always, a doctor).' As far as therapy is concerned, the emphasis is on the form of rationality that prevails in clinical settings. Garfinkel (1967) stresses the practical – rather than theoretical – nature of clinical endeavour, which he defines as an 'artful contextual accomplishment'. Weiland (1975), in similar vein, argues that although medicine relies on the natural and social sciences, the core of medical work is the situational *use* of this knowledge in ever-changing, if routinized, circumstances. The theme of medical dominance comes and goes in phenomenological studies.

Leaving aside the matter of the flawed transcendental phenomenology of Husserl, as fatally *asocial* as Hume's empiricism, a number of criticisms are popularly levied against the 'applied' phenomenological approaches of writers like Schutz and, more substantively, Garfinkel. First, recalling the influence of Parsons, it seems incontrovertible that, however illuminating their work may be in accounting for 'symbolic order', it is less impressive in respect of 'politico-strategic order' (Baert 1998: 88). Second, while they have shown how actors share common stocks of knowledge and work in complex ways to restore order, they are less forthcoming on the (witting) transformation of social structures. In fact, there is a disturbing silence on deliberate action either for or against change. And third, there is a neglect of power, privilege and asymmetrical relations, ironically in that these frequently underpin or shape the social mechanisms under phenomenological investigation. Like interactionism, phenomenology might be said to be more reticent about the system than about the lifeworld, but just as with interactionism, this is, as we shall see, a conclusion in need of qualification.

Conflict theory

The subheading 'conflict theory' is even more of an umbrella term than its predecessors in this chapter; but it will be expedient here to focus on Marx.

Marx, notorious upender of Hegel, was a realist, providing, if Bhaskar (1989a) is to be believed, an early prototype for a critical realist reading of social change. Keat and Urry (1975) usefully distinguish four ways in which Marx was in 'methodological' opposition to the 'vulgar' political economists of the late eighteenth and early nineteenth centuries. First, Marx insists that men act on the external world by means of 'labour', changing both it and themselves, forging a human domain through the production of material objects; and labour and production are inherently social processes. Furthermore, definite stages are identifiable: distinctive types of society exist, each characterized by a distinctive set of human needs met through distinctive means of organizing labour. Marx objects to any political economy focused on isolated individuals, which theorizes society as an aggregate of individuals.

Second, he holds that a phenomenon like capital must not be seen as a natural 'thing'; rather, capital is 'one element in a definite social relationship of production corresponding to a particular historical formation and is only manifested in things, such as the spinning jenny' (Keat and Urry 1975: 99). For Marx, all social phenomena are inherently relational: the category of wage-labour cannot be grasped, for example, without reference to that of capital. Third, Marx maintains that there are no natural or general laws of economic life which are independent of given historical structures (the assertion of which is an example of *commodity fetishism*). Economic laws deal with things which are social rather than natural and need to be seen as specific to a particular mode of production.

Fourth, Marx complains that vulgar political economies trade merely in surface appearances, failing to penetrate deeper to what critical realists term the *real*. He argues that it is commodity fetishism in capitalism that causes this divergence between appearance and reality. Commodities are objects produced which have both a *use-value* – that is, a usefulness to their consumers – and an *exchange-value*. But objects are produced for their exchange-value. People come to see the exchange-value of a given commodity not as a product of men's labour, but as a 'naturally given fixed property of the commodity' (Keat and Urry 1975: 100). Commodities are assumed to have 'thing-like' relations with each other. The social comes to be seen as natural. Thus commodity fetishism means that the real, social relations of production do not appear as they are. Marx regards any – (neo-)positivist – social science stuck at this fetishistic level of appearances as false and distorting.

Marx's espousal of historical materialism is too well known to warrant yet another exposition. In any case, we shall return to his analysis of change and capitalism later. It will be sufficient here to comment on his (relatively underdeveloped) treatment of *relations of class*; on *function* and *contradiction* in the capitalist mode of production; and on his *method of abstraction*.

The commodification of labour-power is the distinguishing feature of capitalism. Wage-labourers may be formally free, but without alternative means of subsistence they are effectively 'wage-slaves'. Moreover, what might be described as 'value-added' is entirely due to labour-power. Whether or not labour-power is in fact a process of value-adding depends on capital's capacity to control workers in the labour process; productivity is critical. Control and productivity are essential for the (exploitative) appropriation of the *surplus value* created by labour. Jessop (1998: 26) puts it well:

> the struggle between capital and labour to increase productivity (by extending the working day, intensifying effort during this time, or boosting output through cost-effective labour-saving techniques) is the fundamental basis of the economic class struggle in capitalism. Class struggle is not simply about relative shares of the capitalist cake. It is rooted in the organization of *production* itself (the labour process) and not just in *market relations* (including struggles over wages) or *distribution* (including distribution through the state). It concerns not only the accumulation of money as capital but also the overall reproduction of capital's domination of wage-labour in the economy and wider society.

Marx certainly deploys a notion of 'functional interdependence' in relation to the capitalist mode of production, even if he rejects functionalist explanation of the kind later employed by Parsons. He recognizes that there are specific functional needs that must be satisfied for a particular mode to exist. The functional interdependencies Marx identifies have to do with the relations of domination that have characterized all forms of society, with the exception of primitive communism. They are based, in short, on the contradiction between the dominant and dominated class.

Consider two of the functional needs of the capitalist mode of production, namely, 'for agents who perform the capitalist function: buying labour-power, directing the use of such power in capitalist enterprises, and so on', and 'for agents who perform the labour function: selling labour-power and producing exchange-value for the capitalist' (Keat and Urry 1975: 115). These functional needs must be met for the capitalist system to sustain and reproduce itself, yet they form a contradiction. Capitalists in competition must strive to expand their profits through accumulation; but this is achieved at the direct expense of those who provide labour-power. In the short term (and holding the level of exploitation constant), anything which increases the proportion of exchange-value that accrues to the capitalist must reduce that received by his wage-labourers. And in the longer term, in Marx's (1933: 39) own words, 'if . . . the income of the worker increases with the rapid growth of capital, there is at the same time a widening of the social chasm that divides the worker from the capitalist, an increase in the power of capital over labour, a greater dependence of labour on capital.' This is a (threatening) structural contradiction at the heart of capitalism.

Finally, it is appropriate, especially in relation to his realism, to mention Marx's discussion of his method of abstraction in *Grundrisse* (Marx 1973). He argues that one cannot adequately analyse a given population in terms of characteristics like its urban–rural divide or occupational structure. Rather, one must ask questions of its classes and all that follows from these. This shifts the analysis from the concrete to 'abstract general principles'. Marx (1973: 101) insists, however, that the scientific method, properly understood, involves using abstract general principles to reconstitute the concrete as a complex combination of many determinations, 'a unity of the diverse'. Keat and Urry (1975: 113) again: 'we analyze how the objects of analysis are determined by the complex combinations of relations between the various abstractly realized notions.' Thus, a given population is not seen abstractly but as determined by the 'rich totality of many determinations and relations' (Marx 1973: 100).

The spotlight has dwelt on selected aspects of the work of Marx but, as mentioned earlier, there are many other conflict theorists. This is recognized in Gerhardt's (1989) two medical sociological models: while one, the *deprivation* (or *deprivation-domination*) model, owes much to Marx, the principal debts of the other, the *loss* model, lie elsewhere. The loss model emphasizes an individual's state of heightened susceptibility to illness due to (socially structured) biographical circumstances indicative of 'loss'. The positive impact of social support on health is often cited. Treatment, in this vein, tends to focus on strengthening those resources which act as social support. The studies of Brown and Harris (1978) serve as exemplars. The deprivation model concentrates on populations rather than individuals. The risks to health and longevity are seen as graded by social strata, as in the long tradition of health inequalities research. Treatment consists in societal rather than individual measures, although these may include calls for 'demedicalization' (see Zola 1972) and 'deprofessionalization' (after the fashion of the polemicist Illich 1975), as well as directly for reductions in material, cultural and other forms of inequality.

It is an even more difficult task to collate criticisms of conflict theory than it was for the paradigms sketched earlier. To say that it tends to be orientated to system and structure rather than lifeworld and agency is more true than false but not particularly helpful. It is a paradigm marked by heterogeneity. As far as Marx is concerned, and notwithstanding an exhaustive critical literature on his continuing (ir)relevance for analyses of high or late modernity/postmodernity (which will be consulted in later chapters), two points stand out at this stage.

First, while Marx (credibly enough) attaches great significance to 'labour', he (less credibly) all but ignores 'interaction', a charge laid most heavily over the years by Habermas (1986). And second, however understandable it may be given some of the propositions contained in his corpus, it will *not* do to assess Marx's theories as if they are (neo-)positivist exercises in 'explaining/predicting' (see above). This said, Marx fails to convince with his alternative account of the scientific method (Keat and Urry 1975). And insofar as his method of abstraction anticipates contemporary critical realism, it remains incumbent on critical realists in particular to make good this deficit.

Loose threads

This opening chapter serves as a reminder of the main paradigms/research programmes that have informed medical sociology through modernity, and of some of the flaws or weaknesses each manifests. But this is only one of its purposes. It is evident that each paradigm/research programme has been founded upon sharp insight and retains value and a capacity to shed light on the social world in general and on health and healing in particular. This suggests a need for *synthesis*, which should be differentiated from mere eclecticism.

What might be called the paradox of *intractable preliminaries* states that sociological explanations of the social world cannot be secure unless they are philosophically grounded, the problem being that to date no attempt, be it foundationalist, like Hume's empiricism or Husserl's phenomenology, or a more recent form of post-foundationalism, has achieved anything like common assent. It seems reasonable to assert that the flaws/weaknesses of paradigms/research programmes matter most for us the more sociological – that is, the less philosophical – they are; but this is not to say that philosophical deficits cannot, on occasions, in practice as well as in principle, undermine the sociological enterprise. The points to stress are that paradigms do not have to be inviolate for us to learn from the work they circumscribe, and that this chapter has identified important theoretical resources for the business of synthesis.

2

Postmodern options: pros, cons and rationality

Sociological analyses around the 'postmodern turn' have gathered momentum since the 1970s and have been a mixed bag; and the use of the word 'around' is deliberate. At one pole are those sceptical of *any* talk of the postmodern unless it be in the form of an account of why there has been so much talk of a postmodern turn of late, culminating in now routinized references to the advent of a postmodern culture ('postmodernism'), or even of a postmodern social formation ('postmodernity'). At the other pole are those who insist on the need for a thoroughgoing – new, radical – postmodern paradigm for sociology.

At each pole, if not as commonly as in between, numerous contributions to the sociological understanding of the social dimensions of health and healing have been proferred. This chapter opens with a characterization of the postmodern turn. The promise of the postmodern for medical sociology is then explored, incorporating in particular postmodern discourses on the body, and a balance sheet of costs and benefits is drawn up. At this juncture a *paradox of disinhibition* is mooted. Brief consideration is given, finally, to the potential for a sociology of the postmodern.

The postmodern turn and its conceptual apparatus

References to the postmodern have a longer and more disparate ancestry than many realize (see Anderson 1998). But what is generally meant by the 'postmodern turn'? Best and Kellner (1997) use the term to refer to a transformation in social life, the arts, science, philosophy and theory which they term 'dramatic'. This, they contend, involves a general shift from modern to postmodern theory, together with a move towards a new paradigm through which the world is perceived and interpreted. The postmodern turn also includes the emergence of postmodern politics, new forms of identities and novel configurations of culture and technology. Many theorists claim too that 'we have left modernity behind, that we have entered a new historical space with new challenges, dangers, and possibilities, while for others, we are experiencing the end of history itself' (Best and Kellner 1997: viii). Best and Kellner's own contribution is intended to sustain the thesis that the many disparate trajectories of the postmodern presently in circulation are in fact coalescing into a Kuhnian 'new paradigm', which they see as 'emergent' rather than dominant, and therefore as the subject of continuing and vigorous dispute. Emergent new paradigm or not, there is a belated, if still somewhat slippery and elusive, measure of agreement among expositors of the postmodern, sympathetic or otherwise, on its defining features. Eagleton (1996), who as it happens is not especially sympathetic, starts with the distinction between postmodernism, understood as a 'form of contemporary culture', and postmodernity, alluding to a 'particular historical period' (although this periodicity is polemically elaborated as a 'style of thought'). His development of his definitions, typically elegant and pithy, warrants lengthy quotation.

Postmodernity, he avers, is a style of thought which is

> suspicious of classical notions of truth, reason, identity and objectivity, of the idea of universal progress or emancipation, of single frameworks, grand narratives or ultimate grounds of explanation. Against these Enlightenment norms, it sees the world as contingent, ungrounded, diverse, unstable, indeterminate, a set of disunifying cultures or interpretations which breed a degree of scepticism about the objectivity of truth, history and norms, the giveness of natures and the coherence of identities. This way of seeing, as some would say, has real material conditions: it springs from an historical shift in the West to a new form of capitalism – to the ephemeral, decentralized world of technology, consumerism and the culture industry, in which the service, finance and information industries triumph over traditional manufacture, and classical class politics yield ground to a diffuse range of 'identity politics' . . . Postmodernism . . . [is a form of culture which] reflects something of this epochal change, in a depthless, decentred, ungrounded, self-reflexive, playful, derivative, eclectic, pluralistic art which blurs the boundaries between 'high'and 'low' culture, as well as between art and everyday experience. How dominant or pervasive this culture is – whether it goes all the way down, or figures just as one particular region within contemporary life – is a matter of argument.
>
> (Eagleton 1996: vii–viii)

There are elements common to most articulations of the postmodern turn, even if there are few if any postmodernists who would subscribe to them all. These can be discerned to varying degrees in the summary statements of Best and Kellner and Eagleton. For present (heuristic) purposes, they might be grouped into four interlinked clusters under the rubrics of the *material*, the *cultural-aesthetic*, the *rational* and the *methodological*.

Material elements

In relation to material elements, accounts are replete, first, with references to inexorable processes of *globalization*, economic as well as cultural (see Waters 1995: Bauman 1998a; Held *et al.* 1999). Economically, such processes are typically explicated in terms of the globalization and abstraction of capital and the ascendancy of financial capital (see Ashley 1997). A prerequisite for globalization, according to Giddens (1990), was the distanciation or separation of time and space, which has permitted the 'disembedding' or 'lifting out' of social relations from their local contexts, principally through symbolic tokens (for example, money) and expert systems (for example, repositories of technical knowledge). Giddens is not alone in insisting too on the simultaneously renewed importance of the 'local'; Robertson (1992) deploys the term 'glocalization' to catch this 'other side' to globalization.

Associated with these dimensions of globalization are, second, claims about the *decline of the nation-state*, and especially of national structures of political and economic regulation. Third, there are many allusions to the irreversible, terminal *'crisis' of postwar welfare statism* (see Carter 1998b; Bauman 1998a). Fourth, it is argued that there has been a *diffusion of power*, with fewer analysing it in terms of readily identifiable loci of 'domination', such as class or state, and more calling on Foucauldian notions like 'surveillance', 'governmentality' and 'technologies of the self'.

Fifth, the analytic emphasis on production in industrial capitalism has been superseded by an emphasis on the reproduction of the conditions of consumption in what is often designated a post-industrial or *consumer society*: references to 'consumerism' or 'consumer economies' are plentiful. A sixth material factor cited is a *destandardization of work*, with patterns of work, adjusted to segmented rather than mass production and oriented primarily to consumerism, described as post-Fordist or 'flexible'. Hand-in-hand with the transition to post-industrial or consumer society, with its innovative and fluid work practices, come, seventh, alleged processes of *class decomposition or dealignment*; and claims to do with the declining salience of class are frequently accompanied by renewed emphasis on other aspects of stratification, like gender, ethnicity and age (see Bradley 1996; Lee and Turner 1996). Eighth, and finally, repeated references are made to the ideas of *identity and difference*, and to the displacement of class identities by consumer identities: in fact, postmodern identities are said to have multiple constituents and to be adapted by individuals more or less continuously in accordance with personal choice (see Bradley 1996).

Cultural-aesthetic elements

What are the main cultural-aesthetic elements of the postmodern? Reference should first be made to postmodernism *qua* aesthetic movement emergent in the 1960s. Postmodernism in this sense is associated with 'the effacement of the boundary between art and everyday life; the collapse of the hierarchical distinction between high and mass/popular culture; a stylistic promiscuity favouring eclecticism and the mixing of codes; parody, pastiche, irony, playfulness and the celebration of the surface "depthlessness" of culture; the decline of the originality/genius of the artistic producer; and the assumption that art can only be repetition' (Featherstone 1991: 7–8). Some consistency with aesthetic modernism is detectable here, leading some to refer to 'second-wave modernism'; but postmodernism appears more radical and has proved more pervasive than modernism. It appears more radical in that while modernism made *representing* reality problematic, postmodernism renders *reality* problematic; and it is more pervasive in that while modernism's influence was largely confined to art, postmodernism's is experienced throughout contemporary culture (witness Baudrillard's (1983) account of the domination of social life by 'simulacra').

Second, it is widely believed that what Anderson (1998: 62) describes as an 'unthinkable' *dedifferentiation of cultural or value spheres*, the 'hallmark of modernity', has occurred. It is not just the boundary between art and everyday life which has been effaced. The boundaries between science, morality and art have become more and more permeable and each has lost its autonomous logic. Science has in this process yielded its privileged status and influence. Third, this dedifferentiation of cultural spheres has been associated, on the one hand, with a *propensity to nihilism* or anarchy in belief and conviction, and, on the other, with a *propensity to fundamentalism*. Much has been made, fourth, of the potency of *glocalization* in a cultural domain more autonomous than hitherto. While there have been well documented tendencies towards a global culture, there has also been, it is claimed, via a kind of 'retribalization', a resurgence of solitary localized activity.

Rational elements

The first rational element of the postmodern unambiguously attributed by commentators is the belated *expiry of all forms of universal reason*. For some, universalism's longstanding logical antithesis, relativism, should be embraced and proclaimed; while for others, like Rorty (1989), no meaningful obligation survives to choose 'between' universalism and relativism. Second, it follows that the flawed (sibling, if rival) secular, progressive and often teleological 'metanarratives' forged in the European (and Eurocentric, as well as colonialist and gendered) Enlightenment of the late eighteenth century, founded initially on a Kantian philosophy of consciousness, are now redundant and must be abandoned. With the *abandonment of metanarratives*, this 'project of modernity' – namely, the application of a Kantian form of universal reason to master the environment for human ends and to create the good society – dies.

What remains on offer in a post-metanarrative postmodern world is, third, an unconstrained choice between what Lyotard (1984) calls 'petit' as opposed to 'grand' narratives, together with a *celebration of fragmentation*, of dissensus over consensus, and a tolerance of the incommensurable. *An altered role for the intellectual*, fourth, is entailed in all this. The 'legislator' cedes ground to the 'interpreter', for whom notoriety has become the chief criterion of public significance (Bauman 1987). Fifth, and lastly, the postmodern turn heralds a *new reflexivity*, leading some theorists otherwise reticent to sign up to a major social transformation to refer to a period of 'reflexive modernization' (Beck 1992; Beck *et al.* 1994). In Giddens's (1990: 38) words, reflexivity 'consists in the fact that social practices are constantly examined and reformed in the light of incoming information about those very practices, thus constitutively altering their character.' It is in this sense that Giddens regards the contemporary world as 'intrinsically sociological'.

Methodological elements

The first methodological element is the pursuit of *polyphony and dialogue*. Lincoln and Denzin (1994: 580) register a move towards pluralism: 'many social scientists now recognize that no picture is ever complete, that what is needed is many perspectives, many voices, before we can achieve deeper understandings of social phenomena'. And later: 'there may not be one future, one "moment", but rather many; not one "voice", but polyvocality; not one story but many tales, dramas, pieces of fiction, fables, memories, histories, autobiographies, poems, and other texts to inform our sense of life-ways, to extend our understanding of the Other . . . The modernist project has bent and is breaking under the weight of postmodern resistance to its narratives' (Lincoln and Denzin 1994: 584). Gibbons and Reimer (1999: 171) refer to 'eclectic mixes' of methods. Tyler (1986) is less inhibited, arguing that postmodern ethnography involves a 'cooperatively evolved text, a pastiche of fragments of discourse allowing both reader and writer a fantasy of possible worlds' (Seale 1999: 169–70). Ethnographic discourse no longer represents, but 'evokes'. The ideals are polyphony and dialogue. A second and related element is a putative *decentring of writers' authority*, a necessary concomitant of the move to allow voices that are 'otherwise suppressed or contradictory to emerge' (Seale 1999: 170).

Clearly this rather formal 'mapping' of the postmodern turn and its aftermath – summarized in Table 2.1 – could have taken different forms (see Scambler and Higgs 1998). There is more than a hint of contingency – some would say, appropriately enough – in *this* summation of the postmodern in terms of *these* material, cultural-aesthetic, rational and methodological elements.

The postmodern in medical sociology

The postmodern turn has had a considerable impact on the conduct of medical sociology in Britain, indirect as well as direct (see Scambler and Higgs, 1998). Self-evidently, the paradigms/research programmes considered in Chapter 1 – (neo-)positivism, structural-functionalism, interactionism, phenomenology and conflict theory – are the issue of, and belong to, modernity;

Table 2.1   Elements of the postmodern

Material
Globalization and the ascendancy of finance capital
Decline of the nation-state and of national regulation
Crises in postwar welfare states
Diffusion of power
Emergence of societies based on consumption not production
Destandardization of work
Processes of class decomposition and dealignment
Displacement of class by consumer identities

Cultural-aesthetic
Postmodernism and the problematizing of reality
Dedifferentiation of value spheres/deprivileging of science
Tendencies to nihilism and fundamentalism
Glocalization in relation to culture

Rational
Expiry of universal reason
Termination of flawed Enlightenment metanarratives
Celebration of fragmentation and dissensus
Intellectuals as interpreters not legislators
New reflexivity

Methodological
Polyphony and dialogue
Decentring of author's authority

---

on the face of it none is equipped to survive the postmodern turn. This dilemma of incommensurability is one we shall return to, but it is important first to convey an illustrated sense of what a postmodern(ized) approach to health and healing might offer us: enter the so-called *sociology of the body*.

There have been concerted attempts over the past generation to reconfigure theoretical approaches to the body. Foucault was certainly not the first to step back from 'biomedicine' and put an accent on the socially constructed nature of illness and medical practice. Freidson (1970), for example, drew in full measure from both interactionism and conflict theory to critique Parsons and to stress that medical professions not only prognosticate on, and legitimate or deny, people's 'acting sick', but actually create the social possibilities for them to do so. But the work of Freidson and others left a 'biological base' beyond the reach of sociology. It was Foucault above all others who drove 'social constructionism' further on, 'right to the heart of the "natural" or "biological"', maintaining that 'what we know as diseases are themselves fabrications of powerful discourses, rather than discoveries of "truths" about the body and its interaction with the social world' (Annandale 1998: 35). Unlike advocates of the paradigms/research programmes spawned in modernity, Foucault (1977: 138) delivers a view in which the subject is 'stripped of its creative role and analysed as a complex and variable function of discourse'. He commences from the notion of the *episteme*, which constitutes subjects during specific historical periods. In *The Birth of the Clinic* (Foucault 1989), he traces the emergence in the nineteenth century of a *clinical gaze* – or new way of conceptualizing the patient's body – the prerequisite for an innovatory form of medical practice. The resultant 'scientific medicine', he argues, was not the product of a reasoned progression in understanding; rather, it represents the displacement of one (incommensurable) 'anatomical atlas' by another (Armstrong 1987). Moreover, and crucially, this process was part and parcel of wider societal change.

The development of European capitalism was accompanied during this time by population expansion and urbanization. In these circumstances historical forms of – coercive, exemplary – social control rapidly became defunct and were superseded by other forms of control, notably *surveillance of self* (or self-monitoring). Bentham's Panopticon epitomized this form of control. A model for prison construction, this consists of a circular building around a central tower: the prisoners cannot know at any given time whether or not they are under observation from the central tower, and so begin to police their own behaviour. Foucault (1979a) sees this panoptic principle as informing a 'whole type of society', the *disciplinary society*, a society underwritten by surveillance of self (Ritzer 1997: 61). The diffusion of this panoptic mode of power throughout society, Annandale (1998: 36) notes, 'is evidenced in the growth of psychiatry and its urge to confess; in the growth of preventive medicine which relies on the internalisation of powerful discourses of healthy diets and fitness regimes; and in self-help techniques (such as weight-control groups).' These 'humanist discourses', she adds, are anything but benign: they exert a 'new and unprecedented kind of power over modern individuals, a form of power ultimately more repressive than any that has gone before.' Foucault (1980: 155) proclaims that there is now 'no need for arms, physical violence, material constraints. Just a gaze. An inspecting gaze, a gaze which each individual under its weight will end by interiorising to the point that he is his own overseer, each individual thus exercising this surveillance over, and against, himself.' What a cost-effective mechanism of social control, Foucault exclaims. The upshot of Foucault's work, then, is that medicine's contribution to social control no longer takes the form of exclusion or repression, but rather of inclusion and normalization.

Foucault's pioneering analyses and relativizing of bodies have served as catalysts for a number of postmodern enquiries into the sociology of the body. Fox's work is an exemplar of the more adventurous of these. The studies of writers within the 'third-wave feminism(s)' of the 1980s and 1990s are among the most political and challenging.

Fox and 'arche-health'

Fox takes his cue not only from Foucault but from Deleuze and Guatteri (see Fox 1993, 1998a, b). His stance is premised in part on a commendation of the postmodern emphasis on open-mindedness, diversity and freedom: it promises exits from taken-for-granted and ritualized forms of categorization and behaviour. It might be said to be concerned, following Foucault (1980), with the 'micro-politics' of the interplay of power/ knowledge texts, with 'texts' here reaching beyond writing to refer to 'any kinds of meaningful systems of communication or behaviour' (Fox 1998b: 10).

Biomedicine and its kin texts or discourses, Deleuze and Guaterri (1984) claim, have 'territorialized' humans as organisms, as 'bodies-with-organs'. They maintain that the body might be grasped in other ways, portraying it as a 'philosophical' surface upon which are inscribed a range of 'knowledgeabilities (texts of power/knowledge), only one of which is the knowledgeability called biomedicine' (Fox 1998b: 12). Thus, while biomedicine constructs the body as a 'natural' organism, whose functioning is defined as 'health' and dysfunctioning as 'illness', the body might be, and in fact is, differently constituted in other discourses. Deleuze and Guaterri term the philosophical surface the 'body-without-organs'.

Unlike the biomedical body-with-organs typifying modernity, the postmodern body-without-organs is free from time and space, only becoming subject to spatial and temporal constraint as the outcome of inscription. While, according to Fox (1997), Foucault allows for no resistance to power/knowledge, Deleuze and Guatteri (1986) purport to do so via their project of *nomadology*. They argue that the body-without-organs is highly contested, with a variety of knowledgeabilities inside as well as outside biomedicine competing for dominance (see Fox's (1994) study of surgeons and anaesthetists). Differentiation and rivalry create possibilities for 'breaking free from discourse altogether, if only for a moment', a moment of nomadic subjectivity (Fox 1998b: 15). Nomadology, for Deleuze and Guaterri, is the repressed's riposte to those who exercise power through their discourses on the human predicament. Nomads are warriors without strategy or goals, 'at war' with those who would territorialize them. Fox (1998b: 16–17) elaborates: 'It is hard to be a nomad; in fact there *are* no nomads, there is only nomadism – it is a process, not an identity. Nomadism is about becoming other, and one never finally becomes other, rather, we lurch from one identity to another. Deleuze and Guaterri (1988: 11) see nomadism as "rhizomatic", a growth which is branching and diversifying, refusing to allow a single line of development.'

It is against this background that Fox has developed his own notion of *archehealth* (echoing Derrida's (1976) 'arche-writing'), which is a becoming other, a freeing of the body-without-organs from discourse, a nomadic subjectivity. While health and illness constrain or territorialize the body-without-organs by their discourses, arche-health is the refusal of, and resistance to, these discourses. 'The ethics and politics of arche-health is deconstructive', Fox (1998b: 36) writes, 'reminding us to ask hard questions of the modernist disciplines which inscribe us into subjectivity through their conceptions of, and preoccupations with, "health" and "illness"'.

Third-wave feminism(s) and 'embodiment'

The 'third wave' feminism of the 1980s and 1990s arose as feminists realized that the theoretical frameworks revised and refined through the first and second waves – resting on doctrines of universality, sameness and scientific methodology – could no longer be reconciled with the increasingly salient concepts of identity, difference, particularity and embodiment (Arneil 1999). In Grosz's (1988: 96) terms, these frameworks (subsuming, naturally enough, the paradigms/research programmes of (neo-)positivism, structural-functionalism, interactionism, phenomenology and conflict theory) are irredeemably 'phallocentric' and must give way to 'entirely new forms of theory based on women's experiences and perceptions rather than men's'.

'Difference', Fox-Genovese (1994: 232) suggests, 'has replaced equality as the central concern of feminist theory.' Difference here refers not only to differences between men and women, but also to differences between women. It is *not* the case, 'third wavers' maintain, that every person is the same by 'nature' and that 'society' creates differences. Moreover the dichotomous pairs so characteristic of Western thought are inherently patriarchal, since 'their very structure is privileged by the male-non-male (i.e., female) distinction' (Grosz 1990: 101). For Cixous *all* dichotomous pairs, or 'binary oppositions', originate in the fundamental duality between men and women.

Annandale (1998: 78) explores the importance of this for health. If we accept that men and women are opposites, then

> all women are colluding in their oppression, since under patriarchy, women's 'opposition position' will always be defined in a negative way. As a fundamental opposition, gendered difference underwrites (i.e. supports) other oppositions which attach to it – for example, men are rational, women irrational; women are caring, men are uncaring, and so on. It is by this process that the positively valued 'health' attaches to men, while the negatively valued 'illness' becomes the province of women.

Consonant with such analyses, theses of the medicalization or 'pathologization' of women's bodies can be read as a form of collusion with biomedicine. Consider, for example, a woman's reproductive capacity (typically regarded within biomedicine's phallocentric and binary logic as her defining feature). It is said that feminists who highlight the iatrogenic consequences of medical interventions in labour and childbirth – involving the accusations of abuse of both 'territorial' and 'technological power' (Scambler 1987) – only end up also echoing 'women's negative experiences' (Annandale 1998). And a similar argument might be made in relation to menstruation (see Martin 1989; Scambler and Scambler 1993).

The postmodern feminist response is to deconstruct the dichotomous pairs/binary oppositions of male/female, man/woman, sex/gender and so on, in order to expose them as 'artefacts of a modernist world-view' rather than 'apt descriptors of men's and women's experience of health and illness'.

Axiomatically, 'if oppositions are dislodged, then men can no longer easily be associated with all that is valued in society and women with all that is devalued' (Annandale 1998: 80). What is required, in the terminology of Irigaray (1985), is the deconstruction of the phallocentric logic which underpins the 'male imaginary' and the creation of a 'female symbolic'.

The postmodern: some observations and qualifications

There is no pretence that this briefest of excursions into postmodern approaches to the body – through Fox and an eclectic mix of third-wave feminists – exhausts, or adequately records, the potential for a postmodern paradigm/research programme in medical sociology. But it provides sufficient basis for useful reflection. And what appears most positive about the postmodern contributions on the body is their *radical potential*, a potential that arises largely out of the interrogation and deconstruction of extant (modernist) theories. The idea of deconstruction is of course pivotal and warrants further comment.

Postmodern thinkers routinely pay homage to Derrida's (1976) explication, even if they tend too often to deploy his terms subsequently in questionable ways. A core thesis of Derrida's is that in Western intellectual traditions 'writing', 'with its intrinsic dangers of loss, dispersal and potentially endless delay of meaning', has been regarded as secondary to, and an inferior substitute for, the spoken word. According to Derrida this is mistaken, and the seeming primacy and immediacy of speech illusory. All language is 'writing' in that the possibilities of both meaning and the recuperation of meaning are intrinsic to it. But if this is the case, Derrida argues, then philosophy, considered as a mode of discourse oriented towards a definitive capture of meaning or truth, will tend to be obstructed and contradicted by its dependence on a medium 'whose dangers it must believe it possible to transcend'.

'Writing', then, has a 'self-undermining' structure. 'It is the activity of uncovering such systematic incoherencies within a text, rather than striving to reveal a unified meaning, which Derrida refers to as "deconstruction"' (Dews 1987: 10). As a process of exposure, deconstruction can be seen as a political act in itself. Foucault's conception of power as a discursive strategy, now frequently discussed and applied in medical sociology (see Peterson and Bunton 1997), is in some ways continuous with Derrida's notion of deconstruction. Thus, as Carter (1998a: 11) expresses it, 'the different ways that groups of people are represented serve to include or marginalize them. So just as conventional histories are said to be written by victors, deconstructionist archaeologies can bring the excluded back into focus by revealing how they were initially peripheralized. Deconstruction therefore can have radical applications, whilst steadfastly rejecting the modernist categories with which the earlier left was constructed.'

The radicalism of deconstruction seems, at first sight at least, assured, with gains for medical sociology, sampled earlier, and an impressive explosion of creative and original thinking, perhaps especially among feminists. But there are qualifications to be made. Take, for example, Irigaray's ambition to deconstruct phallocentric logic and the male imaginary, and her aspiration for a female symbolic. As Annette Scambler (1998: 109) points out, there is an obvious problem here: 'because we are caught in this phallocentric logic we cannot actually define woman at all. To do so would be to enter the logic and to "conceptualise the relationship between the sexes in terms of polarity and opposition", for the dualities are always created from the male imaginary and the woman is only created as other to men and therefore as "lack" in relation to the male subject' (see also Assiter 1996).

If gender is deconstructed and patriarchy has no 'owner', Annandale (1998: 81) observes, it becomes invisible as a target for political resistance. A growing number of feminists are tending to regard (postmodern) deconstruction as a technique, 'an instrument of critique and subversion' (Barrett 1991: 165), but are rejecting the view that there are no (longer any) enduring structural rela-tions – for example, of class, gender, ethnicity and age, or of patriarchal medicine – and, therefore, nothing to struggle against and supersede. The postmodern can end up as a 'view from nowhere' (Bordo 1993).

Linked to these feminist reservations about postmodernism are other general and philosophical sources of difficulty. Consider, first, Lyotard's (1984) semi-nal welcome for the fragmentation and dissensus marked by the postmodern turn. Postmodern thought, in the words of his early and influential text, 'refines our sensitivity to differences and reinforces our ability to tolerate the incom-mensurable'. Sarup (1993) is but one critic who has noted that Lyotard is here displacing one set of metanarratives with another: we are offered a metanarra-tive 'at the end of metanarratives'. Lyotard's commendation of fragmentation and dissensus, which in company with other writers he prescribes as conducive to localized creativity, testifies precisely to the commitment at the level of grand narratives that he takes umbrage at in modernists. What postmodernists in fact do, Harvey (1989: 117) claims, is simply push metanarratives under-ground where they continue to function with 'now conscious effectivity'.

A second and related awkwardness is the relativism implicit in most defini-tions and products of the postmodern. Putnam (1981) is one of many to refer to the 'truism' that a relativistic stance cannot be stated without inconsist-ency, any such statement itself being non-relativistic. There is no escape. It should be self-evident, for example, that neither of Rorty's (1989) defiant tactics, namely to denigrate this critique as modernist, or simply, in liberal ironist mode, to 'change the subject', will suffice. A third difficulty is closely related. It is most often associated with Habermas (1989b). It attests to the neo-conservatism of relativistic postmodernisms, which are unable to mount any 'rationally binding' critiques of existing social relations or to posit alter-natives without what Habermas terms 'performative contradiction'.

A *paradox of disinhibition* might be ventured at this point: it can be expressed in the general proposition that the radical presentation and 'disinhibiting' effects of postmodern theory and practice disguise a deeper and more robust capacity to 'inhibit' change. This is not to claim that truly postmodern interventions

can never have genuinely radical as opposed to (merely) disinhibiting consequences, but rather that such consequences are fortuitous in the necessary
absence of rationally binding support. Nor is it to deny either that sociological interest is appropriately 'engaged' in postmodern analyses despite the (in-
escapable) 'self-refuting paradox' (Jordan 1997); or that there is an urgent
need for a sociology of the postmodern turn and its sequelae (see Lash 1990;
Gellner 1992). To elaborate on this, it is necessary to consider what a sociology of the postmodern might look like.

Sociology of the postmodern

The postmodern turn was earlier epitomized in four clusters of elements
labelled *material*, *cultural-aesthetic*, *rational* and *methodological*. It is expedient
now to return to these rubrics, although in changed order. As far as the
rational is concerned, implicit in the riposte to relativism above is the view
that a concept of universal reason remains tenable. But this is unequivocally
not the reason of the unreconstructed European Enlightenment project, with
its roots in the subject–object relations of the philosophy of consciousness
('be it the "transcendental" unhistorical subject of Kant's "pure reason" or
the global subject behind Hegel's picture of Reasons's "externalisation" and
reabsorption in history, or the privileged historical subject (the working class)
of Marxist thought' (Brand 1990: 10)).

It has been argued elsewhere, following Habermas (1984, 1987), that a
proceduralist concept of universal reason can be adequately grounded in the
subject–subject relations of communicative action (Scambler 1996), as can
certain formal 'moral', as opposed to substantive 'ethical', imperatives pertaining to justice and solidarity (Scambler 1998b). Such a position permits full
recognition of substantive cultural variation in beliefs and values, and of (derivative) 'local' rationalities. One consequence of *this* grounding for a concept
of universal reason is the potential for a newly reflexive and post-legislative –
if not (merely) interpretive – critical medical sociology, consonant with
a *reconstructed* 'project of modernity', with a primary, necessary and moral
obligation to the lifeworld (see Chapter 7).

As little, or less, needs to be said here about the *cultural-aesthetic*, partly
because of the plenitude of discussions in the general literature, and partly
because it is its relation to the *material* that has been neglected. Suffice it to say
that there is fairly clear evidence of a 'cultural shift' roughly captured by the
elements already listed. There is no doubt that this transition to what most
commentators now call a postmodern culture has infused and influenced
medical sociology, prompting conceptual and theoretical innovation and
opening up novel avenues of enquiry and analysis, such as those sampled
earlier, nor that it has brought 'hidden' unacknowledged allegiances to new
or 'adapted' metanarratives, relativism and disguised neo-conservatism. For
all the importance of a sociology of the postmodern turn, any idea of a
postmodern sociology is riddled with antinomies.

The question of the relationship between the material and the cultural-aesthetic is a matter of ongoing dispute. At one pole are a diminishing band of Marxists and others who persist in seeing the latter as epiphenomenal; at the other pole are an increasingly confident group who see the cultural-aesthetic as, at least, an autonomous sphere, and, at most, ubiquitous and invasive of the postmodern consumer society. The argument of this volume lies between these poles, but closer to the first.

Harvey (1989) and Jameson (1991) are among those who have opted for a Marxist framework, albeit refined ones: 'within this structuralist model, postmodernism is understood as the cultural and ideological (including academic) epiphenomenonon of late capitalist modifications, in which citizens are told they are being given choice, options and power when in fact these are legitimations of restriction, regulation and disciplining' (Gibbons 1998: 38). Jameson (1991) has referred to postmodernism as the 'cultural logic of late capitalism', building initially on Mandel's *Late Capitalism* (1975), and latterly on Arrighi's *The Long Twentieth Century* (1994). What Jameson takes from Arrighi's work in particular is the notion that we are currently witnessing a stage of 'finance capitalism', indicative of an 'uncoupling' of the financial and productive circuits of capital and well documented (Ashley 1997), but also that, following Braudel, financial expansion of this type is always 'a sign of autumn'.

What Jameson (1998) seeks and purports to find, with this hint of crisis in the air, is a kind of correspondence between finance capitalism and postmodernism. Finance capital, he suggests, marks a form of 'deterritorialization' (after Deleuze and Guaterri 1984), heralding 'a play of monetary entities' which needs neither production nor consumption:

> which supremely, like cyberspace, can live on its own internal metabolism and circulate without any reference to an older type of content. But so do the narrativized image-fragments of a stereotypical postmodern language: suggesting a new cultural realm or dimension which is independent of the former real world, not because, as in the modern (or even romantic) period, culture withdrew from that real world into an autonomous space of art, but rather because the real world has already been suffused with it and colonized by it, so that it has no outside in terms of which it could be found lacking.
>
> (Jameson 1998: 161)

There is surely no need to search for a correspondence *of this sort* between finance capitalism and postmodern culture. But it is reasonable to suggest that, for all that a dialectical aspect to the relationship between the material and the 'semi-autonomous' cultural-aesthetic needs to be acknowledged, it is the former which, however inconspicuously it may do so, generally leads and prevails. In this context, postmodern contributions to medical sociology, notwithstanding any claims to originality (even if irrationally tendered), may carry heavy *ideological* baggage. This seems true, for example, of postmodern critiques of the postwar modernist 'social conscience' discourse on class-related health inequalities. In fact, such critiques may even serve further to distract appropriate attention from the repeated failures of (system-driven) (neo-)positivists in and around medical sociology to get to grips with health and inequalities (Scambler 1996: see Chapter 5).

The only addendum on the *methodological* at this stage is that, for all the – sometimes grotesque – hyperbole associated with substitute postmodern dealings with the social, an incidental serendipitous effect of the postmodern turn on medical sociology might yet be a freeing up or dereification of largely (neo-)positivist textbook methodological prescriptions. In the light of the complexity of the social world this is overdue. Certainly critical sociological research in an open system, drawing on retroductive and abductive inference to uncover generative mechanisms at the level of real social relations, requires a good deal more imagination, flexibility and triangulation (and, one is tempted to add, patience and modesty of aspiration) than has been associated with the use of orthodox methods.

Final notes

It is a considered premise of the analyses in this book that it is premature to write of postmodernity; that is, of a new social formation. The chapters that follow stress the continuities in relation to the material as a corrective to the recent preoccupation with discontinuity. The preference is to refer to high, over later, modernity. But there are grounds enough to speak of a postmodern turn, of a discernible cultural shift; and it seems churlish to avoid the gloss of 'postmodern culture'. There are two related qualifications, both to do with cultural rather than material continuity. First, it seems apparent that, at least in art, there is sufficient continuity or affinity between modernism – that is, the *avant garde* efforts of the late nineteenth and early twentieth centuries, like Surrealism and Dadaism – and postmodernism to make it tempting to categorize the latter as 'second-wave modernism'. And, second, postmodernism seems at least in part to be an expression or realization of the 'dark' side of modernity (Albrow 1996). Nietzsche, for example, can, and perhaps should, be read as a product of modernity rather than as an architect of the postmodern. For all his genius, the orthodox postmodern fabrication of him as a proto-typical opponent of modernist systems of order and domination is as ludicrous as it is disturbing (Appel 1999).

It might be noted too that medical sociology has been infused and influenced by the postmodern turn in a multiplicity of ways, some of them less than obvious. The number of explicitly postmodern contributions to medical sociology, like Fox's, has been limited. More contributions have benefited from the 'disinhibitions' consequent upon the postmodern turn, like many feminist analyses of the body. But another effect of the postmodern turn has been to undermine the rationally compelling evaluation of paradigms on offer, modernist as well as postmodern. This has given extended lease of life to paradigms/research programmes best regarded as 'degenerating' (Lakatos 1970).

3

Theorizing social change

The period of change that provides a focus for this book might be said to commence with the postmodern turn, although not all sociologists recognize significant social changes over this past generation. Runciman (1997), for example, finds such claims extravagant and unconvincing, preferring to highlight change at the beginning of the twentieth century. Not a few, at the other extreme, have announced the advent of a new social formation, postmodernity. Certainly most sociologists seem committed to the opinion that significant social change has indeed occurred, even if they remain dubious about over-excitable nomenclatures. Introducing their collection of comparative studies, *Continuity and Change in Contemporary Capitalism*, Kitschelt and colleagues (1999: 6) observe just how substantial the change has been – in relation, for example, to the kinds of material elements of the postmodern listed in Chapter 2 – even over the short time since the publication of Goldthorpe's (1984) parent collection on comparative political economy; 'in retrospect', they note, 'it is clear that the Goldthorpe volume gave us a snapshot of a situation that was rapidly changing.'

This chapter is concerned with these changes, affecting not just economy and state but lifeworld as well. In the opening section an outline is given of a critical realist perspective on social structure, relations and change; this provides a philosophical scaffolding to support the substantive theories introduced and defended thereafter and in subsequent chapters. The second section draws on the work of Habermas to 'frame' a general theory of contemporary change. And the third section starts the process of collating theory and empirical studies of change around the economy and state, constituting the system, and the private and public spheres, constituting the lifeworld.

Critical realism, ontology and social structure

It has become a kind of orthodoxy among philosophers and social theorists alike to broach what exists exclusively in terms of what can reasonably be said to be known about what exists; that is, to reduce ontology to epistemology. Bhaskar (1978) refers to this as the 'epistemic fallacy'. What unites 'realists' is the conviction that there exists a natural world independent of our perceptions of it; it stays even if people go. But what of the social world? There is less unity among realists here; and the social world can hardly stay if people go.

Bhaskar (1989a) formulates a 'transformational model of social activity and a 'relational model of society'. Distancing himself from what he sees as Durkheim's 'reification' on the one hand, and Weber's 'voluntarism' on the other, Bhaskar (1989a: 76) writes: 'society does not exist independently of conscious human activity (the error of reification). But it is not the product of the latter (the error of voluntarism).' In fact, there is a real ontological difference, if also a mutual ontological dependence, between *people* and *society*, the latter being defined, after Marx, in terms of a 'network of relations' (hence the relational model of society): 'people are not relations, societies are not conscious agents' (Collier 1994: 147). Bhaskar (1989a: 34–5) again: 'society is both the ever-present *condition* (material cause) and the continually reproduced outcome of human agency. And praxis is both work, that is, conscious *production*, and (normally unconscious) *reproduction* of the conditions of production, that is society. One could refer to the former as the *duality of structure*, and the latter as the *duality of praxis*.'

People do not work to reproduce capitalism any more than they marry to sustain the nuclear family. Yet 'it is nevertheless the unintended consequence (and inexorable result) of, as it is also a necessary condition for, their activity. Moreover, when social forms change, the explanation will not normally lie in the desires of agents to change them that way, though as a very important theoretical and political limit, it may do so' (Bhaskar 1989a: 35).

In another of his books, Bhaskar (1989b: 81) gives a useful, if typically dense, summary statement of the connection between the transformational model of social activity and the relational model of society. It is worth quoting at some length:

> the relational conception does not of course deny that factories and books are social forms. But it maintains that there being social, as distinct from (or rather in addition to) material, objects, consists only in the relationships between persons or between such relationships and nature that such objects causally presuppose or entail. The *social* conditions for the structures that govern the substantive activities of transformation in which human beings engage (and which constitute the immediate explanation of these activities) can thus only be relations of various kinds: between people and each other, their products, their activities, nature and themselves. If social activity is to be given a social explanation it is in this

nexus that it must be found. It is thus in the enduring relations presupposed by, rather than the actual complex motley of, particular social forms, that on this conception, sociology's theoretical interests lies.

Society as the condition of action and society as its outcome both belong to the subject matter of sociology. And society as an object of enquiry is necessarily 'theoretical' in the sense that it is necessarily unperceivable: it cannot be empirically identified independently of its effects. In this respect it is no different from many of the objects of natural scientific enquiry. However, it does differ in another respect: society not only cannot be identified independently of its effects, but it does not *exist* independently of them either (Bhaskar 1989b: 82).

It does not follow that sociology cannot be as scientific as the natural sciences, but it can only be scientific 'in *ways* which are as *different* from the latter as they are specific to the nature of societies' (Bhaskar 1994: 93). Crucially, the objects of sociological enquiry only manifest themselves in 'open systems'; that is, in systems where the 'invariant empirical regularities' sought after by (neo-)positivists do not obtain. This means that sociology, due to an absence of spontaneously occurring 'closures', and the impossibility of creating them (for example through laboratory experiments), is denied, in principle, decisive test situations for its theories. This, in turn, means that the criteria for the rational confirmation and rejection of theories in sociology cannot be *predictive*, but must instead be *exclusively explanatory* (Bhaskar 1989b: 83).

It may not be possible to create artificially closed systems in sociology, but this does not mean that the identification of 'epistemically significant non-random patterns or results' cannot provide the 'empirical controls and contrasts' that laboratory experimentation affords in the natural sciences. Lawson (1997) demonstrates this in his discussion of the significance of demi-regularities for genuinely empirical, as opposed to empiricist, research (for an elaboration, see the consideration of health inequalities in Chapter 5). An awareness of what is often termed 'ontological stratification' is required. Natural and social worlds alike are not composed merely of events (the actual) and experiences (the empirical), but also of underlying generative mechanisms (the real) that exist, independently of whether they are detected, and govern or facilitate events (see Chapter 1).

Bhaskar claims Marx as a pioneer and ally here. Desai (1991: 28) makes the essential point well with reference to Chapter 6 in Volume 1 of *Capital* (on 'buying and selling of labour power'). There is an observable or phenomenal level at which exchange relations are judicially equal and voluntarily contractual. But it is necessary to penetrate to 'the underlying non-observable structural/*real* level to unmask the unequal exploitative class relations' (emphasis added). Reality for Marx is in this sense not directly observable. Moreover, 'reality may be distorted; it may be inverted at the phenomenal level. Thus prices are observable and values are not; exchange is equal but production and extraction of surplus value are unequal. This implies that merely looking at observable facts may be seriously misleading. Sometimes this objection is put as saying that one must not be empiricist.' Desai too notes the difference between empiricist and empirical research: 'good empirical work looks precisely for the interaction of theory and data in a complex dialectical way.' Bhaskar (1998: xv) also contends that the fact that social life is pre-interpreted provides a 'ready-made starting point' for the social sciences. However, as he importantly stresses, 'there are no grounds for treating these data as exhaustive of the subject matter of social science, as incorrigible or their operation as non-causal.' Rejecting Humean causality is a first step in allowing us to see reasons as causes, 'but causes which may, for instance, be rationalizations'.

Critical theory: the decoupling of system and lifeworld

The critical sociology espoused in this volume is informed not only by critical realism, but also by Frankfurt critical theory, especially as developed by Habermas. Habermas is as sensitive to the complex issues epitomized in the dichotomies of agency/structure and lifeworld/system as Bhaskar. Sitton (1996: 168) even suggests that the overriding goal of his theoretical endeavours has been to find a way of combining the two leading approaches to social theory, namely 'the perspective that analyzes society as a meaningful whole for its participants . . . and the perspective that analyzes society as a system that is stabilized behind the backs of the participants.' What Habermas seeks and arguably accomplishes is a theoretical synthesis formed from the insights of the modernist paradigm of interactionism and phenomenology, strong on agency and lifeworld, on the one hand, and conflict theory and structural-functionalism, strong on structure and system, on the other.

Habermas has consistently declared himself to be a Marxist. He has long regarded a credible reconstruction of Marx's historical materialism as a long-term goal, although others have diagnosed a progressive distancing from Marxian orthodoxy and a revised project to 'replace' rather than reconstruct historical materialism (see Rockmore 1989). Outhwaite (1994: 17) defines Habermas's relationship to Marxism as one of 'positive critique'. Be that as it may, from his earliest works Habermas distinguishes between *labour* and *interaction*, charging Marx, as well as Weber and his own mentors at Frankfurt, with a fixation on the former and a fateful neglect of the latter. In the case of Marxian theory, what he takes to be the reduction of interaction (or *communicative action*; that is, action oriented to understanding) to labour (or *strategic action*; that is, action oriented to success) not only dramatically inhibits the scope for the sociological analysis of modernity, but eliminates any potential to ground an acceptable reconstructed project of human emancipation. Habermas (1986: 169) writes: 'to set free the technical forces of production . . . is not identical with the development of moral relationships in an interaction free of domination . . . *Liberation from hunger and misery* does not necessarily converge with *liberation from servitude and degradation*; for there is no automatic developmental relation between labour and interaction' (see Scambler 2001).

One of the major themes running through *Theory of Communicative Action* (Habermas 1984, 1987) involves a focus on the action orientations of society's members, on the one hand, and a focus on how the action consequences are coordinated without necessitating the will or consciousness of the actors, on the other. And this gives rise to the distinction between the *lifeworld*, based on social integration, and the *system*, based on system integration. Habermas's theorization of the lifeworld draws liberally on work from the paradigms of interactionism and phenomenology, and his theorization of the system adapts contributions from the paradigms of conflict theory and structural-functionalism; the result is an invigorating critical synthesis.

The lifeworld does not submit to easy definition. Drawing on the phenomenology of Husserl and Schutz and the interactionism of Mead, Blumer, Strauss and others, Habermas defines it as the 'symbolically prestructured nexus of social interaction that arises in conjunction with the mutually shared interpretations of their situation by social actors'; it functions as an 'indispensable correlate' of his notion of communicative action (Baynes 1990: 57). The lifeworld cannot be 'known' since it serves as the vehicle of knowing. Individuals can no more step outside their lifeworld than they can their language. However, as Sitton (1996: 169) notes, 'although the lifeworld as a whole can never be placed in question, elements of the lifeworld can be and are placed in doubt. In these cases the element is "thematized", made subject to argument as the participants attempt to re-establish their mutual definition of the situation, a pre-requisite for successful cooperation.' Thus the lifeworld can be reproduced through communicative action, but not through instrumental or strategic action. The lifeworld, as Habermas subsequently argues, is the medium, or 'symbolic space' within which culture, social integration and personality are sustained and reproduced (Thompson 1984).

The system has to do with material rather than symbolic reproduction and is characterized by strategic rather than communicative action. Habermas maintains, in a formulation that resonates with Parsons, that social differentiation has delivered four subsystems: the *economy*, the *state*, the *public sphere* and the *private sphere*. Moreover, there has been a fundamental 'uncoupling' between the economy and state, which constitute the system, and the public and private spheres, which constitute the lifeworld. These subsystems are interdependent: each is specialized in terms of what it produces but is dependent on the others for what it does not produce. The economy produces *money*, the state *power*, the public sphere *influence* and the private sphere *commitment*. The products or *media* are traded between subsystems. Crook and colleagues (1992: 28) put it succinctly: 'the economy relies on the state to establish such legal economic institutions as private property and contract, on the public lifeworld to influence consumption patterns, and on the private lifeworld to provide a committed labour force, and itself sends money into each other subsystem.'

The (steering) media of the subsystems are not equivalent in their capacities. With the progressive uncoupling of system and lifeworld, the media, and thus subsystems, of the former come to dominate the latter. Habermas writes in this connection of the 'colonization of the lifeworld'. In a manner owing much to the Weberian theme of rationalization and the Marxian theme of commodification, the lifeworld becomes colonized, 'that is increasingly state administered ("juridified") and commercialized. Possibilities for communicative action in the lifeworld become attenuated as social participation becomes hyper-rationalized in terms of immediate returns. Participants encounter each other as legal entities and as parties to contracts rather than as thinking and acting subjects' (Crook *et al.* 1992: 28). System rationalization has outstripped the rationalization of the lifeworld: in other words, Western rationalization has been 'selective'.

Habermas distances himself from the 'iron cage' pessimism of Weber and others. In fact he accuses Weber of treating the rationalization that has occurred in the Occident as inevitable when it was contingent and selective. Weber, in sum, is charged with conflating the *dynamic* and the *logic* of development. Habermas maintains that the logic of development allows for further rationalization of the lifeworld; that is, for an extension of the scope for communicative action and communicative rationality, and, it follows, for lifeworld 'decolonization'. The most likely present agents of decolonization, and of a reconstructed project of modernity, are the 'new' social movements, as opposed to the 'old' class-based movements. But Habermas sees little prospect of headway in the short term.

We have seen that, like Bhaskar, Habermas defines himself as in the Marxian tradition. So what is left of Marx in his work (Love 1995; and see Scambler 2001)? The capitalist economy, he argues, must be seen as more than an arena within which labour is subordinated and exploited (i.e. in terms of classes). Marx did not distinguish between the level of system differentiation attained in modernity and the class-specific forms in which it has been institutionalized. 'Marx is convinced *a priori* that in capital he has before him *nothing more* than the mystified form of a class relation. This interpretation excludes from the start the question of whether the systematic interconnection of the capitalist economy and the modern state administration do not also represent a higher and evolutionary advantageous level of integration by comparison to traditional societies' (Habermas 1987: 339). The emergence of the discrete media-steered subsystems of the economy and state, Habermas contends, not only increases material reproduction, but also reduces the burden of the processes of communication of a detraditionalized lifeworld.

The institutionalization of 'delinguistified' media such as money and power 'simplifies' social interaction across many spheres of life by reducing the conditions necessary for coordinating action. Thus prices, for example, representing the medium of money, can transmit information that 'automatically' coordinates the interactions of strategically acting individuals or businesses.

Habermas argues that the economic subsystem is constituted by formal law. Within it, individuals are free to act strategically in accordance with legal definitions which exclude other normative considerations: the law marks off domains of 'norm-free sociality'. The economic subsystem procures the performances required for its functioning via the legal institution of the labour contract. Labour has to be 'monetarized' because the economic subsytem, *qua* subsystem – and there is more than a hint of the systems theory of Luhmann (1982, 1995; see Scambler 1998c) here – 'can relate to its environment only via its own medium', money (Habermas 1987: 292). This monetarization of labour permits the functioning of the subsystem, which delivers goods and services to be exchanged for monetary demand.

Habermas (1987) recognizes that the economy is 'crisis-ridden' or subject to 'disequilibria'. Disequilibria are to be expected in a subsystem adapting to changing environments. In a capitalist economy these disequilibria are handled by another subsystem, the state; that is, by a bureaucratized administration steered by the medium of power.

Why have there been excesses of system rationalization and increasing lifeworld colonization? Why, to put it differently, have the subsytems of economy and state trespassed beyond what is strictly necessary for the institutionalization of money and power? Like Offe (1985a), Habermas (1987) maintains that the welfare state emerged to fill in the 'functional gaps' of the capitalist economy caused by the economic disequilibria of 'crisis-ridden growth', such as business cycles and paucity of infrastructural investment. The welfare state also occurred because of the potential for class struggle over distribution. This potential is blocked by a variety of corporatist devices resulting in wage scales set through bargaining mediated by the state, and by the direct state provision of use-values like health care. In this way 'the social antagonism bred by private disposition over the means of producing social wealth increasingly loses its structure-forming power for the lifeworld of social groups, although it does remain constitutive for the structure of the economic system' (Habermas 1987: 348). With the steady rise in standard of living, plus other state-sponsored protections from system imperatives, 'conflicts over distribution also lose their explosive power' (Habermas 1987: 349–50).

The rising standard of living and protective policies of the welfare state reduce the salience of the role of employee and enhance that of consumer. In this way, in Sitton's (1996: 173) phrase, 'class structuration in the lifeworld is obliterated'. McCarthy (1984: xix) refers here to 'the disappearance of the proletariat into the pores of consumer society'. The welfare state also transforms citizens into clients. The subsystem of the state requires legitimation, which it attains in the form of mass loyalty by providing use-values and other services that are not forthcoming from the economic subsystem that operates through exchange values. The state 'thereby transforms citizens into clients responding to legally anchored power. Habermas even refers to this clientalization of citizens as the "model case" of "colonization"' (Sitton 1996: 173–4). This is Habermas's version of the 'welfare state compromise' that has characterized postwar advanced capitalist societies.

Habermas maintains that the continued effectiveness of the welfare state compromise remains dependent on the growth of both market and welfare state. This growth results in the expansion and increasing density of the 'monetary-bureaucratic complex'. This happens where 'socially integrated contexts of life are redefined around the roles of consumer and client and assimilated to systematically integrated domains of action' (Habermas 1987: 351). Further colonization of this sort is possible, and resistance weak, because the lifeworld has been detraditionalized; its rationality potentials are 'encapsulated' in expert cultures; and it lacks the cultural resources, mobilized by an intact public sphere, to halt the intrusions of media-steering. As a consequence, 'phenomena of alienation and the unsettling of collective identity emerge' (Habermas 1987: 386).

Habermas continues to insist that the economic subsystem retains its primacy for social evolution; but he maintains too that its problems are manifested elsewhere: 'I still explain these pathologies ("loss of meaning, anomic conditions, psychopathologies") by referring to the mechanisms driving capitalism forward, namely economic growth, but I assess them in terms of the systematically induced predominance of economic and bureaucratic, indeed of all cognitive-instrumental forms of rationality with a one-sided or "alienated" everyday communicative practice' (Habermas 1992b: 250). 'Pathologies' displace social crisis.

Ultimately, for Habermas, the classical socialist project has to be amended. The importance of media-steered subsystems for social evolution has to be accepted. Sitton (1996: 71) again: 'a further rationalized lifeworld – one in which culture, social order and socialization are increasingly based on a consensus achieved through reasoned discourse rather than on traditional understandings – requires an unburdening of social coordination that can only be actualized by maintaining areas of social interaction steered not by communicative action but by media-steered subsystems.' This is an issue dealt with in depth in Chapter 7.

There is much in Habermas's reformulations of Marx, system/lifeworld dichotomy and notions of selective rationalization and lifeworld colonization which is helpful. But there are also weaknesses and lacunae, some of which will become apparent in the next section, which is focused on key changes within and across the four subsystems of economy, state, private sphere and public sphere.

Changes in system and lifeworld

The argument in this section touches on many of the material, and some of the cultural-aesthetic, elements of the postmodern turn listed in Chapter 2, although the term high modernity, indicating change within the existing social formation, is preferred to that of postmodernity, which would indicate a transition to a new social formation. Habermas's theoretically grounded, analytic distinctions between the subsytems of system and lifeworld frame the argument (but not, I hope, to the extent of inhibiting it).

Economy and state

It has become commonplace for sociologists to supplement their accounts of a historical progression from 'liberal' capitalism (characterized by a 'facilitative' state) to 'organized' capitalism (characterized by an 'interventionist' state) with assertions of a more recent shift to 'disorganized' capitalism (with states typically remaining more interventionist than facilitative) (Offe 1985a; Lash and Urry 1987). Habermas is one of many to chart the growth of welfare state interventionism consequent upon the progression from liberal to organized capitalism, and to note that this functioned to take the sting out of conflicts of class; to supply those use values and other services required for the reproduction of capitalist activity but beyond the capacity of the economy itself to provide; and, increasingly, to restructure and support private capital. The disorganization of capitalist production can be dated – politically at least – from the 1970s, from which time nation-states started to dismantle their interventionist and planning structures and to promote the 'deregulation' of many areas of economic activity.

Scott (1986, 1997: 264–5) notes that while state expenditure during organized capitalism was associated with an increase in the productivity of capital, a portion of this productivity was (and is) required to finance current and future state expenditure, 'and unless private productivity grows along with the growth of state expenditure there will be a decline in the rate of capital accumulation . . . State expenditure becomes a necessary support for private capital that nevertheless poses problems for private profitability and so makes further public expenditure more difficult to finance.' The expansion of state intervention and collective provision also results in political dislocations within the state itself. To cite Habermas (1976) once more, economic 'crisis tendencies' do not vanish with welfare statism but instead become displaced into the state's own structure. States seek to accommodate their budgetary problems through regulatory policies, but in a private enterprise system there are determinate limits to state power. Scott (1997: 265) again: 'rather than securing an independent and autonomous policy or one that is in the "general interest" of capital, states are likely to pursue policies that reflect a balance of power among the various capitalist interests represented within their agencies. Consensual state policies, to the extent that they occur, are consequences of the dominance of particular fractions of capital within the state apparatus.'

In the stage of disorganized capitalism, born out of what Sklair (1998a: 152) calls the 'devastation of the 1970s', the economies of nation-states have become disarticulated: in particular, economic interests have become more globalized. Capitalist families and capitalist enterprises alike are 'locked into a globalized circus of capital and investment' no longer organized around distinctively national economies (Scott 1997: 298). That globalization has occurred over the past generation seems beyond dispute, although there exist confirmed 'sceptics' as well as, at the other extreme, 'hyperglobalizers' (Giddens's 'geewhizzers': see Giddens and Hutton 2000). In their thorough review of the evidence on global production networks, Held *et al.* (1999) testify to the pre-eminence of multi- or transnational corporations in world output, trade, investment and technology transfer. Around 53,000 transnational corporations account for between 20 and 30 per cent of world output, and up to 70 per cent of world trade.

Contrary to the sceptics, multinational corporations are not simply 'national firms with international operations', nor are they, as the hyperglobalizers argue, 'footloose corporations' which wander the globe in search of maximum profits . . . Rather multinational corporations play a much more central role in the operation of the world economy than in the past and they figure prominently in organizing extensive and intensive transnational networks of coordinated production and distribution that are historically unique.

(Held *et al*. 1999: 282)

Small and medium-sized enterprises too are increasingly engaged in globalized business.

The story of global *finance* is even more remarkable. The same authors document an exponential growth in global finance since the 1970s, such that the extensity, intensity, velocity and impact of global financial flows and networks are unprecedented. The eras of the classical Gold Standard and of Bretton Woods are long gone. 'More currencies, more diverse and complex financial assets are traded more frequently, at great speed, and in substantially greater volumes than in any previous historical epoch. The sheer magnitude of capital movements, relative to either global or national output and trade, is unique' (Held *et al*. 1999: 235). With this has come a highly institutionalized infrastructure permitting 'twenty-four-hour real-time cross-border financial trading'. Whereas, historically, trading in foreign exchange was a result of international trade, now trade accounts for only 2 per cent of global currency movements. Global financial flows have a life of their own: largely liquid, they are attracted by short-term speculative gains. Besides currency trade, new financial instruments such as bonds, mutual funds, global depository receipts and derivatives have emerged as contributors to the globalization of finance (see Singh 1999). Moreover, as Polito expresses it to Hobsbawm (see Hobsbawm 1999: 78), financial markets can occasion 'irrational and domino-effect reactions' with potential to 'transform part of the world into a gigantic financial crash of global proportions, in the flicker of an eyelid.'

Some have argued that as relations of class have also become more global, national capitalist classes have become increasingly fragmented (e.g. Arrighi *et al*. 1989). Others, like Sklair (1995, 1998a, 2001), have asked whether it is appropriate now to refer to a *transnational capitalist class*. Sklair's (1998a: 136) neo-Marxist global system theory is rooted in the notion of transnational practices; that is, 'practices that are abstracted from national class systems in that they cross state boundaries and do not necessarily originate with state agencies or actors.' He argues that the dominating forces of global capitalism are the dominating forces of the global system, adding that the building blocks of this theory – in the economic, political and cultural-ideological spheres respectively – are the transnational corporations, an embryonic transnational capitalist class, and the culture-ideology of consumerism. He divides the transnational capitalist class analytically into four principal constituents: the executives of transnational corporations, globalizing bureaucrats, globalizing politicians and professionals and consumerist elites. His thesis is that those who prevail in these groups, taken together, constitute a 'global power elite, ruling class or inner circle in the sense that these terms have been used to characterize the class structures of specific countries' (see Domhoff 1967; Useem 1984; Scott 1996; Sklair 1998a: 137).

Scott (1997: 313) suggests that it is premature of Sklair to deploy concepts like 'transnational capitalist class' and 'global power elite'. For all his (Weberian) caution, however, Scott himself reveals that, despite the transition from organized to disorganized capitalism, propertied families remain a powerful economic and political force; these families, he attests, 'are far from having their privileges usurped by upwardly mobile career managers' (see also Haseler 2000). And he concludes:

> wealthy families have diversified their income-earning assets, and many now participate in strategic control on the basis of mechanisms other than direct inheritance of a place in the family firm. In the stage of disorganized capitalism . . . the members of this class have become involved in the more extensive transnational economic practices that are disarticulating their national economies. National capitalist classes have themselves become more fragmented and 'disorganized', and their futures may – though this is, as yet, unclear – involve the formation of a global capitalist class.

The role of Britain's 'strongly globalized capitalist-executive' will be explored in detail in relation to issues of health and healing in subsequent chapters.

Elsewhere, Scott (1991) maintains that state power in Britain has a class character. Adopting Therborn's (1978: 144) phrasing, state power has a class character when what is accomplished through the apparatus of the state 'positively acts upon the (re-)production of the mode of production, of which the class in question is the dominant bearer.' A state operates in the interests of a capitalist class, Scott (1991: 139) writes, 'when its activities reinforce the conditions for the reproduction of that class and it fails to act in ways which undermine these conditions.' Britain, he concludes in his *Who Rules Britain?* (1991), is ruled by a 'capitalist class whose economic dominance is sustained by the operations of the state and whose members are disproportionately represented in the power elite which rules the state apparatus' (for further detail, see Monbiot 2000).

The claim that there now exists an embryonic transnational capitalist class has often been linked with the view that the nation-state is 'in decline'. Jessop (1994a) refers to the post-Keynesian and post-Fordist, 'hollowed out', Schumpeterian workfare state typical of disorganized capitalism. But the reality is more complex. Not all nation-states share the same properties. Coates (2000: 9–10), for example, distinguishes between: the 'market-led' capitalism of countries like the USA and, since 1979 at least, Britain ('Anglo-Saxon capitalism'), in which decisions on capital accumulation are largely left to private companies; the 'state-led' capitalism of countries like Japan and South Korea ('Asian capitalism'), where decisions on accumulation are taken by private companies but in close liaison with public agencies; and the 'negoti-ated' or 'consensual' capitalism of the Scandinavian countries and (West) Germany ('European welfare capitalism'), where decisions on accumulation are taken in the context of strong worker rights and welfare provision.

Weiss (1999) similarly discriminates among nation-states, placing them on a continuum of 'managed openness'. Echoing Coates's comments on Anglo-Saxon capitalism, Weiss (1998: 3) observes that 'if American and British analyses generally project passive or ineffectual states as victims of external forces, this is because their authors daily confront such a reality: that is to say, political institutions with weak capacities for *domestic* adjustment strategies.' It is unfortunate, she adds, that 'state denial' has been peddled with quite such enthusiasm and lack of subtlety by English-speaking social scientists. The ability of nation-states to adapt to globalization will, she predicts, heighten rather than diminish differences in 'state capacity' over the next generation. The applicability of such analyses to Britain, and the changing role of Britain's 'weakly globalized power elite' in relation to its strongly globalized capitalist-executive, will be addressed in the context of health and health care in Chapters 4 and 5.

Two phenomena routinely associated with the newly globalizing economy – arguably overseen by an embryonic transnational capitalist class – and putative state decline ought at least to be mentioned here, although they too will be analysed more comprehensively later, namely the so-called 'crisis of welfare statism' (see Chapter 4) and the 'new inequality' (see Chapter 5).

The state production of welfare has been a conspicuous source of political concern in all developed societies since 1970; and in almost all far-reaching welfare reforms have occurred, notably in Britain. Neo-liberal political regimes, like Britain's Hayek-educated 'Thatcherite' governments from the 1980s onwards, 'driven by the conviction that markets are almost always more efficient than states, that public-sector workers shielded from effective competition will always conspire against consumers and that overall levels of taxation are too high, have sought to address the problem of cost by extending market disciplines to state welfare activity' (Pierson 1996: 101). Predictably, these reforms have failed to address deepening social inequalities (except, that is, with ideological sophistry), and have almost certainly contributed to them.

Disorganized capitalism has been linked with growing social inequality. In terms of the distribution of income and wealth in Britain, Atkinson (2000: 376) recognizes the advent of the first Thatcher government as a 'turning point', identifying 'distinct phases' in the two decades after 1979: 'widening inequality arising from earnings and an increased proportion of families with-out work up to the mid-1980s, followed by a more rapid rise in inequality associated with a reduction in redistribution.' And Britain has not been alone (see Atkinson's *Poverty in Europe* (1998), in which he stresses the significance of the relations between poverty, unemployment and the notion of social exclusion).

The deteriorating circumstances of the socially excluded who constitute what is (arguably unadvisedly) termed an 'underclass' have been well documented.

Less investigated and discussed are the members of what Haseler (2000) (perhaps also unadvisedly) calls the new, and largely global, *overclass*. Those in this category comprise the 'super-' or 'mega-rich'. And the statistics are truly staggering. According to the *Sunday Times* Rich List 2000, the world's richest man, Bill Gates (software, Microsoft), is worth £53.12 billion. Twenty-seven of the world's richest 50 people are American (i.e. American passport holders); Britain's richest, Hans Rausing (packaging), just misses the top 50 on £4 billion (Beresford and Boyd 2000). Haseler (2000: 9) reports that the combined wealth of the world's super-rich – that is, those worth US\$1 million or more – was around US\$17 trillion in 1997, more than double the gross national product of the USA. It will be argued later that it is vital to understand the activities of the (global) rich, whom Bauman (1998a: 9) aptly describes as 'absentee landlords, mark II' (characterized by a diminishing sense of national obligation – 'the corporation is an ingenious device for acquiring rights and shedding responsibilities': Monbiot 2000: 11), if we are to explain the durability and deepening of (national) inequalities.

Private and public spheres

As we have seen, Habermas (1987) argues that in what he calls 'economically constituted class societies' system and lifeworld have become uncoupled. From the perspective of the system, the subsystem of the economy 'exchanges wages against labour power and goods and services against consumer demands'; and the subsytem of the state 'exchanges organizational achievements against taxes and political decisions against mass loyalty.' Complementary lifeworld roles crystallized around these exchanges are those of employee and consumer (in relation to the economy) and client and citizen (in relation to the state). Actors who fulfil the roles of employee and client 'have to free themselves from lifeworld contexts and adapt to formally organized realms of action. The roles are juridically defined.' This does not apply, however, to actors *qua* consumers and citizens (i.e. participants in the formation of public opinion). 'The relevant juridical norms do not define these roles but only provide the scope, within which they can take shape on the basis of preferences and value orientations which have been formed in the private and public realm of the lifeworld. These cannot be "bought" as labour power or "raised" as taxes' (Brand 1990: 58–9).

But what is left for the lifeworld? Its complementary private and public spheres are limited to social integration. The institutional core of the private sphere, according to Habermas, is the *nuclear family*, the focus no longer for economic tasks but for socialization; and the institutional core of the public sphere is to be found in the *culture industry*, the *press* and the *mass media*.

It is of course easier to distinguish analytically between system and lifeworld, together with their respective subsystems and media, than it is to 'recognize' them in the social world. This is in part a function of selective rationalization and lifeworld colonization. Habermas (1987: 325) writes:

To the degree that the economic system subjects the life-forms of private households and the life conduct of consumers and employees to its imperatives, consumerism and possessive individualism, motives of performance, and competition gain the force to shape behaviour. The communicative practice of everyday life is one-sidedly rationalized into a utilitarian life-style; this media-induced shift to purposive-rational action orientations calls forth the reaction of a hedonism freed from the pressures of rationality . . . As the private sphere is undermined and eroded by the economic system, so too is the public sphere by the administrative system. The bureaucratic disempowering and desiccation of spontaneous processes of opinion- and will-formation expands the scope for engineering mass loyalty and makes it easier to uncouple political decision-making from concrete, identity-forming contexts of life.

As far as the private sphere is concerned, socio-demographic changes bearing on the nuclear family unit have been monitored by (neo-)positivist forms of social accounting. And the parameters are important. The contrast between the start and finish of the twentieth century in terms of households and families is striking and worth rehearsing briefly (see Jackson 1999). Britain had only just begun its fertility transition by 1900. Average family size was almost four children. Expectations of life at birth were about 50. Population size was (still) growing at a rate of about 1 per cent per annum; almost 30 per cent of the population were aged under 15, and those over 65 barely numbered 5 per cent. Poor infant survival and child and maternal welfare remained problematic. Socio-economic differences in birth and death were beginning to be measured and to cause concern. 'Husbandry servants' had gone, but apart from this household structures had not decisively broken with the pattern of previous centuries. Widowhood was common, but illegitimacy was exceptional and declining; divorce was all but unknown; and cohabitation was 'the exclusive and rare pursuit of the lowest social classes and of the more adventurous radicals and bohemians' (Coleman 2000: 85).

Things were very different in 2000 (see McCrae 1999). Problems of high infant and child mortality had been all but resolved, with 98 per cent of children now being expected to survive to the age of 50. By 1997, life expectancy at birth was approaching 75 years for men and 80 years for women (ONS 2000a: 117). A century of low fertility has led to worries about aged dependency rather than large families. If fertility is further reduced from its current level of 1.7 then early twentieth-century concerns over low birth rates could be revived. Coleman (2000: 86) also highlights the fact that while households have become 'smaller and simpler', they have also become 'more varied and disrupted'. Britain, he suggests, has become 'an enthusiastic participant in the "second demographic transition", becoming Europe's leader in divorce and lone-parent families.' In European terms, Britain is now exceptional in respect of high teenage births, lone-parent families and divorce; and it also shows upward trends in immigration and asylum-seeking (Coleman and Chandola 1999).

Most of these socio-demographic shifts have occurred gradually and/or cannot be accounted for in terms of the transition to global or disorganized capitalism and/or to a postmodern culture. Some changes, however, coincide quite closely with the period of focus of this volume. At the time of publication of the first edition of *Social Trends* in 1970, two-thirds of single-person households comprised people over pensionable age. By 1998–9 this proportion had fallen to about half. The increasing proportion of one-person households involving people under pensionable age reflects the decline in marriage, an increase in the average age at marriage and the rise in the rate of separation and divorce (ONS 2000b: 34).

Since the early 1960s too there has been a decline in the proportion of 'traditional' nuclear households in Britain. In 1961, 38 per cent of households conformed to this type, but by 1998–9 this had decreased to 23 per cent. The proportion of lone-parent households with dependent children, however, almost trebled over this same period, reaching 7 per cent of all households in 1998–9. In 1971, 7 per cent of families with dependent children were lone-mother families; by 1998–9 this had trebled to 22 per cent. By 1998–9, 23 per cent of dependent children lived in lone-parent families. Before the mid-1980s, it seems, the rise in lone-parenthood was mostly due to divorce, but since then single lone-motherhood (i.e. never married, non-cohabiting women with children) has grown at a faster rate (ONS 2000b: 35).

The rate of cohabitation has also increased significantly over this period. Only 2 per cent of women who married in the late 1960s had lived with their future spouses before marriage; by the early 1990s more first marriages were preceded by cohabitation than not. There has also been an increase in the numbers of people cohabiting, irrespective of whether or not the cohabitation led to marriage. The peak age for cohabiting for women in 1998–9 was 25–29, with 39 per cent of women cohabiting, while for men it was 30–34, with 44 per cent of men cohabiting (ONS 2000b: 40).

These figures are suggestive of quite rapid change in household and family composition. There are a number of themes consonant with them which might be signposted. The first of these concerns changes in *gender relations*. These are, as Walby (1990, 1997) shows, extremely complex. Moreover, the contrast between private and public spheres itself has strong negative connotations for feminists. It is sufficient for now to record evidence both of 'convergence' and of 'polarization' (Walby 1997). Convergence between genders is occurring among some younger people as a result of improved access for some young women to education and the labour market. Among women, polarization is occurring 'between those, typically younger, educated and employed, who engage in new patterns of gender relations somewhat convergent with those of men, and those, particularly disadvantaged women, typically older and less educated, who built their life trajectories around patterns of private patriarchy.' At the tail end of a comment on the trend towards lone-mother families, Walby (1997: 3) writes: 'women are more independent from men, but poorer'. It remains generally true that patriarchal relations which long antedated – but have been 'adapted' during each of

– capitalism's liberal, organized and disorganized stages continue to oppress or constrain women across the subsystems of economy and state and in both the private and public spheres of the lifeworld.

A second theme is that of *individualization*. Beck and Beck-Gernsheim (1995: 76) have argued that an extended process of individualization has characterized high modernity. They identify three general historical phases: in the first the family was essentially an economic unit, with neither partner possessing an individual biography; in the second men were expected to take the initiative in organizing their own lives, family cohesion remaining intact at the expense of women's rights; and in the third, roughly since the 1960s, both men and women have been faced with 'the blessings and burdens of making a life of their own'. Beck and Beck-Gernsheim (1995: 61–2) write: 'we are witnessing a new period in the history of women, and therefore in the history of men and women. Now for the first time two people falling in love find themselves both subject to the opportunities and hindrances of a biography designed by themselves.' This is an era of 'do-it-yourself-biography' (Berger *et al.* 1973). Beck and Beck-Gernsheim maintain that this accent on individual biography, part and parcel of a detraditionalized culture often designated postmodern, militates against stable, monogamous, loving relationships (paradoxically, at a time when individuals are searching ever more anxiously for stability in precisely such partnerships).

The third theme acknowledges something of a *sexual revolution* during this same period. Giddens (1992) suggests this would have been unthinkable without the creation of what he calls 'plastic sexuality'. This refers to sexuality unharnessed from any intrinsic relation to reproduction. Together with plastic sexuality, of course, phenomena like the ready availability of contraception and divorce should also be noted. These interconnected themes of gender relations, individualization and plastic sexuality suggest a new fluidity and dynamic around the 'core institution' of the private sphere.

The concepts of 'civil society' and 'public sphere' are highly fashionable, the more so since the implosion of the Soviet Union in 1989, but tend to be used as synonyms and with imprecision. Habermas (1996: 367) distinguishes them. For him civil society exists at the interface of the private and public spheres of the lifeworld. It consists of those 'more or less spontaneously emergent associations, organizations and movements that, attuned to how societal problems resonate in the private life spheres, distil and transmit such reactions in amplified form to the public sphere.' Elsewhere it has been suggested that it may be helpful to distinguish further between two 'sectors' of civil society (Scambler and Martin 2001). What might be called the *enabling sector* of civil society is located in, or derives its impetus from, the private sphere. It is within the enabling sector that – as part and parcel of the ordinary everyday intercourse of the lifeworld (and typically in what Oldenberg (1997) has analysed as informal meeting, or 'third', places) – issues of potential concern arise and are often identified. The protest sector of civil society is located in, or is directed towards, the public sphere. It is within the *protest sector* that people come together, or are mobilized, in networks, campaign groups, (new) social movements and other forms of association in pursuit of influence for purposeful change (third places often being important here too) (see Chapter 7).

The public sphere generates influence, a conception Habermas took over from Parsons. It is a 'warning system' with 'sensors' that operate throughout society. From a vantage point of democracy, the public sphere must, additionally, 'amplify the pressure of problems, that is, not only detect and identify problems but also convincingly and *influentially* thematize them, furnish them with possible solutions, and dramatize them in such a way that they are taken up and dealt with by parliamentary complexes' (Habermas 1996: 359). Political influence supported by public opinion is only translated into political power – that is, 'into potential for rendering binding decisions' – when it affects the behaviour of voters, legislators, officials and so on.

The 'bourgeois' public sphere first emerged in eighteenth-century Europe (Habermas 1989c). It was not part of the state but, on the contrary, a sphere in which activities of the state might be confronted and criticized. 'The medium of this confrontation was itself significant: it was the public use of reason, as articulated by private individuals engaged in argument that was *in principle* open and unconstrained' (Thompson 1993: 176). While the concepts of civil society and public sphere have traditionally been counterposed to the state, Habermas and others distinguish them too from the economy (see Cohen and Arato 1992). However, the nascent bourgeois (white, European, male) public sphere came fairly rapidly to be dominated 'by mass media and large agencies, observed by market opinion research, and inundated by the public relations work, propaganda, and advertising of political parties and groups' (Habermas 1996: 367). Further discussion of this process, as well as its present-day sequelae and the (limited) promise of a rejuvenated public sphere, can be postponed since they are reviewed quite comprehensively in Chapter 7.

A final point needs to be emphasized before the framework and body of substantive theory outlined in this chapter are used to address the alleged crisis of welfare statism and the new inequality, namely the nature of the colonization of the private and public spheres of the lifeworld by system imperatives.

Habermas, as was noted above, defines clientalization as a model case of colonization. He acknowledges, but understates, the importance of consumerism in this regard. Discussing globalization, Sklair (1998a: 140) makes the key point: 'the culture-ideology of consumerism is the fundamental value system that keeps the system intact.' And later: 'the point of the concept of the culture-ideology of consumerism is precisely that, under capitalism, the masses cannot be relied upon to keep buying when they have neither spare cash nor access to credit.' 'The modern world system', Wallerstein (1998: 10) writes, 'was, and is, a capitalist system, that is, a system that operates on the primacy of the endless accumulation of capital via the eventual commodification of everything.' The generation of a culture-ideology of consumerism, therefore, is bound up with the self-imposed necessity that capitalism must be ever-expanding on a global scale. This expansion rests crucially on selling more and more goods and services to people whose basic needs (a somewhat ideological term anyway) have already been met, as well as to those whose needs have not been satisfied (Sklair 1998a: 148–9). Consumerism, as well as clientalization, is a direct threat to citizenship (Hobsbawm 1999). It will be argued in later chapters that relations of class are critical for grasping the ideological role of consumerism, as they are indeed for a proper appreciation of the state's substitution of clients for citizens. It is astonishing how frequently those wishing to record a change from productivism under organized capitalism to consumerism under disorganized capitalism have neglected these ideological properties. And this is as true, as we shall now see, of the health domain as it is of other sets of social institutions.

PART TWO

Structural divisions in health and health care

4

Health care reform

Passing reference has been made to the improvement of the public health through the twentieth century, if only in terms of crude indicators like longevity. This might be elaborated with a further paragraph or two of (neo-)positivist social accounting. The increase in life expectancy was in fact steady throughout the twentieth century (in continuance of a trend apparent by the middle of the nineteenth century) (Charlton 1997). However, improvements in mortality begin at different times for different age-groups (see Fitzpatrick and Chandola 2000). The first marked improvement occurred in the 5–24 age-group around 1860. Infant mortality fell steadily from 1900, with notable accelerations in the period immediately after the Second World War, and again in the 1970s; in 1900, one-quarter of all deaths in the population occurred in the first year of life, but by the end of the century this had declined to 1 per cent. Mortality rates for the 15–44 age-group improved in the course of the twentieth century, although with interruptions from the influenza epidemic of 1918 and for the two world wars. Improvements for those aged 45–54 also started at the beginning of the century; for those aged 55–74 mortality declined from the 1920s; for those aged over 74 the decline began after the Second World War. For older age-groups the most marked improvements in mortality took place from the 1970s.

As far as the changing causes of mortality are concerned, there is, as Fitzpatrick and Chandola (2000: 101) note, a broad consensus: 'from the beginning of the twentieth century infectious diseases have been responsible for a diminishing proportion of all deaths. Instead, the so-called degenerative diseases, particularly heart disease, strokes and cancer, have become the major causes of death.' And, as these same authors (2000: 102) add: 'the declining significance of infectious diseases was the single main reason for the dramatic increase in life expectancy . . . Conversely, the main reason for the increase in heart disease, strokes and cancer has been that individuals were increasingly likely to reach the older ages at which these diseases typically, although not exclusively, occur.'

In 1900 medical experts regarded tuberculosis (TB) as 'the greatest single threat to health' (Webster 1994: 38). McKeown (1976) has famously argued that the decline in mortality from infectious diseases like TB, enteric fever, typhus, cholera, smallpox and scarlet fever – collectively responsible for 20 per cent of deaths in 1900, but only 0.5 per cent in 2000 – typically occurred for reasons other than the accessibility and uptake of medical care. Crucial factors, he suggests, were improvements in standard of living, better nutrition, cleaner water supplies and improved personal hygiene and sanitation, related in part to reduced overcrowding consequent upon smaller family size (Fitzpatrick and Chandola 2000).

In some ways McKeown's classic high-impact study serves as an exemplar of an expanding body of research – yielding numerous rival 'models' – on the social and environmental determinants of life-threatening (and other) disease, and long since incorporating the major killers in 2000: heart disease, strokes and cancer (see Siegrist 2000). It is often inferred, on the basis of an increasingly confident assertion of the causal power of social and environmental factors, that medical care, for all the alleged potency of the biomedical armoury at its disposal, has contributed little to the past century's decline in mortality. This is a partial truth. While the (professionally convenient) 'myth' that biomedicine alone bestowed the gift of enhanced longevity has been wholly debunked, medical care has nevertheless played *a*, if not *the decisive*, part in this process. Moreover, it has contributed also to curing/caring in relation to a wide range of non-life-threatening diseases and conditions. As Fitzpatrick and Chandola (2000: 124) point out, joint replacement surgery over the past 30 years has transformed the lives of tens of thousands. Medical care has to be assessed against the criterion of health-related quality of life as well as mortality.

So if the impact of modern medical care has been less than has been claimed by its spokespersons, it remains hugely important. This chapter focuses on the delivery of medical care, as well as of nursing and other forms of health care, in Britain, and for comparative purposes the USA, during the phase of disorganized capitalism. In the opening section the putative 'crisis of welfare statism', routinely associated with a 'need' to 'reform' health care systems in advanced societies, is briefly revisited, using the framework described in Chapter 3. The remainder of the chapter is committed to a series of analyses of aspects of health care and systems of delivery. These analyses, which are tentative and provisional, are attempts to apply the perspective of critical realism as well as that of critical theory. After some preliminary remarks on 'models', involving the triad of 'logics', 'relations' and 'figurations', analyses are proffered of: (a) Thatcher's introduction of the 'internal market' into the British National Health Service and its sequelae; (b) the rise and demise of Clinton's health reform package in the USA in the early 1990s; and (c) the influential concept of a 'Third Way'.

Crisis and reform

The growth of welfare state interventionism with the progression from liberal to organized capitalism has been noted. It has been widely argued that the progression from organized to disorganized capitalism has precipitated a crisis in (at least this form of) welfare statism and an urgent need for policy reform. Certainly the early 1970s was the period, most especially in Anglo-Saxon capitalism, when the idea of the crisis of welfare statism took grip. OPEC's fivefold increase in oil prices in 1973 precipitated, if it did not cause, an economic slump throughout the advanced capitalist world. Economic growth, low inflation, full employment and balance of trade all suddenly seemed beyond easy accomplishment. Increasing state indebtedness and public expenditure, most acute between 1973 and 1975, led to generalized concerns about the costs of welfare provision. Early theories tended to construct notions of crisis as *external shock*, typically citing the increase in oil prices. These were soon superseded by theories of crisis as *longstanding contradiction*, posited from both the New Right and neo-Marxism, each discerning structural weaknesses at the heart of the postwar consensus. The bolder of these theories raised the spectre of crisis as *turning point* (Pierson 1998: 137–8; see also Fitzpatrick 1987).

O'Connor's (1973) *Fiscal Crisis of the State* offered a neo-Marxist account of longstanding contradiction, emphasizing that the capitalist state has to try to fulfil two basic and often contradictory functions, accumulation and legitimation. Thus: 'a capitalist state that openly uses its coercive forces to help one class accumulate capital at the expense of other classes loses it legitimacy and hence undermines the basis of its loyalty and support. But a state that ignores the necessity of assisting the process of capital accumulation risks drying up the source of its own power, the economy's surplus production capacity and the taxes from this surplus' (O'Connor 1973: 6). O'Connor argued that a combination of the socialization of costs and the private appropriation of profits creates a fiscal crisis, or 'structural gap', between state expenditures and state revenues, resulting in a tendency for state expenditures to increase more rapidly than the means of financing them. In the USA, the focus of O'Connor's reflections, growing resistance to paying taxes, intensifying hostility to government authority, the mobilization of welfare recipients by (new) social movements and heightened politicization in an increasingly unionized workforce had all, he claimed, pressured the state and made a fiscal crisis imminent 'by the late 1960s'.

New Right critics worked with other premises of contradiction. *Neo-conservatives* argued that sustained postwar economic growth, the institutionalization of the welfare state and the 'bidding up' processes of adversarial democratic politics had given rise to a 'revolution of rising expectations'. A whole range of goods and services had come to be seen, quite inappropriately, as non-negotiable 'rights'. Pierson (1998: 143) summarizes, 'decline of authority and mutual responsibility within the family meant that social welfare functions traditionally met within the private and family sector generated new claims upon the state and a population increasingly dependent upon state beneficence.'

For the *neo-liberal* element in the New Right the principal problem lay in the relationship between liberal representative democracy and the market economy. Brittan (1975) attributed the risk of the former's self-destruction to two endemic threats: the generation of excessive expectations; and the disruptive effects of organized sectional interests, notably trade unions, in the market place. Rising inflation might be a short-term consequence, 'but in the last analysis the authorities have to choose between accepting an indefinite increase in the rate of inflation and abandoning full employment to the extent necessary to break the collective wage-push power of the unions' (Brittan 1975: 143). But high rates of *either* unemployment *or* inflation are incompatible with the survival of liberal representative democracy.

The 'troubles' of the 1970s were serious enough and were to herald significant change; but they did not in the event issue in the irrecoverable depth of crisis envisioned by some theorists. The external shock of the quintupling of oil prices quickly lost its early salience. Although there are undoubtedly longstanding contradictions in disorganized capitalism, the diagnoses of around-the-corner turning points made by O'Connor (who predicted socialism) and Brittan (who predicted the collapse of liberal representative democracy) are far from being confirmed.

From the late 1970s there have been numerous derivative, novel and rival theories of the putative crisis of welfare statism, and, increasingly, in marginally less heady times, of what Taylor-Gooby (1985) has termed 'crisis containment'. There is no space to review these here (see O'Brien and Penna 1998; Pierson 1998). Instead, one additional theory pertinent to the arguments of this volume will be briefly outlined, that of Jessop's (1994a, b, 1995) state-theoretical analysis of the Schumpeterian workfare state.

Jessop draws on neo-Marxist state theory and the multifaceted 'regulation approach'pioneered by French political economists interested in the dynamics of long-term cycles of economic stability and change. The regulation approach distinguishes between *regimes of accumulation* and *modes of regulation*. Regimes of accumulation refer to relationships between production and consumption existing during given periods of economic growth; thus Fordism as a regime of accumulation was characterized by the congruence between mass production and consumption. Modes of regulation refer to 'frameworks' that support a given growth period; thus, in the Fordist period, expectations of life-long, full-time male employment and the social wage (that is, extensive welfare provision), which functioned to provide the social conditions and stability necessary for the accumulation process, were central to the mode of regulation (Allen 1992). According to Jessop (1995: 1623), the regulation approach is more concerned with 'the emergence over time of reproducible structural coherence in accumulation regimes in and through regulation than it is with the genesis of specific policy measures and their implementation in specific institutional or organizational sites.'

Like others (for example, Lash and Urry 1987; Esping-Anderson 1990), Jessop (1994a) argues that different nation-states are responding differently to the shift from the Fordism of organized to the post-Fordism of disorganized capitalism. He defines 'flexibility' as the key feature of post-Fordism. The response of the British state, he argues, has been to regard welfare policy as subservient to the demands of labour market flexibility. There has occurred a general reorientation of economic and social policy to the needs of the private sector and a broad range of measures to 'remodel' social institutions along the lines of commerical enterprises (O'Brien and Penna 1998). The Keynesian welfare state, according to Jessop (1994b), has been transmuted into a Schumpeterian workfare state, in which social policy is not geared to 'meeting need, ameliorating hardship or rational humanistic planning', but is instead subordinated to the demands for competitiveness in the global economy. Moreover, 'no amount of objective social scientific research on social problems will set the policy agenda at the level of the state, for social policy is seen as strategically implicated in the social regulation of the new growth regime' (O'Brien and Penna 1998: 158) (see Chapter 7). In short the displacement of the Keynesian welfare state by a Schumpeterian workfare state is *necessary* to achieve the requisite degree of 'fit' between roles, norms and expectations and the means by which capital accumulation is secured in the new growth regime.

So where has Jessop's analysis left us? Was there, and is there yet, a crisis of welfare statism? Have we witnessed a generation of crisis containment since the 1970s which has necessarily led to 'structural adjustment'? Or is talk of a crisis of welfare statism a mere rhetorical or ideological device to cover a potentially hazardous transition to a new mode of regulation to match a new regime of accumulation without incurring a crisis of legitimation? The rest of this chapter comprises a circuitous attempt to respond to these questions. But, first, a few paragraphs of conceptual preparation are indicated.

Models of logics/relations/figurations

Efforts to develop substantive sociological theories on the twin bases of critical realism and critical theory are predictably and understandably rare. For this reason the analyses of aspects of health and health care in this and later chapters are presented as partial and provisional. They are, as it were, pieces of a jigsaw, contributing (albeit differentially) to the overall picture. Not all the pieces will be provided, but I hope that those that are will fit; and there is a sense in which the assorted analyses in this and the next two chapters are cumulative, with later examples enriching, as well as complementing, their predecessors.

The concept of models in natural and social science has a varied pedigree (see Morgan and Morrison 1999). It will be used here to refer *to a particular mode of assembly of theory and data of heuristic value.* It comprises three elements: *logics*, *relations* and *figurations*. These elements are perhaps best articulated through an example linked to the previous discussion. The subsystems of the economy (primarily) and the state (secondarily), which together of course constitute Habermas's system, possess their own 'logics', most significantly those associated with production and regulation respectively (in Jessop's terms, deriving from the prevailing regime of accumulation and mode of regulation). These logics require, order and/or establish the parameters for (*real*, in Bhaskar's sense) 'relations'. It is real relations that supply the 'generative mechanisms' underpinning critical sociology's explanatory thrust. The most significant relations arising from the logic associated with production (and 'filtered through' that associated with regulation) remain those of class. Relations of class are expressed in networks or 'figurations'. Figurations may be defined, following Elias (1978), as spatio-temporal interdependency chains or networks. These are fluid and diachronically changing (van Krieken 1998). They may occur at the global level as well as at the levels of the nation-state and the local.

Two general principles may be associated with this model. The first is the *principle of compatibility*. This states that, *ceteris paribus*, while, in any given figuration, different – even multiple – behavioural or policy options may be possible (that is, there is typically an element of contingency), only those options which are compatible with the prevailing logics and relations are likely to be realized. The second is the *principle of advantage*. This states that, *ceteris paribus*, in any given figuration, the advantage from any behavioural or policy option exercised is likely to accrue disproportionately, and without conspiracy, to the principal beneficiaries of the prevailing logics and relations. Importantly, both principles may, in exceptional circumstances, be subverted. Intermittent reference to these two principles will be made in succeeding analyses.

The example of logics-relations-figurations given above is especially pertinent to the first, tentative application of the model; that is, to Thatcher's health policies through the 1980s, leading to the introduction of an internal market into the British National Health Service in 1991. The logics associated with production and regulation are paramount, as are relations of class (although not to the exclusion of all other relations); and the figuration is the nation-state.

Health care reform in Britain

A few paragraphs of background social history will have to suffice (for more detail, see Carrier and Kendall 1998). The British state was not a pioneer of welfare or personal health service prevision, at least by European standards. Its initial direct engagement, not unrelated to rumbling public unrest as well as to observed high rates of work absenteeism and lack of fitness for war duty among working men, came with Lloyd George's Liberal government's National Health Insurance Act of 1911. This Act, through the agency of Approved Societies, cushioned a section of the *male* working class from the costs of sickness. The scheme – a contributory one by state, employer and employee – entitled beneficiaries to free primary care by an approved panel doctor (that is, by a local GP), and to a sum to compensate for loss of earning power due to sickness; it did not cover hospital services. The rest of the population, including better paid working men, women, children and older people, either had to secure their primary (as well as their secondary) care on a fee-for-service basis, or, if too poor, fell back on a limited and fragmented system of 'public' (state-funded) or 'voluntary' (charitable) care. The Act covered 27 per cent of the population in 1911, and this had only been extended to 45 per cent by the beginning of the Second World War. Well before this time, gathering momentum through the 1920s and 1930s, it had been widely recognized that Britain's socially and geographically maldistributed health services provided too little too arbitrarily to too few and were in urgent need of an overhaul (Webster 1998).

It was during the Second World War, in 1942, that the nature of this overhaul was agreed in principle by Churchill's coalition government. It was to evolve out of Beveridge's (1942) painstaking blueprint for an assault on the 'five giants' hindering social progress (namely, Want, Disease, Ignorance, Squalor and Idleness), which incorporated plans for a National Health Service. The postwar return of Atlee's Labour Party (1945–51) saw not only the realization of the concept of a welfare state, but, following the National Health Service (NHS) Act of 1946, a skilful piece of midwifery by the Health Minister, Aneurin Bevan, the actual birth of the NHS in 1948 (see Eckstein 1958). Based on the principles of collectivism, comprehensiveness, universalism and equality (plus that of professional autonomy) (Allsop 1995), the state was thenceforth committed to provide primary and secondary health care free at the point of service for those in need. These services were to be funded almost exclusively out of central taxation.

The 1946 Act, like its predecessor in 1911, involved compromise, chiefly with history and the medical profession. The form the NHS took was a product of past health care and of the honed power of professional interests. Notably, GPs avoided becoming salaried employees, instead emerging as independent contractors paid capitation fees based on number of patients; the prestigious teaching hospitals won a substantial degree of autonomy; and GPs, and more significantly (salaried) hospital consultants, won the 'right' to continue to see private patients. The survival of private practice meant that from its inception, 'the NHS was weakened by the fact that the nation's most wealthy and private citizens were not compelled to use it themselves and by the diluted commitment of those clinicians who provided treatment to them' (Doyal and Doyal 1999: 364; see also Rivett 1998).

The cross-party consensus on the principles and practices of the NHS held for a generation, its original tripartite division into hospital, GP and local authority services intact through minor, episodic piecemeal engineering; and private practice remained marginal in terms of patient numbers. By the end of the 1960s, however, it was apparent that the NHS, with growing numbers of people with chronic and disabling conditions, had a caring role in the community as well as a curative one within hospitals, and that this challenge required both better integrated services and a more efficient, planned allocation of resources. The result, in 1974, was a thorough, bureaucratic reorganization of the NHS by Heath's Conservative government, involving the creation, under the Department of Health and Social Security (DHSS) (newly formed in 1968), of 14 regional health authorities (RHAs), 90 area health authorities (AHAs) and 200 district management teams, each – in their specialist domains of planning, implementation and day-to-day management respectively – functioning by 'consensus management'. GPs remained independent contractors but were integrated at each level; and in each district there was a community health council (CHC) to act as the public's 'watchdog'. Other consequences of the Act included the introduction of a limited list of drugs available to GPs to prescribe on the NHS, and of competitive tendering for support services (involving the private sector).

By the mid-1970s the economic slump was occasioning a serious rethink about cost containment (not just in Britain – see Saltman and Figueras 1997). In the first year of stability in spending, 1950–1, the NHS had absorbed 4.1 per cent of gross domestic product (GDP). This proportion fell steadily to 3.5 per cent of GDP in the mid-1950s; by the mid-1960s it had regained and passed the level of 1950–1; and by the time of the NHS reorganization of 1974 it had risen to 5.7 per cent of GDP. In fact, public expenditure as a whole reached a peak in 1975, accounting for nearly a half of GDP (Webster 1998).

The Wilson/Callaghan Labour governments from 1974 to 1979 took steps to contain public, including health, expenditures. When Thatcher was elected in 1979, she brought to office convictions suited to the notion of a burgeoning crisis in welfare statism. Galbraith (1992) has observed that, most conspicuously in Anglo-Saxon capitalism, bureaucracies in the public sector have been more readily identified and condemned than those – arguably, no less prevalent – in the private sector. In 1983 Thatcher invited Roy Griffiths from Sainsbury's to undertake an enquiry into NHS management practices. The result was a new hierarchy of general managers on fixed-term contracts and an end to consensus management. Thus, from 1985, there was a general manager of the NHS itself and of each RHA and district health authority (DHA), the latter having replaced the AHA tier, abolished in 1982. This streamlining allowed for greater central control over activity at all levels. The rationale was enhanced efficiency and 'value for money' (DHSS 1983). The levels of NHS spending, if not of perceptions and rhetorics of crisis, remained fairly constant during the 1980s, at about 6.5 per cent of GDP.

In 1988, amidst much talk of crises of expenditure and delivery, Thatcher announced a wide-ranging confidential review of the NHS. A White (not a Green) Paper, *Working for Patients*, was published the following year (Secretary of State for Health 1989). This document concentrated on *the means of delivery of health care*, the only direct financial innovation being the introduction of tax relief on private health insurance premiums for those over 60 (but one of Thatcher's bids to promote the private sector during the 1980s). The four main proposals in the White Paper (extending to a new contract for GPs in 1990) were: the introduction of an 'internal' or 'quasi-market' into the NHS; extra provisions for professional accountability (especially in relation to audit); a further streamlining of the management hierarchy along 'business lines'; and the development of general practice (for example, by altering GPs contracts to foster activities like information-giving and screening, and by making it easier for patients to change GPs) (Mays 1997: 200). The White Paper proposals were largely enacted in the NHS and Community Care Act of 1990, which was implemented in 1991.

The most radical measure, the internal market, designed to facilitate 'managed competition', entailed the separation of the roles of *purchaser* and *provider* in a manner recommended by the American analyst, Enthoven (1985). DHAs became primarily purchasers not providers, buying hospital and community health services for their populations from providers in the public or private sectors. A DHA's budget was set on the basis of 'weighted capitation'; that is, according to the size and age structure of its population, weighted for differences in morbidity between areas. GP practices with more than 11,000 patients were encouraged to become 'fundholders', permitted to buy diagnostic, outpatient and selected non-emergency surgical procedures for their patients from providers, including the private sector. Hospitals and other directly managed units were prompted to become self-governing NHS 'trusts', enjoying more managerial discretion. The income of NHS trusts was based on ability to market services to purchasers; that is, to DHAs (on behalf of patients of non-fundholding GP practices), to fundholding GP practices and to private insurers. Through all this the NHS was to remain (in principle, if somewhat less in practice) a relatively centralized, tax-funded service accessible to all on the basis of need and largely free at the point of use (Mays 1997).

Major's conservative government more or less defended Thatcher's legacy. In 1991 the *Patient's Charter* was introduced, setting out a number of standards patients might expect from the NHS (for example, waiting times for initial outpatient appointment and for admission for a planned treatment); the Charter was 'updated' in 1995. And in 1992 the Private Finance Initiative (PFI) was launched, with the objective of attracting private capital to public schemes; the perceived political advantage of PFIs was that the public sector would contract to buy services, not assets, and thus the capital expenditure achieved would not be part of the public sector borrowing requirement (PSBR) (Salter 1998). By the time of Major's departure in 1997 expenditure on health had topped 7 per cent of GDP.

For Blair (1997), the welfare state is 'encouraging dependency, lowering self-esteem and denying opportunity and responsibility in almost equal measure . . . The more demands that are put upon it, the essential passive nature of too much provision – especially benefits – is revealed.' Unsurprisingly, the 'New' Labour government – of the 'Third Way' – has so far shown little inclination to abandon Thatcher's experiment with managed competition, although it has tried some piecemeal social engineering of its own, prominent examples being the introduction of a new system of purchasing, or commissioning, by means of some 500 primary care groups (PCGs); and a series of – largely ineffectual (Hutton 2000) – initiatives on patient empowerment. There has been something of a switch of rhetoric too, from efficiency to quality, giving rise to evidence-based National Service Frameworks for major care areas and disease groups; a National Institute for Clinical Excellence to foster clinical guidelines and good practice in audit; and a Commission for Health Improvement to monitor quality in the delivery of services. An emphasis on improving health (beyond the delivering of health care), and on closer collaboration with local authorities, is also evident (Klein 1998).

In the March 2000 Budget, following growing public disaffection, Blair undertook to raise spending on the NHS by 6.1 per cent annually in real terms over a four-year period in order to lift spending towards the European Union average. In July of the same year he published 'The NHS Plan', which detailed a range of service targets, conspicuously reductions in 'queuing', said to be achievable as a result of this extra investment. Among the further reforms anticipated in this document were: a new system of 'earned autonomy' to devolve power from the centre to local health services; 'modern contracts' for GPs and hospital doctors to reward quality and productivity (and also to proscribe private work for newly qualified hospital consultants 'for perhaps seven years'); the extension of rights to prescribe medicines to non-doctors; a 'concordat' with private providers to enable the NHS to make better use of private facilities; and new care trusts to commission health and social care in a single organization. The jury has yet to retire on these changes, let alone pronounce, but it seems that there has been little effective discontinuity in policy since Thatcher's heyday (Iliffe and Munro 2000).

On the face of it Thatcher's imposition of an internal market on the NHS was odd. First, it was not a meaningful market (West 1998). Second, there was no prospect of *either* a meaningful market *or* her lesser option of an internal market realizing her stated goals of more cost-effective care and/or patient choice. Moran (1999) observes that from the mid-1970s onwards, and in every advanced capitalist society, health care reform was dominated by the language of cost containment. He is worth quoting at some length:

> it seemed to follow from this that the most radical reforms would take place in those health care systems where the problem of containment was most acute. That expectation made the British experience in the late 1980s and early 1990s unfathomable. In those years Britain underwent major institutional changes in health care. But as far as cost containment was concerned the evidence was compelling in a way rare in social inquiry: the UK had an outstanding record in delivering cheap, cost-effective health care; and that record was due to the command and control system of the NHS, the very elements that were being modified by the Conservative government's 'reforms'.
>
> (Moran 1999: 171–2)

The failure of the reforms to deliver on patient choice (purchasers made choices on their behalf, thereby predefining and foreclosing their options), or on local public or patient accountability (Milewa *et al.* 1998: Hutton 2000), was no less predictable. But analysis at the policy level is of course not enough.

It has often been observed of health (and other) policy that, in ascending order, its formation, implementation and outcome all tend towards the unpredictable: moreover, even in its formative phase, it is rarely (only) what it seems. So it was with Thatcher's reforms. This, at least, should not take a critical realist unawares. In her discussion of 'policy transfer' (in this instance from the USA to Britain), O'Neill (2000: 61) rightly asserts that the internal market was from the start 'an abstraction that had no concrete existence in the American, or indeed any other, health care system.' Its appeal can only be appreciated in the light of Thatcher's political agenda. O'Neill (2000: 61) puts it well: 'while the nature of the "crisis" was ostensibly financial, the government had to focus on options that would transform the service without being unduly burdensome on the public purse (given its desire to reduce the PSBR). More importantly, the government had to find a way to transform the NHS which did not challenge its founding principles in a politically explosive way. As policy makers looked around for solutions to this dilemma the high profile that American market-centred theories of health care had assumed within policy-making circles provided an accessible and acceptable source of ideas to build upon.' These ideas: purported not to contradict the founding principles of the NHS; seemed – according to neo-liberal economic doctrine – to herald efficiency gains; built on the managerial reforms initiated in 1983; were consistent with the reforms enacted in other public services, like education; and appealed to the 'ideological foundations of the Thatcher government'.

The salience to this particular policy enterprise of the logics of the regime of accumulation and mode of regulation of disorganized capitalism, and of relations of class (deriving from the subsystem of the economy) and of what, adapting Scott's (1996) usage, I shall hereafter refer to as *relations of command* (deriving from the subsystem of the state), can now be addressed, albeit with caution.

Three theses on the transition from organized to disorganized capitalism are pertinent. The first maintains that the threat of a 'legitimation crisis' associated with the shift to a new mode of regulation compatible with, and increasingly conducive to, a newly emerging regime of accumulation has receded, at least for the time being. While Habermas (1976) was perspicacious in the early 1970s to signal the potential for a crisis of legitimation, what has happened *since* has served to militate against its imminent realization. In general terms, in the disorganized capitalism of the last generation the logic of the subsystem of the economy (i.e. of accumulation), enacted through relations of class, has occasioned a reformulation of the logic of the subsystem of the state (i.e. of regulation), enacted through relations of command (and, as a subset of command relations, *relations of welfare*) which both *(further) privileges class relations over command (and welfare) relations* and, perhaps temporarily (and certainly paradoxically), *diminishes the prospect of a legitimation crisis*).

The reduced likelihood of a crisis of legitimation is tied in with the 'disenfranchising' nature of the new inequality noted at the close of the previous chapter. For example, those Bauman (1998b) refers to as the 'new poor' and others as constituting an underclass, together with many members of the working class, can, against the background of high unemployment and underemployment, governance by neo-liberal (and later 'Third Way') career politicians, destandardized work practices and trade union disempowerment, be neglected (and further, in the context of a renewal of *relations of worth* reminiscent of the Victorian poor law system, be held personally culpable for their deprivation and impaired health and longevity) 'in the interests of a competitive national economy' *without the state's legitimacy being called decisively into question.*

That Thatcher was unable to undermine the British National Health Service as speedily or efficiently as she might have hoped, or as comprehensively as she did other aspects of welfare, like public housing, was largely a function of the (cross-class) public regard for, and commitment to, this most odd and unlikely by-product of organized 'Anglo-Saxon capitalism' – which is not to say she did not try (Beck *et al.* 1992).

The second thesis affirms a shift in the public–private mix in health care consonant with both the enhanced salience of class over command relations (allowing for a redefining of relations of welfare and worth) and the reduced threat of a legitimation crisis. The NHS was from its inception a hybrid, an amalgam of public and private sector provision. It was also critically dependent on the private sector for such items as equipment and, notoriously (via transnational corporations), pharmaceutical products (see Abraham 1995). But after the urgent economic troubles of the early 1970s many health policy analysts and advisers, convinced of a mismatch between the demand for state welfare and the finite supply of public finance from taxpayers (that is, of a welfare state crisis), argued for one or more of three political options: to limit or reduce demand by means of restrictions on social rights; to divert demand by inducing people to finance their welfare privately; or to attempt both by blurring the boundaries between public and private welfare. All of these have been tried (Salter 1998).

The shift towards commodification and the private sector that characterized British health care through the 1980s and 1990s – for all that public sector provision remains dominant – has led Gabe and Calnan (2000: 268) to refer to a 'marketized state'. Thatcher promoted the private sector by a raft of measures: by relaxing controls on private hospital development and limiting local authorities' powers to object (the number of private hospitals increased by 39 per cent during Thatcher's time in office, and private beds by 58 per cent: Calnan *et al.* 1993); by revising NHS consultants' contracts so they had more scope to undertake private practice; by relaxing controls on 'paybeds' (for private practice) in the NHS; by encouraging (more ambitious and commercial) private health insurance by making premiums paid by employers and low-paid workers with individual subscription plans tax deductible (the proportion of the population with private health insurance increased from 5 to 13 per cent while Thatcher was in government: Calnan *et al.* 1993); by providing tax relief on private health insurance for those over 60; by permitting a rapid expansion of private nursing home provision ('prompted by the discovery of open-ended social security support for the elderly and the corresponding decrease in NHS provision', a 'loophole' belatedly closed in 1992: Salter 1998: 199); and by encouraging, for example through 'competitive tendering', the privatization of a range of NHS hospital services (a process since reversed in favour of in-house personnel) (see Gabe 1997; Gabe and Calnan 2000).

The implementation of the internal market, not least through what Salter (1998: 207) terms 'boundary obfuscation', further boosted the private sector. It aped the private sector in its new managerialism and in the key role accorded to annual purchaser–provider contracts; and, more directly, it allowed for DHAs and GP fundholders to contract clinical and other services from private providers. Less obviously, hospital trusts began to deploy their paybeds against their commercial rivals. However, of all the neo-liberal measures taken – which have in the round left the NHS more intact than Thatcher might have planned, due to the electoral politics of public loyalty – perhaps Major's PFIs, inherited with some enthusiasm from 1997 by Blair, will in the medium and longer term best facilitate a recommodification of British health care. For this reason they warrant an additional word.

Salter (1998: 201–2) is right to observe that the big PFI ventures are 'not so much building contracts as very large, long-term service contracts involving a multiplicity of participants organized in consortia which generate quite novel regulatory problems for the state. PFI is about considerably more than simply "private finance". It is about the detailed web of commercial relationships which must exist in order to render the use of that finance viable for both private and public partners.' Boundary obfuscation is apparent here too. Pollock and her colleagues (Gaffney *et al.* 1999a, b, c; Pollock *et al.* 1999; Pollock and Vickers 2000) maintain that under PFI 'the private sector designs, builds, finances, owns, and operates services. Hospitals funded by the private finance initiative are leased back to the public sector for periods of up to 60 years . . . these hospitals, said by the government to comprise "the largest hospital building programme in the history of the NHS", will be funded through extensive hospital closures and resources generated by NHS trusts, not by new government funds' (Gaffney *et al.* 1999a: 48). These authors support their case in their detailed report on the Worcester Royal Infirmary PFI (Pollock *et al.* 2000). In a separate piece they 'warn' that, as PFI schemes are mooted for primary as well as for acute hospital facilities, private insurance companies like the Norwich Union are 'tapping into NHS funds' and 'blurring the boundaries between private and public health provision in search of greater profits' (Player *et al.* 1999: 28). Monbiot (2000: Chapter 2) pulls fewer punches as a result of his investigations of the PFI scheme in Coventry. He concludes:

among the many costs of the Private Finance Initiative is the transfer of control and ownership of the nation's critical infrastructure to private business, whose interests are often wholly distinct from those of the electorate. Complicated and confidential, it has been able to penetrate areas of public life whose overt privatization would be politically impossible. It has enabled companies to harness the great untapped resources they coveted, sustaining their share prices by turning public capital into private cash. The purpose of the Private Finance Initiative is to deliver the assets of the state to the corporations.

(Monbiot 2000: 92)

Finally, the third thesis postulates changes of *habitus* in the British population leading to a (postmodern) ambivalence toward welfare statism. It was Elias who pioneered the idea of habitus (as 'second nature' or 'an automatic, blindly-functioning apparatus of self-control': Elias 1994: 113, 446). Defining 'national character' as 'a habitus problem par excellence', he famously used it in his last published volume to throw light on the recent course of German history (Elias 1996). But the contemporary – and present – use of habitus is more commonly associated with Bourdieu (1977: 78), who writes: 'the habitus, the durably installed generative principle of regulated improvisations, produces practices which tend to reproduce the regularities imminent in the objective conditions of the production of their generative principle, while adjusting to the demands inscribed as objective potentialities in the situation, as defined by the cognitive and motivating structures making up the habitus.' This requires elucidation.

There is in each of us, Bourdieu (1977: 79) insists, 'part of yesterday's man'; in fact, and he cites Durkheim approvingly here, 'it is yesterday's man who inevitably predominates in us, since the present amounts to little compared with the long past in the course of which we were formed and from which we result.' And this history, much of which is 'forgotten' (that is, part of the unconscious), incorporates 'the objective structures it produces in the second natures of habitus'.

Another point stressed by Bourdieu (1977: 81–2), who is more interested in class than national habitus, is that, contrary to the paradigms of interactionism and phenomenology, interpersonal relations are never solely 'individual-to-individual', but are always informed by 'the objective structure of the relations between social conditions' (see Chapter 6 on doctor–patient relations).

Habitus can be understood as a system of 'lasting, transposable dispositions'; or as a 'subjective but not individual system of internalized structures, schemes of perception, conception, and action common to all members of the same group or class.' Bourdieu (1977: 85–6) elaborates on the idea of a specifically class habitus as follows:

the objective structures which science apprehends in the form of statistical regularities (e.g employment rates, income curves, probabilities of access to secondary education, frequency of holidays, etc.) inculcate, through the direct or indirect but always convergent experiences which give a social environment its *physiognomy*, with its 'closed doors', 'dead ends', and limited 'prospects', that 'art of assessing likelihoods', as Leibniz put it, of anticipating the objective future, in short, the sense of reality or realities which is perhaps the best-concealed principle of their efficacy.

But there are many social structures/relations, groups and, it seems, forms of habitus; as well as national and class habitus, for example, gender, ethnicity and age must be taken into account. In a contribution to an intriguing collection entitled *Complicating Categories: Gender, Class, Race and Ethnicity* (Boris and Janssens 1999), DeVault uses Sartre's concept of *seriality* in a way pertinent here. In explicating his concept, Sartre notes that individuals waiting for a bus in the morning constitute a 'series'; others may see them as having something in common but they are unlikely to see this themselves. If, however, a bus fails to stop, making them late for work, they may acknowledge their commonality through conversation. At this point the 'series' becomes a 'group'. DeVault (1999: 34–5) continues: 'it is only when these individuals begin to take action (perhaps combining to take a taxi to work) that the "group" becomes a "fused group". If this "group" were to organize a boycott of the bus, they would become a "pledged group".' Sartre, like Bourdieu, was concerned with class, but these notions have been applied also to gender (Young 1994).

We can now clarify the contention that there have been changes of habitus in the British population which have encouraged a (postmodern) ambivalence towards welfare statism. Allied to the postmodern cultural turn (see the discussion of the cultural-aesthetic, but also the rational, in Chapter 2) and the theme of individualization (introduced in Chapter 3), many have written of a new 'postmodern self'. Gibbons and Reimer (1999: 57) record the shift to a postmodern culture and note that 'the connectedness of individuals and groups to the lifeworld of general society' has betrayed a 'loosening' as a result of individualization. They write:

> the production, reproduction and consumption of self-narratives has blossomed in a way and to an extent that was previously unimaginable, witnessed in the thousands of items available on the shelves of every newsagent and within the covers of most of these products. Through this enlargement of sources of the self, the very possibility of mass self-production, -reproduction and -consumption is diminishing, whether at the level of class, gender, the national or the international.

Talk of a postmodern self is perhaps more understandable than justified. But it is surely plausible to argue that while real (objective) social relations in Britain continue to underlie and inform the habitus of nation, class and so on, there is yet a novel, postmodern propensity towards seriality. It is a feature of the putative postmodern self, in short, that consciousness is fragmented and cognition tends to lack the coherence and constancy of stance demanded of it by the modern, which of course diminishes the potential for 'groups' to become 'fused' or 'pledged'. But, again, the question of the extent to which this is a function of the ideology of disorganized capitalism must be raised; and the principle of compatibility certainly applies. It is not that people are no longer committed to the welfare state in general, and the NHS in particular, but rather that commitment itself has become, if not less intense, then relativized, incoherent, inconstant and pliable.

In summary, and slotting in only one piece of a daunting jigsaw, it has been argued that class relations in disorganized capitalism in Britain have gained ground over command and welfare relations, but without occasioning a crisis of legitimation. As a result the NHS has experienced some recommodification. While the habitus of the people remains rooted in class relations, the – partly ideological – shift to a postmodern culture has been marked by seriality, fragmented consciousness and relativized cognitions. Such recommodification as has taken place around health care has occurred largely by class activity and default.

Clinton and the question of reform in the USA

As the phrase 'Anglo-Saxon capitalism' implies, Britain and the USA share important features. The recent welfare and NHS reforms have often been described as an 'Americanization' of the British system, and not only in relation to the neo-liberal Reagan/Thatcher era (Walker, 1999). It will be instructive to consider briefly the context and fate of Clinton's health care proposals in the early 1990s. The model of logics/relations/figurations used for the NHS remains broadly appropriate, as do the concepts of legitimacy, class–command relations and habitus.

The origins of American health care have been comprehensively analysed by Starr (1982). It will suffice here to outline its four main 'building blocks' or components, namely Blue Cross and Blue Shield (the 'Blues'), commercial or 'for-profit' insurers, health maintenance organizations (HMOs) and Medicare and Medicaid (see Weitz 1996), before reflecting on Clinton's reform proposals.

At the start of the twentieth century a mix of private fee-for-service medicine and institutionalized philanthropic care met the needs of most US citizens. It was not until the depression of the 1930s that health insurance took off. The Wall Street collapse in 1929 prompted the American Hospital Association, alarmed at the prospect of hospital bankruptcies, to found a non-profit company, Blue Cross, to sell insurance to individuals to underwrite the payment of hospital bills. Blue Cross was, then, designed to protect hospitals, not patients. The American Medical Association founded Blue Shield to cover medical bills, a measure to safeguard doctors, not patients. The 'Blues', as they are known, set their premiums on the basis of 'community rating' (that is, individuals paid according to the risk level of the community *as a whole*), thus spreading costs. Individuals pay fee-for-service, then apply for reimbursement. Typically, they pay a deductible, and are reimbursed for the remainder of their hospital and/or medical bills. Lifetime, or annual, maximums are usually imposed. By the time of Clinton's intervention in the early 1990s, nearly one in five Americans had Blue Cross or Blue Shield coverage.

Beginning in the 1940s, commercial or for-profit insurers entered the market, their numbers rapidly expanding. They offered lower premiums than the Blues through the use of 'actuarial risk rating' (that is, by identifying and insuring only those with low health risk); individuals with poor health profiles either paid higher premiums or were excluded. Those in supposedly high-risk occupations, like construction, also paid higher premiums. Losing out in increasingly fierce competition with these rapacious for-profit insurers, a number of Blue Cross/Blue Shield companies later switched from community to actuarial risk rating.

The 1930s and 1940s also saw the rise of HMOs. Unlike the Blues and the commercial insurers, early HMOs, like Kaiser Permanente and the Group Cooperative of Puget Sound, were run by people intent on providing affordable, high-quality care to local communities. Whereas the Blues and commercial insurers used fee-for-service and retrospective reimbursement, the HMOs relied on salaried doctors and prospective reimbursement: they paid doctors a set salary, regardless of the number of times they saw their patients or the number of procedures performed. The onus was on keeping patients healthy. HMOs also paid the full cost of preventive care. Patients paid nothing beyond the cost of their insurance premiums providing they used only doctors affiliated with their HMO and saw specialists only if referred by their primary care doctor.

Health expenditure represented 7.3 per cent of GDP in the USA by 1970. Seeing their potential for cost containment, Nixon threw his support behind HMOs, and in 1973 federal legislation made grants available to help to trigger HMOs and required firms with 25+ employees and providing health benefits to offer an HMO option. HMOs grew quickly, with one in five Americans with health insurance belonging to one at the time of Clinton's election. But by this time HMOs had changed: co-payments (that is, fees paid per visit) had become standard, and two-thirds had become for-profit. The original or 'staff' model, according to which HMOs hired doctors who worked for a salary and exclusively for their HMO, was now exceptional. In the 'group' model, HMOs contract with a single group practice to provide services to HMO patients, but members of the group see private patients as well. In the 'network' model, contracts are placed with multiple group practices. In group and network models doctors are typically paid by capitation. And in 'individual practice associations' (IPAs), the fastest growing HMO model, individual doctors see HMO patients on a fee-for-service basis, with the fees negotiated in advance with the HMO.

From the late 1970s onwards there was something of a convergence in the practices of health care providers. In order to retain clients who might be attracted to the lower than average costs of HMOs, many Blues and commercial insurers have added 'preferred provider options' (PPOs). In a PPO, individual doctors, working from private offices on a fee-for-service basis, contract with the insurer to provide care for insured patients at pre-negotiated fees. Patients can still see any doctor, but their insurance will pay a significantly higher proportion of their bill if they see doctors belonging to their PPO. HMOs, meanwhile, have extended their patients' choice by an option known as 'point of service' (POS). Patients can still receive care from the HMO doctors, but under POS can also see other doctors in exchange for higher co-payments. DiMaggio and Powell (1983) have termed this tendency to convergence 'institutional isomorphism'.

The final component of US health care consists of Medicare/Medicaid. These programmes were enacted by Congress in 1965 during the Johnson administration and were designed to reach out to those without access to insurance coverage, whether through the Blues, commercial insurers or HMOs. Medicare covers all Americans over the age of 65, plus some with disabilities, and is funded through social security taxes. Part A, which is free, is a hospital insurance programme: for the first 60 days all costs are covered (minus deductibles); for the next 30 days a daily co-payment is required; and for 90+ days a higher daily co-payment must be paid, up to a lifetime maximum of 60 additional days of care. Part B is a medical insurance programme. It is not free, but conditional on optional monthly premiums deducted from social security retirement payments. It covers 80 per cent of the costs of medical care, outpatient hospital services and diagnostic tests, but does not cover prescription drugs, long-term nursing care at home or routine minor costs. Many people purchase additional private insurance – 'medigap policies' – for their retirement. Those on very low incomes may get extra help through Medicaid.

Medicaid provides coverage primarily on the basis of income and physical disability, and covers approximately one-eighth of those under the age of 65. Low income is insufficient to guarantee cover: individuals must be both poor and aged, blind, disabled, pregnant or the parent of a dependent child. Sixty per cent of those in relative poverty (that is, with incomes below the federal poverty line) do *not* qualify. Medicaid is funded through a mix of federal and state sources, which means that states have leeway to determine eligibility and benefits within broad federal guidelines. Federal regulations allow states to offer preventive and therapeutic care, and inpatient and outpatient medical care, but many states err on the side of parsimony. However, states *must* provide Medicaid for children under six, and for pregnant women whose family incomes fall below 133 per cent of the federal poverty line (Weitz 1996).

This is an appropriate juncture to mention the gradual emergence and rapid spread of *managed care*. 'Faster than almost anyone expected', writes Anders (1996: 244), 'managed care has become the *de facto* national health policy of the United States.' Managed care is a mechanism of cost control. It refers to 'any system that controls costs through closely monitoring and controlling the decisions of health care providers' (Weitz 1996: 333). 'Utilization review' is one such mechanism: in many plans doctors are now required to call a utilization review office for approval before they can hospitalize a patient, order an expensive diagnostic test, perform surgery and so on. A utilization review office may also tell doctors how many days they can hospitalize a patient with a given diagnosis. By the time Clinton's reform package was put together, half of insured Americans belonged to some form of managed care plan (Iglehart 1994).

This simplified account of the genesis of the Blues, commercial/for-profit insurance companies, HMOs and Medicare/Medicaid, and of managed care, provides a backcloth to the rhetoric of crisis, more insistent from the 1970s onwards, that led ultimately to Clinton's intervention in the health arena. The crisis was attributed to *rising health care costs* and *declining coverage*.

By 1980, health expenditure in the USA had risen to 9.2 per cent of GDP, and by 1990, to 12.2 per cent. In 1990, the USA spent $2,750 per capita on health care, compared with Britain's $910 per capita (US Congressional Budget Office 1993). The effect of rising costs on individuals was marked, experienced in relation to both the cost of insurance and costs 'in addition' to insurance. Employers too had shifted costs to consumers. Starr (1994) has debunked four myths about the immediate causes of rising costs. They were not due, he shows, to especially high expectations of health care, to the propensity for malpractice suits, to the ageing population or to advanced technologies. Comparing American with Canadian health care, he concludes that rising costs in the former were a function: of high administrative costs, accounting for between a third and a half of the difference in costs between the USA and Canada; of doctors' fees (with unfettered fee-for-service, more specialists and self-referral; that is, to self-owned facilities), accounting for a further third of the difference; and of hospital costs, accounting for the remainder of the difference.

Rising costs have led to declining coverage. Approximately 15 per cent of Americans lacked health insurance on any given day in 1993, more than at any time since the initiation of Medicare/Medicaid nearly 30 years previously (one in five lacked health insurance for part of the year) (US Bureau of the Census 1994). Because of Medicare, health care coverage is primarily a prob-lem for the young and middle aged. But being in work may not be enough: in 1993, one in nine of those aged 18–29 and in full-time employment was uninsured (in fact, they and their dependants accounted for over 50 per cent of the uninsured). And then there are the underinsured: it was estimated in 1993 that 20–25 per cent of Americans had coverage inadequate to protect them against financial ruin in the event of major illness. Finally, there are the precariously insured: figures for the same year show that a quarter of US households contained someone who could not switch jobs for fear of losing their insurance. Divorce, loss of job, becoming ill and being chronically ill can all lead to loss of health insurance (Weitz 1996).

'It all began with such marvellous intentions' (Barer *et al.* 1995: 453). When Clinton was elected to the presidency in 1992 he determined to take advant-age of the strong and widespread public support for health care reform. His rhetoric anticipated a fusion of a Democratic impetus for universal coverage with a Republican impetus for cost containment. 'Single payer' options for reform enjoyed little political support outside the ranks of the Democratic Party and were quickly discarded. Largely Republican schemes of 'market incrementalism' were predictably given short shrift. Skocpol (1997) has termed the compromise scheme Clinton eventually adopted – shaped by the political need to gain cross-party and public backing and to placate the 500+ lobbyists in Washington – *inclusive managed competition*.

Clinton's scheme might be summarized as follows. At its core was the commitment to universal coverage and a 'guaranteed baseline package' equivalent to that offered by many large American corporations (although it was recognized that this might have to be cut back as a result of political trading). There would be substantial employer contributions: 80 per cent for larger businesses, with subsidies and limits on contributions for smaller businesses (the level of employer contribution averaged out at 57 per cent). The scale of these employer contributions was essential in lieu of general increases in taxation. Large corporations/businesses (that is, those employing 5,000+) could 'opt out' and purchase their own insurance; all other businesses would be part of 'mandatory health purchasing alliances', through which they would purchase insurance. These 'regional' health purchasing alliances would be a mechanism for harnessing competitive market forces to produce true price reduction in health care, as well as for inducing insurers to compete over quality and efficient of delivery. They would use community rating. There would be 'regionally adjusted contingent premium caps', a device of last resort if health alliances and market forces failed to hold prices down. Medicare would remain, although with efficiency gains. Medicaid would be reduced in the light of employer contributions/health alliances, but federal and state governments would subsidize coverage for the unemployed. It was a scheme whose time had come but it failed, leaving, it seemed, only the possibility of refining managed care plans, which by 1998 had expanded to cover four out of five insured Americans, and other relatively unpromising cost-saving devices and varieties of piecemeal social engineering or incrementatlism (Churchill 1999). Yet, as Kirkman-Liff (1997: 37) observes, 'what killed the Clintons' reforms was both the past history of incremental reforms that created a powerful network of groups interested in preserving the current system and a decline in faith of the public in the ability of government to successfully provide sound structural reform.' There is, he suggests, an inherent contradiction: 'the US system needs fundamental, comprehensive structural reform if it is to achieve universal coverage and cost-containment. However, only incremental piecemeal reform is politically and economically feasible, and incremental piecemeal reform will only make the systems increasingly difficult to reform and increasingly complex.' In fact, health care at the time of writing represents in excess of 14 per cent of GDP (compared with an OECD mean of 8 per cent), which means that close to 2 per cent of the US economy is composed of the profits from health insurance and medical care organizations. Moreover, the evidence is that more American citizens are moving into the categories of uninsured, underinsured and precariously insured. It has been estimated that the numbers uninsured are currently increasing by one million per annum (Fletcher 1999).

If Thatcher's insertion of an internal market into the NHS lacked either public support or a compelling rationale, Clinton's reform plan, although a politically compromised hybrid, wanted for neither. Why, then, was his Health Security Act dead in the water well before the close of the 'health debate' of 1993–4? The 'surface' reasons are multifold (Kirkman-Liff 1997). For example, the Hilary Clinton/Ira Magazina team adopted dubious tactics: the initial proposal was perhaps too long, intricate and polished, allowing for too little subsequent bipartisan trading and haggling. And the electorate was predisposed to cynicism and declining faith and trust in (partisan) government (King 2000), exacerbated by topical issues of political fund-raising and lobbying. But it is suggested here that less obvious or 'beneath the surface' issues of legitimacy, class and habitus are also salient.

Many of the trends designated as postmodern were discernible in the USA before they had an impact in Britain. Nor, typically, did they take off from the same baselines in the two societies. This certainly applies to processes of individualization and to the new inequality. The American poor were not so new – although they too have endured further disenfranchisement, and for much the same reasons – in the generation of disorganized capitalism (Galbraith 1992). Yet a crisis of legitimation (if not of public disorder) is probably more unlikely in the USA than it is in Britain. This is due both to the more marked (and enhanced) salience of relations of class over relations of command (as well as welfare and worth) and to the more pronounced, and arguably deepening, suspicion of the dark Orwellian potential of the state (which remains a prime feature of the American habitus).

Barer and colleagues (1995) are among those to explore the role of 'vested interests' and of the 'disinformation' accomplished by 'spin doctors' in scuppering Clinton's reforms. 'Those concentrated interests with the most to lose', they write (1995: 456), 'have far more powerful incentives to get their case across, than does anyone to make the case for the effect of reform on the average American.' Ironically, Marmor (1994) cites Enthoven – key advisor to Thatcher's class-driven NHS reforms – on this issue: 'the US political system', the guru avers, 'is incapable of forcing change in such power institutions as the insurance industry, organized medicine, the medical devices industry and the pharmaceutical industry.' Navarro (1995: 459) is more blunt: 'the reality is that the United States lacks a national health programme because of its specific class relations.' We should not write about 'interest group behaviour' but instead about class. He argues that (proven) single payer options were 'politically unfeasible' because they were unacceptable to the corporate and upper middle classes.

The staggering power of the capitalist class and enormous weakness of the working class explains why health care reform failed again. The United States, the only major capitalist country without government-guaranteed universal health care coverage, is also the only nation without a social-democratic or labour party that serves as the political instrument of the working classes and other popular classes. These two facts are related. In most advanced countries, the establishment of universal entitlement programmes has also been based on the political alliances of the working class with the middle classes, through the election of social-democratic governments or through their pressure on non-social-democratic governments.

It is a case, again, of baselines being different.

Churchill's (1999: 406) comment on current American health care is empirically unexceptional: 'instead of leading to health security, market forces lead to health insecurity. Instead of building solidarity among citizens, market competition and the commercialization of health services further divide and fragment society.' Marmor and Mashaw (1995) contend that these forces, once grasped by the American public, will return health care reform to the political agenda. This may be, but in the meantime there seems little prospect either of a legitimation crisis or of any effective interruption to the dominance of class relations over those of command, welfare and worth.

It is of course in large measure ideological, but overlaying class habitus in the USA are *national* 'lasting, transposable dispositions'. These militate directly against health care reform. Americans, in their earliest days 'runaways from authority' who invented rather than inherited their form of government (Lipset 1977: 58), have always been suspicious of government *per se*; and there is evidence that this suspicion, or distrust, has grown stronger – and at a faster rate than in comparable Western nations, including Britain (Dalton 1999) – during disorganized capitalism (Putnam *et al.* 2000). 'The typical American', Churchill (1999: 409) observes, 'believes that government can do little right and the market can do little wrong'. And he continues, 'yet another factor in society's failure to address these problems (that is, of health care delivery) is the tendency to moralize about those who are not winners in the market competition, that is, to see the uninsured and underserved as victims of their own poor health practices and personal failings.' Blaming victims is a convenient way to rationalize inequality, as will become apparent in Chapter 5.

The collapse of Clinton's initiative for inclusive managed competition, which represented a partial but significant attempt to decommodify health care in the USA, has to be understood, paradoxically, with reference to the same logics and relations that informed Thatcher's more successful market-oriented reforms, which represented a partial recommodification of health care in Britain. It is the historical baselines which are different. Class relations in the USA have ceded little to, and have gained important concessions from, relations of command and welfare since the 1970s, not solely in frustrating Clinton, but also, for example, in subverting managed care plans (an instance of the principle of advantage in operation); and this has again been accomplished, despite rising health care costs and declining coverage, without risking a legitimation crisis (in part perhaps because the USA has a record of absorbing or 'tolerating' inequality which is second to none in the Western world, although Britain is in hot pursuit). Moreover, individualism and ego-centrism remain at the heart of the American national habitus, which continues to be class-compatible and largely ideological, notwithstanding tendencies towards the postmodernization of culture and self.

Tocqueville's judgement of the (white, male) American citizen decades after the American Revolution still resonates in the national habitus: 'freed from the king, feudal traditions, roots, and connections, he saw himself simply as an entity rather than part of a larger social or moral whole . . . he owed nothing to any other and expected nothing: he stood alone, confident he controlled his whole destiny, thrown back forever upon himself alone' (quoted in Takaki 1990). Failure is a personal matter.

Initial reflections on the 'Third Way'

The brief observations on the 'Third Way' in this section once more summon the logics of the regime of accumulation and mode of regulation and real relations of class; but the figuration of the nation-state is displaced by that of the Anglo-Saxon capitalism typified by the USA *and* Britain.

The concept of the Third Way, according to Giddens (1994, 1998, 2000), announces the arrival of a 'radical politics' which is 'beyond left and right'; that is, in the British context, one which supercedes both the classical social democracy of the 'old' or pre-modernized Labour Party and Thatcherite neo-liberalism. He posits 'as a prime motto for the new politics': '*no rights without responsibilities*' (Giddens 1998: 65). Unsurprisingly it is a politics which requires us to 'rethink the welfare state in a fundamental way' (Giddens 1994: 17). In organized capitalism the welfare state was a 'class compromise' or 'settlement' designed to provide security against external risk; but this is no longer appropriate, especially when so much risk is manufactured. Moreover, the neo-liberals have exposed key deficiencies in the Keynesian welfare state, including: its ineffectiveness in countering poverty and as an agency of income or wealth redistribution; its reliance on a model of traditional gender roles, presuming male participation in paid labour, with a 'second tier' of support for families lacking a male bread winner; its bureaucratic inflexibility; and its creation and fostering of welfare dependency. Disorganized capitalism, in short, requires a new 'settlement', and as a matter of urgency.

Building on the work of Inglehart (Inglehart and Abrahamson 1994), Giddens (1994: 18) commends what he terms *positive welfare*: 'the welfare state grew up as a mode of protecting against misfortunes that "happen" to people – certainly so far as social security is concerned it essentially picks up the pieces after mishaps have occurred. Positive welfare by contrast, places much greater emphasis on the mobilizing of life-political measures, aimed once more at connecting autonomy with personal and collective responsibilities.' The notion of personal responsibility not only has a special appeal for thinkers of the Third Way, but underpins the (substantially inherited) communitarian rhetorics of both Clinton's Democratic and Blair's New Labour governments. 'Labour is being Americanized', Pilger complained in 1995. He traces Blair's rhetorical themes back to Clinton's early speeches. Blair's terminology and vision, he adds, endorse Thatcher's view of the 'bootstraps' society, according to which the 'unemployed, the low paid, single parents, the sick and the homeless are to assume "responsibility" for decisions in which they have taken no part.'

Swanson (2000) documents how in the USA the discourse of personal responsibility is linked to two key events in the 1950s and 1960s: the white middle-class fear of moral degeneracy and the 'discovery of poverty'. This is worth quoting at some length:

> like earlier in American history the white middle-class image of the poor, who were (and are) disproportionately people of colour, came to represent what the middle-class feared most in itself; softening of character, a lack of firm internal values. The poor were (and still are) assigned character traits opposite from those that the middle-class claimed for itself; the poor person lived for the moment, unable to think ahead, to save or plan for the future, while the middle-class person was imagined to have self-discipline, a strong superego, an ability to plan ahead to meet self-imposed goals. Such images have a significant impact on how poverty and social problems, particularly those associated with the poor, are conceptualized and addressed.
>
> (Swanson 2000: 34)

In the 1970s and 1980s American conservatives, and subsequently many liberals, began to maintain that most social problems were caused by a decline in 'traditional values' in certain segments of the population. This decline had its origins in the nature of government activity, and especially in government aid to the poor. Notoriously, Murray argued that 'the expanded social-welfare measures of the 1960s created poverty by undermining the fragile assumption . . . that adults are responsible for the state in which they find themselves' (cited by Swanson 2000: 36). A parallel emphasis on culture and values can be found in both Clinton's and Blair's espousal of welfare reform. Echoing Pilger, Swanson (2000: 36) summarizes: 'Clinton's (and Blair's) rhetoric and policies have much in common with Reagan's (and Thatcher's) in terms of locating the solution to economic and social problems in the reform of individuals' character and not in government or community efforts to alter structural conditions or relations.'

Three remarks on the Third Way will have to suffice to close this chapter. First, it seems incontrovertibly the case that the Third Way fulfils precisely the same ideological functions as neo-liberalism; that is, both philosophies constitute adequate rationalizations for a mode of regulation appropriate to the new regime of accumulation of disorganized capitalism. In fact, this provides a paradigmatic application of the principle of compatibility. And real relations of class, it has been argued with reference to British and US health care, have assumed renewed salience relative to those of command and welfare in the present phase of disorganized or global capitalism, despite a possible, and perhaps temporary, reduction of the potential for class consciousness and class-based collective action.

The second remark is that, for all the prepotency of (rapidly globalizing) class relations, command and welfare relations at the level of the nation-state

remain significant. But as well as becoming more answerable to class, they
have changed their nature during disorganized capitalism. More attention will
be paid in Chapters 5 and 6 to the new parameters of the relationship between
state and citizen and to concepts like *governmentality*, *surveillance*, *risk* and *tech-nologies of the self*. Higgs (1998: 193–4) is one who has analysed this relationship.
His summary is clear and succinct:

> the new citizen learns to engage with risks constructively because if he
> or she doesn't there is no collective security net waiting to make good
> the damage. Here risk takes on the form of 'dangerousness' and the sur-
> veying processes that have become the core of the modern state have a
> need to identify such potential trouble. The nature of such potential 'risks'
> range from the failing school to the delinquent child, from the welfare
> mother to the unmotivated jobless teenager, and from the discharged
> psychiatric patient to the frail house-bound older person. Each of these
> categories is a failure in social policy terms and it is the role of the state to
> provide methods of reasserting the proper order of things. Even with
> the physically frail and potentially mentally confused older person, the
> lesson to be learned is to make provision earlier in life so that recourse to
> the limited resources of the state is not necessary.

Third, it needs reiterating that what Taylor-Gooby (1997: 171) calls the
'traditional agenda of social policy', namely 'class inequality, the strength of
capital and the policy programme of the nation-state', continues to matter
(see also Hay's (1998) critique, and Taylor-Gooby's (1999) rejoinder). Navarro
(1999: 676), likewise focusing on Britain, is less circumspect than Taylor-
Gooby:

> social democracy as the major instrument of the European labour move-
> ment established the welfare state in western continental Europe. The
> UK welfare state, with the exception of the National Health Service, is
> underdeveloped. Most social transfers are quite low by European stan-
> dards and frequently are means-tested. What seems to be needed is not
> for a social democracy to learn from the Third Way, but rather the Third
> Way to learn from what Giddens derisively calls 'classical' social demo-
> cracy. Its 'break' with the latter condemns the Third Way to becoming a
> step back rather than a progressive step in the proper direction.

What is required, arguably, is a *reconstruction of the welfare project* (Habermas
1989a).

5

The new inequality and health

Changes in the distribution of wealth and income in Britain in the recent past, from 1900 to the present, are complex to fathom (see Scott 1994; Atkinson 2000). Capital income, or wealth, is the smaller part of total national income, but is more unequally distributed than earned income. There has been a trend towards greater equality in wealth distribution over the century as a whole, especially during the period from 1950 to 1980 (Atkinson 2000: 358–9). In 1911, the top 1 per cent of the population held over two-thirds of personal wealth; by 1950 this had fallen to just under one-half; and by 1980 it had declined to under one-quarter (Scott 1994). However, wealth inequality remains marked. As late as 1996, for example, out of a total UK marketable wealth of £2,042 billion, the top 1 per cent still owned 19 per cent (with the top 5 per cent owning 39 per cent and the top 10 per cent owning 52 per cent), *while the bottom half shared only 7 per cent between them* (ONS 2000b: 97) (although the 7 per cent owned by the bottom half rises to 17 per cent if state and occupational pension wealth is included: Atkinson 2000: 360).

In the *Sunday Times* Rich List 2000, Beresford and Boyd (2000: 4) ranked Britain's top ten billionaires as follows.

1   Hans Rausing (£4 billion).
2   The Duke of Westminster (£3.7 billion).
3   Sir Richard Branson (£2.4 billion).
4=   Lakshmi Mittal (£2.2 billion).
4=   Lord Sainsbury (£2.2. billion).
6=   Bernie and Slavica Eccleston (£2 billion).
6=   Joseph Lewis (£2 billion).
8   Sri and Gopi Hinduja (£1.9 billion).
9=   Philippe Foriel-Destezet (£1.5 billion).
9=   Bruno Schroder (£1.5 billion).

Putting these extraordinary figures into some kind of context, it is worth noting that in 1997–8 over 50 per cent of British households reported having less than £1,500 pounds in savings, with 30 per cent reporting no savings at all. And in particular, 71 per cent of single-parent households and 41 per cent of single adult households had no savings (ONS 2000b: 97).

Material living standards as a whole have of course risen considerably since 1900 (Dilnot and Emmerson 2000). In fact the magnitude of the growth rate in per capita disposable income over this period has been such that even supposing, hypothetically, that the share of the bottom fifth in total income had halved, this fifth would still be nearly twice as well off today in purchasing power as their counterparts at the start of the century (Atkinson 2000: 349).

It is often assumed that the distribution of earnings remained reasonably stable for the first three-quarters of the twentieth century, only to show widening dispersion from the 1970s. In fact, it seems that through the 1970s the bottom decile rose relative to the mean, and the top decile fell (possibly a function of high rates of inflation or government interventions like incomes policies: Atkinson 2000). From the late 1970s, however, the distribution began to widen steadily, with wage inequality reaching the highest levels experienced in the twentieth century (for a conclusive discussion of Gini coefficients for hourly and weekly wages for men and women, based on data from the General Household Survey, the New Earnings Survey and the Family Expenditure Survey for the period 1975–96, see Machin 1999). Atkinson (2000: 354) writes, 'the bottom decile fell as a percentage of the median, losing some but not all of the ground gained in the 1970s. The deterioration in the position of the bottom decile appears to have stopped in the 1990s. More marked, and continuing in the 1990s, is the rise of the top decile, which increased from 167 per cent of the median to 187 per cent in the 15 years after the election of Mrs Thatcher. Overall, the decile ratio increased from 2.87 in 1977 to 3.41, 20 years later.' In summary, the rapid rise in wage inequality in the 1980s was characterized by 'an opening out of both ends of the distribution with the highest earners doing much better than those in the middle, but in turn the middle doing much better than the bottom' (Machin 1999: 189).

Definitions of 'low income', or relative poverty, vary. The threshold adopted to define low income in *Social Trends 30* is 60 per cent of median equivalized household disposable income (equivalization here denoting adjustment for size and composition of household); this is one of the thresholds used in the Department of Social Security's anti-poverty strategy. The proportion of the British population living in households with an income below this level fluctuated between 10 and 15 per cent during the 1960s, 1970s and early 1980s. It rose steeply from 1985, reaching a peak of 21 per cent in 1992, since when it has fallen slightly (down to 18 per cent in 1997–8). Children are disproportionately represented in low-income households; in 1997–8, two out of five of these children were living with one parent only, and more than half were living in households where no one was in paid work (ONS 2000b: 93).

In the spring of 1999, 18 per cent of those aged under 16 were living in work-less households (ONS 2000c: 87).

These figures suggest a phase of disorganized capitalism in Britain characterized by a dramatic and continuing inequality of wealth, and a less dramatic but *widening* (hence 'new') inequality of personal and household income. In comparative terms, Britain is not alone among the advanced nations, with the USA, Japan, Australia, Sweden and the Netherlands also showing substantial increases in income inequality in the 1980s and 1990s. Various factors, like changing demographics (for example, more single-parent families), have played their part, but the main driving force behind this growth of income inequality has been the growing inequality of earnings (earnings constitute more than 70 per cent of market income: Gottschalk and Smeeding 1997). While in most countries strong social safety-nets, represented by tax and transfer offsets, have meant that the growth of market-income inequality has not led to sizeable increases in relative poverty, the USA and Britain are clear exceptions (Faux and Mishel 2000).

The new inequality in Britain is linked intimately with a changing, globalizing labour market. This chapter begins by considering the changing nature or 'destandardization' of work. The second section focuses on the multifarious – and largely (neo-)positivist – attempts to track the relationship between work, 'occupational (social) class', or socio-economic group (SEG) or status (SES) (often presumed proxies for class), and health. It is argued that the resultant contrastive demi-regs need to be put to more imaginative sociological use (see Chapter 1). The third section settles on Wilkinson's (1996) *Unhealthy Societies: The Afflictions of Inequality* and the debate it has precipitated. The virtue of Wilkinson's contribution is that it goes beyond the rather tame and tedious hunt for statistical associations between measures of SEG/SES and health to postulate a strong causal rationale. Wilkinson is criticized, however, for neglecting real relations of class.

In the fourth section it is argued that relations of class remain vitally important if the production and reproduction of health inequalities in Britain are to be accounted for. To this end, a critical realist and neo-Marxist retheorization of class is put forward. This theory then informs a consideration of what has, provocatively but without apology, been called the 'greedy bastards hypothesis' (GBH), which asserts that health inequalities in Britain can plausibly be regarded as the (largely unintended) consequences of the ever-adaptive behaviours of members of its (weakly globalized) power elite, informed by its (strongly globalized) capitalist-executive (Scambler 2001). This is once more framed in terms of the model of logics-relations-figurations. The fifth section contains some reflections on the salience of other social relations, like gender, ethnicity and age, to health inequalities – in ways complementary to, as well as independent of, relations of class. This involves establishing a typology of generative mechanisms serviceable for research in an open system. And the chapter ends with further remarks on health inequalities through the lens of the Third Way.

Destandardized work practices

Sometimes theory forges ahead faster than the data warrant, and this may be true of the sociological investigation of changing patterns of work. For all its insightfulness and shrewdness, for instance, Beck's (2000) diagnosis of the 'Brazilianization' of occidental work seems premature. But if there is continuity, there is discontinuity too. Another brief exercise in (neo-)positivist social accounting is in order here. In 1971, around the outset of disorganized capitalism, 91 per cent of men and 56 per cent of women in the UK were economically active (that is, either in work or seeking work); by 1999, these figures had changed to 84 per cent of men and 72 per cent of women. More than 60 per cent of married or cohabiting women with pre-school children were economically active in 1999, compared with fewer than 40 per cent of lone mothers. Seventeen per cent of households in 1999 were workless (ONS 2000b: 68) (see also Gregg *et al.* 1999).

More and more people are working part-time, although women are far more likely to do so than men. Since 1984, the earliest date for which reliable figures are available, the rate of increase in part-time working has actually been higher among men: it has doubled for men, and increased by a quarter for women (ONS 2000b: 70). Nevertheless, only 8 per cent of men's jobs were part-time in 1999, compared with 43 per cent of women's (Stationery Office 2000: 30). Temporary work is becoming more common: 7 per cent of workers (around 6 per cent of men and 8 per cent of women) were in temporary jobs (that is, on fixed-term contracts, agency temps, casual workers or seasonal workers) in 1999 (ONS 2000b: 73). Flexible working patterns are also more prevalent, especially for women: around 16 per cent of men in full-time work and 15 per cent in part-time work experienced some form of flexible working in 1999, compared with 24 per cent of women in both full- and part-time work (ONS 2000b: 74). Self-employment too is on the increase: 7 per cent were self-employed (10 per cent of men and 3 per cent of women) in 1998. The striking expansion in self-employment has come among people with specialized and highly marketable skills (Gallie 1999: 299).

There are many definitions of unemployment. The International Labour Organization (ILO) regards a person as unemployed if she or he is working less than 1 hour per week, wants to work more and has taken active steps to find work in the previous four weeks, or is waiting to take up a job, and is able to start work in the next two weeks. According to these criteria, the unemployment rate in Britain was 6.1 per cent in 1977, peaked at 11.7 per cent in 1984 and was back to 6.1 per cent in 1998. If, however, 'discouraged workers', those wanting jobs but unable to start in the next two weeks, plus all those who want jobs, are included, the 1984 peak rises to 18 per cent and the 1998 figure rises to 12.8 per cent (Nickell 1999: 10). The very considerable rise in unemployment after the mid-1970s, it seems, was not due to any substantial increase in turnover. The average worker in Britain is only slightly more likely to become unemployed in 2000 than thirty years ago. Once a person enters unemployment, however, he or she remains without a job for nearly three times as long. Unemployment is especially high for young men, and for men (less so in women) without qualifications (Nickell 1999).

Finally, union membership warrants a comment. In fact, union membership has fallen each year since it peaked in 1979, with the largest fall occurring in 1992. Since 1989, when the Labour Force Survey began, membership has fallen by 21 per cent. In 1998 only 31 per cent of men and 28 per cent of women were members of a trade union (ONS 2000b: 79).

There is empirical evidence, then, of what appear to be changing work patterns; that is, in addition to the increase in income and earnings inequality already noted. In particular, there is now more part-time, temporary and flexible labour; more self-employment; more chronic unemployment; more work-less households; and union membership has declined. Many see these trends gaining pace over the next decade, with novel information and communication technologies (ICTs) prompting 'virtual' and other 'non-standard' forms of work, including, for example, 'hot-desking', 'hotelling' and significant extensions of home-working (Scase 2000). How are these changes to be theorized?

In organized ('solid', 'heavy', Fordist) capitalism, Bauman (2000: 145) maintains, 'capital and workers were united, one may say, for richer for poorer, in sickness and in health, until death them did part.' People's mentality was long term: it was an era, in Sennett's (1998: 23) terms, of 'strong unions, guarantees of the welfare state, and large-scale corporations'; and 'relative stability'. The properties of disorganized ('liquid', 'light', post-Fordist) capitalism are quite different:

> and the crucial ingredient of the multi-sided change is the new 'short-term' mentality which came to replace the 'long-term' one . . . Flexibility is the slogan of the day, and when applied to the labour market it augurs an end to the 'job as we know it', announcing instead the advent of work on short-term contracts, rolling contracts or no contracts, positions with no in-built security but with the 'until further notice' clause. Working life is saturated with uncertainty.
>
> (Bauman 2000: 147)

Beck (2000: 70) refers to organized capitalism as 'first modernity' and disorganized capitalism as 'second modernity'. He characterizes the latter as the 'risk regime', emphasizing a new political economy of 'insecurities, uncertainties and loss of boundaries'. In many ways echoing Bauman, Beck (2000: 70–1) writes:

> with the risk regime, people are expected to make their own life-plans, to be mobile and to provide for themselves in various ways. The new centre is becoming the precarious centre. Poverty is being 'dynamized': that is, cut up and distributed across life-sections. It is becoming a 'normal' – less and less often just a temporary – experience at the centre of society. Whereas Fordism and political Keynesianism presupposed the

boundaries of the national state, and thus the standpoint and tax-raising potential of national politics and society, this orderly framework is superseded in the risk regime by a compulsion to relocate and prevail on the world-market and in world society.

There are many analyses in this vein. They should be treated with a measure of caution since they offer easy, neat, often hyperbolic representations of present and future worlds on the strength of bold extrapolations from recent, typically American (see Beck 2000: Chapter 7), empirical trends. But the point in sampling them here is to stress that work patterns do seem to be changing, in Britain as well as America, and that it is part of the sociological task to account for these with references to real, continuous, as well as discontinuous, social relations associated with the transition from organized to disorganized capitalism. This will re-emerge as a major theme later in the chapter. As a prolegomenon, however, the vast (neo-)positivist body of research on work, 'class' and health inequalities needs to be addressed.

Work, 'class' and health inequalities research

Crompton and Mann (1986: xi) have observed that quantitative researchers have retained a commitment to class *analysis* in the face of a growing sociological scepticism about class *theory*: 'the need for class measurement endures, even when class theory becomes unfashionable.' The most enduring instrument in health inequalities research in Britain has been the Registrar General's occupational measure of class (RGOC), which allocates the range of occupations to five groups: class I (professional), class II (managerial/technical), class IIINm (skilled non-manual), class IIIM (skilled manual), class IV (partly skilled) and class V (unskilled) (OPCS 1991). For many decades, however, its users have denounced it – after the manner of Cartwright and O'Brien (1976: 82) – as 'more of a blunderbuss than a carefully calibrated instrument'. The RGOC, in Wilkinson's (1986: 180) opinion, is no more than 'an undefined proxy for the effects of unknown socio-economic differences'. Some researchers have preferred to use socio-economic group (SEG), which combines information on employment status, authority and establishment size with the occupational data (see Annandale 1998).

One of the most impressive and influential attempts to collate the evidence concerning linkages between the RGOC and SEG and morbidity and mortality was the 'Black Report' of 1977–80 (DHSS 1980; Townsend and Davidson 1988), which was commissioned by Callaghan's Labour government and published and sidelined by the new Thatcher regime. This report showed, in the later words of one of its authors, 'that inequalities in health had been widening since the 1950s, that this trend was principally related to inequalities of material resources, and that a programme of higher social security benefits and more equal distribution of income, as well as action on housing and services, was required' (Townsend 1999: x). The elimination of child poverty was flagged as a priority for the 1980s. Adopting an essentially (neo-)positivist mode of explanation/prediction, as well as of social accounting, the report concluded, more formally, that the association between class and health was real, not artefactual (that is, it was not a function of measurement decisions), and that it could be most adequately explained in terms of material factors (like level of income and quality of housing), although cultural/behavioural factors (like smoking, alcohol consumption, diet and exercise) and, to a lesser extent, social selection (that is, downward mobility occasioned by poor health) were also of salience.

The years since the Black Report have been rich in (more and more dense and statistically intricate) updates: from Whitehead's (1987) *The Health Divide: Inequalities in Health in the 1980s*; via Davey Smith and colleagues' (1990) revisitation of the Black Report 'ten years on'; to the data collation edited by Drever and Whitehead (1997); *The Independent Inquiry into Inequalities in Health* ('Acheson Report', 1998, plus its published 'evidence' (Gordon *et al.* 1999) commissioned by a pristine Blair government); and comprehensive reviews of the data like that by Shaw and her associates (1999). While it would be unfair, even churlish, to downplay what has been discovered since the Black Report, two consistent findings should not surprise us. First, it is apparent that health inequalities have continued to increase – there is a 'widening gap' (in terms of the RGOC/SEG, a kind of 'stretching' of stepwise gradations). Second, the Black Report's emphasis on material factors has proved justified: what is still needed, Shaw *et al.* (1999: 102) insist, is more research which 'determines the precise routes through which material disadvantage causes poor health', a need which continues to leave the 'research establishment' largely and unsurprisingly unmoved (Blane 1985; Blane *et al.* 1997).

There are seemingly endless expert and textbook compilations of data on the widening gap, so we can be selective and brief. Referring to data for 1992–6 from the ONS Longitudinal Study, Townsend (1999: 5) describes the life expectancy gap between men in RGOC I (professional) and RGOC V (unskilled) of 9.5 years (for women, it is 6.4 years) as 'staggering'. The full data are given in Table 5.1 (see Hattersley 1999).

Table 5.1 Expectation of life by RGOC for men and women, England and Wales, 1992–1996

Social class	Men	Women
I	77.7	83.4
II	75.8	81.1
IIINM	75.0	80.4
IIIM	73.5	78.8
IV	72.6	77.7
V	68.2	77.0
All	73.9	79.2

Note: For this analysis social class is as of entry into the study (usually 1971).
Source: Hattersley (1999).

Among both men and women aged 35–64, overall mortality rates fell for each RGOC group between 1976–81 and 1986–92; but at the same time the gap between RGOC I/II and IV/V increased. In the late 1970s, mortality rates were 53 per cent higher among men in IV/V compared with those in I/II; and in the late 1980s, they were 68 per cent higher. Among women, the differential increased from 50 to 55 per cent (Harding *et al.* 1997). These growing differences were apparent too for many of the major causes of death, including coronary heart disease, stroke, lung cancer and suicides among men, and respiratory disease and lung cancer among women (Stationery Office 1998).

Despite the overall fall in mortality rates and rise in life expectancy, standard measures suggest a slight increase in self-reported longstanding illness and limiting longstanding illness. Again, socio-economic differences are compelling: in 1996 among those aged 45–65, for example, 17 per cent of professional men reported a limiting longstanding illness, compared to 48 per cent of unskilled men (the figures for women were 25 and 45 per cent). The same pattern obtained for younger adults, older men and children (ONS 1998).

Tables 5.2 and 5.3 are eloquent on links between mortality and unemployment and relative poverty respectively (adapted from Harding *et al.* 1999:

Table 5.2   Trends of mortality rates per 100,000 by employment status and RGOC V among men aged 36–64, 1971 Cohort, England and Wales

Social class	Follow-up period			
	1976–81	*1981–5*	*1986–91*	*1991–5*
Employed				
Non-manual	3,361	2,518	2,178	1,642
Manual	4,105	3,281	3,281	2,455
Unemployed				
Non-manual	4,689	3,980	2,500	2,889
Manual	5,917	4,505	6,059	4,113

Source: Harding *et al.* (1999).

Table 5.3   Inequality ratios of SMRs for deaths under 65 in Britain and percentage of households below half average income (HBAI), 1959–1995

Decile	*1959–63*	*1969–73*	*1981–5*	*1986–9*	*1990–2*	*1993–5*
Ratio 10:1	1.75	1.58	1.70	1.78	1.87	1.98
HBAI (%)	11	9	11	17	24	23

Note: No HBAI figures are available for 1950–3. The minimum estimate has been taken for each period. SMR data are only available for certain years before 1981 from the Decennial Reviews.
Source: Shaw *et al.* (1999).

Shaw *et al.* 1999). Table 5.2 relays trends in mortality rates per 100,000 persons by employment status and RGOC among men aged 36–64. It shows that over the past two decades mortality was consistently lower among men in RGOC I/II/IIINM than among men in IIIM/IV/V, regardless of employment status. In each period, and in each RGOC grouping, mortality was higher for those unemployed than for those employed.

Table 5.3 gives inequality ratios (bottom : top deciles) of standardized mortality ratios (SMRs) for deaths under 65 in Britain, and the percentage of households below half average income, throughout the stage of disorganized capitalism. Shaw *et al.* (1999: 116) point out that inequalities in mortality were lowest when inequalities in income were lowest; that is, between 1969 and 1973 (after the Labour governments of 1964–70). 'It was only in the 1980s that both inequalities in health and inequalities in income rose dramatically, rose together and rose to unprecedented levels.' They infer that reductions in health inequalities can be accomplished within short timespans, but only in tandem with reductions in income inequalities.

The (neo-)positivist programme of research to explain/predict health inequalities has gathered momentum steadily since the Black Report and led to an abundance of published papers. The sociological input has on the whole not been impressive: too many have been content merely to follow social epidemiological 'exemplars' (like the rightly celebrated Whitehall studies), as well as their hypotheses and cues; and too few have been ready to pose more authentic (one might say, classical or modernist) sociological questions about the production, reproduction and persistence of health inequalities, and about the generative mechanisms involved, and to adopt post-positivist methods to seek answers (the critique of positivism in Chapter 1 is central here (see also Forbes and Wainwright 2001), the espousal of critical realism less so) (Higgs and Scambler 1998).

Nor are the RGOC, SEG or SES classificatory schemes adequate proxies for relations of class, as is often tacitly assumed (even when explicitly denied). Wohlfarth (1997) rightly argues that SES measures (focusing on prestige) have their origins in the (structural-)functionalist perspective on stratification (Davis and Moore, 1945), while measures of class (focusing on ownership and/or control of the means of production) stem from (neo-)Marxist conflict theory. Comparing measures of SES and a neo-Marxist operationalization of class based on the early work of Wright (Wright and Perrone 1977; Wright 1979), he found SES and class to be far from 'interchangeable'. Using a limited neo-positivist methodology, he found associations between *each of* SES and class and psychopathology, *speculating* that the causal pathway between SES and psychopathology may be quite different from the causal pathway between class and psychopathology. SES inequality might be incorporated into the personality in the form of self-esteem; while class inequality might be incorporated into personality in the form of locus-of-control.

It does not, of course, follow from the fact that both (neo-)positivism itself and measures like the RGOC and SES/SEGs are problematic that no explanatory headway has been made. But it remains the case both that demi-regs have frequently – and erroneously – been regarded as *intrinsically* worthwhile, and that better investments of sociological time and effort are available. Four 'gains' from extant research (that is, beyond documentary and telling social accounting) are pertinent to the position developed later in the chapter.

The first is the empirical affirmation and reiteration of the abiding importance of material factors for health inequalities. Moreover, attention is beginning to be paid to what might generally be described as the indebtedness of agency to structure (as epitomized in Bourdieu's concept of habitus, explicated in Chapter 4). In the terminology adopted in the Black Report, cultural/behavioural factors are not easily distinguished from material factors (see Bartley *et al.* 1998a). For example, as Graham (1995, 1996) makes clear in her work on women and smoking, buying a packet of ten cigarettes can be a cheap, pleasurable, understandable and *rational* option for someone struggling with the ugly mundanity of day-to-day material scarcity. Popay and her colleagues (1998: 80) make the general point well:

what we are suggesting – to coin an old fashioned phrase – is that people make their own history (and future) – but not always in conditions that they have themselves chosen. In order to further our understanding of the causes of health variations we need to study directly the experiences of individuals and their biographies, and link these to the social organization of places and their histories. This analysis requires, in turn, an awareness of the influence of national and global socio-economic change.

Second, a range of factors beyond the RGOC/SES/SEG have been incorporated into health inequalities research and have yielded a promising array of contrastive demi-regs. Apart from such obvious factors as gender, ethnicity and age, for example, studies are currently under way on the roles of 'space' and 'time' (see Bartley *et al.* 1998b). Although social relations in these studies frequently appear to be undertheorized, some, at least, are postpositivist. In her review of recent work on time and biography, Blaxter (2000) distinguishes between 'social', 'calendar' and 'personal' time. Social time acknowledges the fact that societal change takes place irregularly, such that the collective experience of one generation can differ significantly from that of its successor (each carries its own 'imprint of time': Wadsworth 1991). Calendar time refers to 'clock' time, according to which childhood proceeds through adolescence to adulthood and thence to the third and fourth ages. Personal time is time as it is experienced and perceived by an individual. This more subtle appreciation of time is fostering a processual (birth cohort, longitudinal) as opposed to a static (cross-sectional) orientation in the sociology of health inequalities.

Third, reflecting this sharper awareness of time, there is a growing interest in health and the life course (Wadsworth 1997; Blane 1999). The life course, Bartley and colleagues (1997: 1195) maintain, combines the biological and the social. They argue that 'individuals' biological development takes place within a social context which structures their life chances, so that advantages and disadvantages tend to cluster cross sectionally and accumulate longitudinally.' (Neo-)positivist researchers are almost compelled by their commitment to a Humean perspective on causation to exaggerate the potential for, and their attainment of, experimental closures; but life course research at least suggests that specific diseases and causes of death may relate to the life course in quite different ways (Davey Smith *et al.* 1998).

Wilkinson, Coburn and the health inequalities debate

Wilkinson's work on income inequality and health, and especially his book, have had a catalytic effect on the field. Although his methods remain firmly within the (neo-)positivist paradigm, unlike so many of his more unadventurous colleagues he has put forward a distinctive substantive theory of health inequalities. He argues that, once certain levels of GNP per capita have been attained (approximately US$5,000), the principal determinant of level of health status within a nation-state is degree of income inequality. In his own words, 'apparently regardless of the fact that health differences within societies remain so closely related to socioeconomic status, once a country has passed through the epidemiological transition, its whole population can be more than twice as rich as any other country without being any healthier' (Wilkinson 1996: 3). Nor is Wilkinson (1996: 107) afraid to be precise, calculating that a difference of only about 7 per cent in the share of income going to the bottom 50 per cent of the population would result in a two-year increase in life expectancy.

Why is this? What is known as 'the Wilkinson hypothesis' draws on the seminal work of Putnam (1983) to assert that *social cohesion/trust* is the dominant mechanism linking a nation-state's degree of income inequality with health. Wilkinson (2000: 998) contends that income inequality involves 'not only the effects of changes in the burden of low social status but, perhaps less obviously, also the effects of poor social affiliations.' He suggests there is firm evidence that where income differences are more marked, social divisions tend to be exacerbated; 'levels of trust' and 'the strength of community life' tend to be lower; rates of 'social anxiety' and 'chronic stress' tend to be enhanced; rates of hostility, violence and homicide tend to be higher; and there tends to develop a 'culture of inequality' characterized by 'a more hostile and less hospitable social environment' (Wilkinson 1999a, b). In many of these respects, he adds, humans are less unlike many other animals than they might suppose.

Wilkinson (2000: 998–9) goes on to conclude that 'although we used to assume that the direct effects of poorer material circumstances accounted for the social gradient in health, it now looks as if a major part of the association between low social status and poorer health springs from *the experience of low social status or subordination itself*' (emphasis added). Moreover, this general conjecture sits well with 'the increasing success of psychosocial factors in explaining health inequalities'.

Wilkinson's hypothesis raises numerous issues, ranging from the adequacy of his measurement of changing national rates of income inequality, to his definition of social cohesion/trust, to his privileging of psychosocial pathways, to the appropriateness of his inferences from animal to human behaviour. The critique here remains general, taking Coburn's (2000a) entry into the health inequalities debate as its cue. Coburn (2000a: 136) notes, appositely and depressingly, that 'almost all the attention within the SES-health status tradition has been devoted to attempts to explain why and how SES is related to health . . . There has been an overwhelming tendency to focus on the possible social/psycho-biological mechanisms through which social factors might be tied to health rather than on examination of the basic social causes of inequality and health.' This neglect of the determinants of SES and income inequality incites Coborn (2000a: 137) to argue that, 'rather than income inequality producing lowered social cohesion/trust leading to lowered health status, neo-liberalism (market dominance) produces *both* higher income inequality and lowered social cohesion . . . and, presumably, either lowered health status or a health status which is not as high as it might otherwise have been' (see also Muntaner and Lynch 1999).

Coburn (2000a: 138) identifies three basic assumptions of neo-liberalism: 'that markets are the best and most efficient allocators of resources in production and distribution'; 'that societies are composed of autonomous individuals (producers and consumers) motivated chiefly or entirely by material or economic considerations'; and 'that competition is the major market vehicle for innovations.' Economic globalization, he argues, was abetted by neo-liberals, and neo-liberalism benefited from globalization. And in consequence, society in global or disorganized capitalism has been 'restructured', notably by means of a (partial) recommodification of state welfare. With the possible exception of Japan, Coburn (2000a: 140) maintains that 'the more market-oriented or neo-liberal the regime the greater the income inequality.' He (2000a: 142) goes on to contend also that 'the more market-oriented the society, the higher the social fragmentation and the lower the social cohesion and trust.'

Coburn is quite right to find Wilkinson at fault for calling off his search for causes too early (although Wilkinson is at one with almost all other (neo-)positivists in this respect). But it is incongruous – as Coburn (2000b: 1010) seems later to recognize in response to a series of commentaries on his paper – that he both insists that class relations are fundamental for SES and income inequality, and focuses almost exclusively on the putative causal role of neo-liberalism. Paul Higgs and I have argued that it is neo-liberalism's *class-generated ideological properties* – that is, its potential to rationalize core capitalist-executive action – that matters; and as has already been noted, consistently with the principle of compatibility, the contrasting doctrines of the Third Way possess functionally equivalent properties and potential (Scambler and Higgs 2001). In the next section an attempt is made to complement the reinvigorating contributions of Coburn, Muntaner, Lynch and others by suggesting a retheorization of the linkage between real class relations and health inequalities.

Class relations and the GBH

The transition from organized to disorganized capitalism has entailed (one might say 'noisy') discontinuity; but not surprisingly given that Britain remains an unequivocally (Anglo-Saxon) capitalist society, there is more ('quiet') continuity than there may appear to be. Seabrook (1982: 47) has a point: 'in the end, it is the static nature of society that stares us in the face, in spite of all the upheavals. All the talk of change turns out to be changing people so that they fit the modified needs of cold economic processes.' Sympathetic to Seabrook, Webster (2000: 70) argues that 'while there is undoubted change taking place, and this at a speed and with a reach hitherto unimaginable, it is for the most part a matter of continuity, consolidation and extension of established relations.' It is with the extension of established relations of class that we are concerned here.

It has become apparent in the course of Chapters 3 and 4 that a critical realist and neo-Marxist theory of class relations underpins many of the analyses and arguments of this volume. It is time to clarify the substance of this theory, not least because, first, ('hard') class theory, as opposed to ('soft') class analysis (Higgs and Scambler 1998), has all but disappeared from medical sociology; and, second, many mainstream sociologists, impressed by discontinuity (which for some heralds a new social formation of postmodernity), have announced the supercession or even the 'death of class' (Pakulski and Waters 1996; for recent debates on class, see Lee and Turner 1996).

Bhaskar (1989a) regards Marx as providing an early statement of both a transformational model of social activity and a rational model of society, which he combines with an additional premise of historical materialism, namely that it is material production that ultimately determines the rest of social life. Adapting Bhaskar's Kantian transcendentalism, Paul Higgs and I have argued elsewhere that given the 'social patterning' consistently exposed by social researchers deploying a mix of what Crompton (1993) terms 'nominal', 'weakly relational' and 'strongly relational' class schema (for reviews, see Adonis and Pollard 1997), notwithstanding exaggerated (postmodern) assertions of class decomposition or dealignment (see Chapter 2), there *must* exist *real relations of class* hinging on the ownership/control of the means of production (Scambler and Higgs 1999: 281).

Clement and Myles (1997) have developed a neo-Marxist perspective on class which provides a useful starting point for further discussion. It has much in common with Wright's early (strongly relational) formulation, if not with his later (weakly relational) 'principal assets' model (Wright 1985). They utilize the insights of Carchedi (1977), maintaining that classes are formed at the point of production and reproduced throughout social life. Central to class formation are the criteria of 'real economic ownership of the means of production' and the 'appropriation of surplus value and/or value through control and surveillance of the labour of others' (what Charchedi terms the 'global function of capital'). The exercise of control and surveillance with regard to the labour process is distinct from the accomplishment of 'coordination and unity', which is part of 'creating surplus value/labour' (in Carchedi's terms, part of the 'global function of the collective worker') (Clement and Myles 1997: 12).

The distinction between control/surveillance on the one hand and coordination/unity on the other is crucial. While the latter are essential for any large-scale system of production, the former follow from the requirement to 'impose discipline' on workers in the interests of extracting surplus value and/or surplus labour from them. This extraction of surplus value and/or surplus labour is particular to maintaining members of the *capitalist-executive*, who have 'specific powers that are called real economic ownership' (Clement and Myles 1997: 13). The work of control and surveillance represents an extension of real economic ownership; and in nation-states like Britain becomes 'the task of a complex, hierarchically organized ensemble of people who collectively perform what used to be the function of the individual capitalist' (Carchedi 1997: 70). These tasks of capital are now the responsibility of people who are themselves separate from real economic ownership, the *new middle class*.

The principal criterion for the capitalist-executive class is real economic ownership; that is, 'the power to direct production to specific purposes and dispose of its products' (Clement and Myles 1997: 14). This entails command over 'strategic decision-making'. Individuals belong to the new middle class if they are involved in 'tactical decision-making' in administrative processes affecting others or if they exercise control and surveillance over the labour power of other employees, including the right to discipline those workers. Those who (only) coordinate and lend unity to the labour process, 'and are therefore productive of surplus value and/or value', do not belong to the new middle class but with collective labour.

The *old middle class* owns its own means of realizing its labour: its members work 'outside' the dominant relations of production. Whereas the classic petit bourgeoisie owned its own property and enjoyed independence from the capitalist class, 'a more intensive analysis of the fate of the old middle class under advanced capitalism reveals that many members retain their formal ownership of their means of production and possession of their immediate labour process but have often lost control over real economic ownership (thus becoming dependent commodity producers), experiencing proletarianization without becoming proletarian' (Clement and Myles 1997: 15).

But the primary relationship for Clement and Myles is between the capitalist-executive class and the *working class*. And the working class is the class that has no command over the means of production, the labour power of others, or its own means of realizing its labour. It is a class with only its labour power to sell; it is the subject of capital as mediated by the new middle class.

Missing from this theoretically plausible schema are more focused considerations of the existence/structural characteristics of what were earlier dubbed an 'underclass' and an 'overclass', the first a putative product of the new inequality, the other its beneficiary. Each will be considered in turn, but neither term will survive.

The concept of an underclass

There has been much debate in sociological circles on the existence or otherwise of an underclass in Britain; that is, of a sizeable 'outsider' (Bradley 1996) or 'surplus population group' (Esping-Anderson 1993) which is materially, and perhaps culturally, adrift. The emergence of such a group has variously been attributed to: the growth of chronic unemployment; the decline in industrial jobs; women's changing labour market position; the collapse of working-class communities; and attempts to dismantle the welfare state (Bradley 1996: 50). But there is relatively little agreement on the defining criteria of an underclass. Buckingham (1999) distinguishes three approaches. The *behavioural* approach contends that recent increases in the illegitimacy rate, male labour market inactivity and serious crime affirm the existence of an underclass of welfare dependants (Murray 1990). As for causes, the incentive effect of welfare benefits, a breakdown in traditional morality leading to an anti-work culture and individual genetic factors are emphasized. *Labour market* approaches focus on structural factors like the destandardization of work practices and labour disadvantage: 'forced into long-term unemployment and poverty, a spatially concentrated and socially excluded underclass is created, which develops a culture that rejects mainstream values . . . the culture follows but does not cause the problem' (Buckingham, 1999: 50). *Critical* approaches deny the existence of an underclass: they accept the emergence of a 'periphery of part-time, temporary and long-term unemployed *class situations*', but argue that these do not constitute a 'homogeneous and distinctive *social class* called the underclass' (Buckingham, 1999: 51; see Gallie 1988).

Analysing longitudinal data from the National Child Development Study, Buckingham himself finds pros and cons in all three approaches, although he takes pains to insist that behavioural factors, like 'weak work attachment' (so often sought and found solely among the underprivileged: Gans 1995), may well be significant. Ultimately, he concludes that there may be an emerging underclass in Britain. This judgement may yet be premature. The term underclass suggests a group literally underneath the class structures of society (Bauman 1998b). Novak (1996: 190) rightly argues that class position, 'at least in the Marxist sense', is not decided by whether someone is 'employed or unemployed, poor or poorer'; instead, 'the unemployed, the old, the sick, the "economically inactive" constitute part of the working class.' Chronic and long-term unemployment and its associated immiseration is a periodic feature of capitalist economies. It is too early to discern a qualitatively different phenomenon warranting the use of the concept of an underclass. It makes sense in the interim to refer to a (perhaps temporarily) *displaced segment* of the working class (Scambler and Higgs 1999: 285).

Core capitalist-executive/power elite

Less, and less rigorous, attention has been paid by researchers to rich capitalists than to poor workers; and this is even more true of medical sociologists interested in the maldistribution of health than it is of sociologists in the main-stream. In the course of their participation in the 'Comparative Project on Class Structure and Class Consciousness', launched at the turn of the 1980s by Wright, Clement and Myles (1997: 19) analysed class distributions for samples from five nation-states: the USA, Canada, Norway, Sweden and Finland. The breakdown for the USA, which was distinctive for its high proportion of members in the capitalist-executive and new middle class, was as follows: capitalist-executive (10.2 per cent); new middle class (28.3 per cent); old middle class (7.8 per cent); and working class (53.7 per cent). Clearly only a small core of those belonging to the capitalist-executive in the USA are *significant players* in the US economy, let alone in the global economy or as part of a nascent transnational capitalist class (see Chapter 3). Similarly in Britain's less potent economy. Scott (1991: 89–90) has identified what he calls a 'capitalist class' in Britain composed of entrepreneurial capitalists, 'passive' rentiers and executive capitalists, together with an 'inner circle' of finance capitalists 'with directorships in two or more very large enterprises in the system of impersonal capital'; he estimates the size of this group at 0.1 per cent of the population, or about 43,500 individuals.

Scott (1991: 151) argues that Britain is ruled by a capitalist class whose economic dominance is sustained by the state and whose members are 'dispro-portionately represented in the power elite which rules the state apparatus'. He specifies three preconditions for the existence of a 'ruling' capitalist class: first, a power bloc dominated by a capitalist class; second, a power elite recruited from this power bloc, and in which the capitalist class is dispro-portionately represented; and third, mechanisms which ensure that the state operates in the interests of the capitalist class and the reproduction of capital. If such a power bloc is to endure, it must attain 'consciousness', 'coherence' and a capacity for 'conspiracy'; that is, 'it must evolve some awareness of common interests and concerns, it must achieve some degree of solidarity and cohesion, and its leading members must be capable of pursuing some kind of coordinated policy of action to further these interests' (Scott 1991: 122; see also 1997).

If there is a small, dynamic and strongly globalized core of significant players in the British capitalist-executive, how might the power elite govern-ing the state apparatus, permeated and informed by these leading capitalists, be characterized? Helpful here is the ESRC Whitehall Programme on 'The Changing Nature of Central Government in Britain', and especially Smith's *The Core Executive of Britain* (1999). Drawing on the work of Rhodes (1995a, b), Smith argues for the displacement of the simplistic 'Westminster model', founded on theories of the vertical distribution of power and parliamentary sovereignty, by a 'core executive model', founded on theories of the hor-izontal distribution of power and of a core executive epitomized by overlap-ping networks. While some networks, like the connections between Prime Minister, cabinet and departments, are relatively permanent, others exist only for the lifetime of a particular policy, such as Welfare to Work.

Power is defined by Smith in terms of resource dependency. He writes:

power depends on relationships between actors and not on command. Frequently, outcomes can be a positive-sum game rather than a zero-sum one. In order to achieve goals, actors have to negotiate, compromise and bargain. Consequently, power does not just exist in conflicts between cabinet and Prime Minister but, as Foucault suggests, it is in every situation and relationship as actors develop belief systems, strategies and alliances in order to exchange resources and achieve goals. There is no need to adopt a discourse or post-modern approach to see the core executive as a field of micro-politics, where power is exercised through a multitude of agencies and coherence imposed through the 'adoption of shared vocabularies'.

(Smith 1999: 33–5)

Smith acknowledges that both the British parliament and its core executive have lost power with globalization, although, like Weiss (1999), he emphasizes the continuance of 'state capacity'. What seems apparent both from the analyses of previous chapters and from the remarks in this section is that the case for the *effective and decisive* penetration of Britain's small, dynamic and weakly globalized core executive/power elite by significant players and their allies from its small, dynamic and strongly globalized core of the capitalist-executive seems incontravertible (sceptics might consult Monbiot 2000). Crudely symptomatic of 'overlapping networks' is the behaviour of Thatcher's former chancellor and health secretary, Ken Clarke, who apparently receives £100,000 per annum as deputy chairman of British American Tobacco (BAT), the world's second biggest tobacco company, and a concern at the time of writing under investigation over smuggling allegations (Maguire 2000).

It is now time to turn to the GBH, the background to which has been prepared elsewhere (Scambler 2001). Britain's greedy bastards (GBs) are numbered among Scott's (1991) 'capitalist class' of 43,500. Of particular significance, without doubt, are the chairmen and chief executives in the FTSE 100 companies surveyed for the *Sunday Times* (Waples *et al.* 2000).

A few eloquent facts on their appetites will have to suffice. For the second year in succession Colt Telecom's Paul Chisholm was Britain's best (and most over-) paid Footsie boss. His package over the previous year, including salary, bonus and share-option gains, totalled £146.5 million (whereas according to the investigating team he should have received £6.9 million 'had he been paid strictly according to Colt's size, complexity and share performance', an overpayment of 1,994 per cent). Britain's 'most underpaid' Footsie boss was Robin Saxby, chief executive of ARM: his package worked out at £6.6 million when according to the journalists' calculations he 'should have been paid £11.6 million' (fortunately for Saxby, he also owns 2.4 per cent of his £6.8 billion company). It is noted that over the previous year a clearer relationship between fixed pay and company size emerged. Waples and colleagues write: 'there has only been a small rise in the median fixed pay from £497,000 to £515,000, while the upper quartile has increased from £605,000 to £698,000. The big increases have come in variable pay, in the upper quartile. The median total pay has increased from £920,000 to £1.4 million and the upper quartile from £1.5 to £2.9 million.' This shows, they add, 'that pay is now increasingly linked to performance'. Further comment would be superfluous.

The GBH states, without a hint of hyperbole, that Britain's persisting – even widening – health inequalities might reasonably be regarded as the (largely unintended) consequences of the ever-adaptive behaviours of members of its (weakly globalized) power elite, informed by its (strongly globalized) capital-executive. The GBH will be considered in terms of the model of logics/relations/figurations used in Chapter 4. The logics are again those of the regime of accumulation and mode of regulation of disorganized capitalism, the relations those of class, and the figuration that of the British nation-state.

It has been implied throughout the preceding discussion that relations of class have gained a new prominence in disorganized capitalism relative to those of command (and welfare); and, relatedly, that the disenfranchisement of the 'new poor', in particular, has reduced any imminent threat of a legitimation crisis. Many would be sympathetic to the general postulate that class affects health. The GBH pinpoints one, maybe even *the*, prepotent *sociological* mechanism. But how can the strategic decisions of leading representatives of the capitalist-executive, however indirectly or circuitously, bear on the health and longevity of their fellow citizens?

It should be clear that real class relations are very different from the relations implicit in the RGOC or in versions of SES or SEG. It is not of course the object of 'taking class seriously' that this delivers a steeper and more satisfying gradient for morbidity/mortality than the RGOC or SES/SEG. Indeed, the (neo-)positivist obsession with gradients may have become counter-productive for the sociological imagination. It would be absurd to suggest too that core members of the capitalist-executive are, by virtue of their extraordinary wealth and influence, predisposed to enjoy the longest lives, replete with health and well-being.

But it is entirely plausible to argue that strategic decision-making conducted by a small, focused and – if necessary – conspiratorial core alliance of the global GBs of the GBH, for the most part facilitated by the state's globalizing power elite, is a vital – direct and intended – determinant of the changing distribution and pattern of labour and of income/social transfers in Britain; and, therefore, a no less vital – indirect and largely unintended – determinant of its enduring and widening health inequalities. In short, the destandardization of work and the new inequality (as well as derivative processes like the new individualization), *and therefore the widening of health inequalities*, all of which have marked the transition from organized to disorganized capitalism, have their genesis in, although they cannot be reduced to, the adaptive behaviours of the GBs. 'Organizational downsizing', to take a topical as well as a symbolic example, is unambiguously bad for employees' health (Kivimaki *et al.* 2000). It is the GBs, above all others, who bear causal responsibility for what Gorz (1999: 1) describes as a 'new system':

a new system has been established which is abolishing 'work' on a massive scale. It is restoring the worst forms of domination, subjugation and exploitation by forcing each to fight against all in order to obtain the 'work' it is abolishing. It is not this abolition we should object to, but its claiming to perpetuate that same work, the norms, dignity and availability of which it is abolishing, as an obligation, as a norm, and as the irreplaceable foundation of the rights and dignity of all.

Recent government propaganda about training schemes and falling unemployment should not be permitted to disguise the changed nature of work in Britain; or the growth of inequality; or the ideological taint of the Third Way.

It seems unlikely that there are discrete and identifiable 'pathways' running from class relations (incorporating the GBH) via – taking Wilkinson's prescribed route as but one example – income inequality and low social cohesion/trust through to enhanced morbidity and mortality; rather, there are likely to be innumerable, different and changing routes to the same end points. Nor does the notion of a 'web' appear especially helpful (even if, following Krieger's (1994) suggestion, the spider is identified as class). Pathways and webs smack of (neo-)positivism and underanalysed demi-regs.

The concept of *capital flows* used here builds on previous research (notably on the significance of material factors and of time and the lifecourse), and may have advantages over pathways/webs (as well as being an ironic echo of the flow of finance capital so symbolic of disorganized capitalism). It is suggested, in a nutshell, that relations of class (allowing for the hugely disproportionate sway of the GBs) systematically affect the flows (typically *variable*, and arguably of special salience for particular conditions at *critical periods* of the lifecourse: Bartley *et al.* 1997) to individuals of different types of capital with potential to impact on health and longevity. The point of intersection between these capital flows and the individual is the class habitus. It is important to acknowledge, of course, that class relations are not the only relations to affect these capital flows; and that uninterrupted flows do not in any case guarantee health and longevity, nor (even heavily) interrupted flows rule them out. Six types of capital will be mentioned, although only a comment or two of clarification on each will be possible: *biological capital, psychological capital, social capital, cultural capital, spatial capital* and *material capital*. It is not a definitive list and there are other potential candidates for inclusion, like 'emotional capital' (S. Williams 1998, 2000a). The popular notion of 'health capital' has been omitted since its deployment here would be tautologous (van de Mheen *et al.* 1998).

The flow of biological (or 'body') capital may be affected by class relations even prior to birth. Low-income families, for example, are more likely to produce babies of low birthweight (Power *et al.* 1996); and low-birthweight babies may have an increased risk of – among other things (Bartley *et al.* 1994) – chronic disease in adulthood, possibly even through biological programming (Barker 1992). Psychological capital flows afford a generalized capacity to cope, extending to what Rutter (1985) once described as 'resilience in the face of adversity'. The 'vulnerability factors' that Brown and Harris (1978) found reduced working-class women's capacity to cope with certain categories of 'life event', thus rendering them more susceptible to episodes of clinical depression than their middle-class counterparts, are, in a sense, class-induced interruptions to the flow of psychological capital.

Social capital flows, which have to do with social integration, networks and support, are well researched in respect of health. They also represent a significant theme in Wilkinson's specification of 'psycho-social pathways', associating income inequality via social cohesion/trust with (premature) mortality (although it has been argued that his indicators minimize or exclude forms of social cohesion and trust emergent in working-class communities: Muntaner *et al.* 1999). Flows of cultural capital are typically generated initially through processes of primary socialization and go on to encompass formal educational opportunities and attainment; class-related (early) arrests to these flows can have long-term ramifications for employment, income levels and, therefore, health (Plesis 2000; Smith 2000).

Area-based studies are beginning to map the relevance of spatial capital flows for health with some precision (Curtis and Jones 1998). There are clear indications too that areas with high mortality tend to be areas with high rates of net out-migration; and it tends to be the better qualified and more affluent who exercise the option to leave (Shaw *et al.* 1999). Prime significance, finally, should be attached to flows of material capital. There may be a ready interaction between the capital flows, but it is self-evidently the case both that the flow of material capital is fundamental and an influence on all others (for example, without material capital, the flow of spatial capital is likely to dry up), and that it is the flow most directly responsive to class relations. In this respect, the Black Report got it more right than wrong.

If then, as many now argue, there is a clustering of advantage or disadvantage over time and place, then one way of pursuing this empirically may be by developing a concept of capital flows, *with priority accorded to material capital*, variably affected by class relations as a generative mechanism. But if class is important, it is of course not the only provider of pertinent generative mechanisms.

'Categorical', 'derivative' and 'circumstantial' mechanisms

It has been argued that class relations (featuring the GBH) provide the single most important generative mechanism for explaining health inequalities, and that a fruitful avenue of investigation of this mechanism might be through its affects on types of capital flow of known significance for health and longevity. Class has been understood, it might be said, as a *categorical* mechanism. But for all that the model of logics/relations/figurations adopted here is of signal importance, it far from exhausts sociology's contribution to explaining health inequalities. A model rooted in the logic of patriarchy, gender relations and the figuration of the nation-state, for example, would add significantly to our grasp of the maldistribution of health and health care in contemporary Britain. For this model, gender would be the categorical mechanism.

Models, like Weber's ideal types, are devices; but more subtlety and differentiation is required than has yet been allowed for. In the realities of structured everyday interactions, of course, the biographies and repertoires for action of, say, a young man of Indian descent working as a junior doctor in the British NHS, or a pregnant 14-year-old from a white low-income household, are a dynamic, fluctuating, non-deterministic amalgam of – to curtail a daunting list non-arbitrarily – class, gender, ethnicity and age relations, each with its corresponding habitus (affording opportunities for seriality, fusion or pledging) (see Chapter 4). So, if it remains reasonable to deploy models, as devices, to stress ways in which, say, class or gender relations can be categorical, it needs to be recognized too that a whole range of relations – which, as Bhaskar (1989b) puts it, are not only *real*, but also *intransitive* (that is, they exist independently of their identification) and *transfactual* (that is, they are relatively continuous and enduring despite the variability of their outcomes in open systems) – may be exerting (interactive) objective effects, accompanied or not by subjective awareness.

A threefold typology of generative mechanism might enhance the model of logics/relations/figurations without compromising its usefulness. Mechanisms are described as *categorical* if in their own right they bear a strong causal responsibility for the outcome of interest (for example, class relations in respect of health inequalities in Britain). They are described as *derivative* if their causal relevance is apparent, but is in large part a function of the causal power of another (categorical) mechanism (for example, command relations as derivative of class relations in respect of health care reform in Britain and its failure in the USA). And they are described as *circumstantial* if their causal role is apparent but neither categorical nor derivative; it may even be fortuitous in the context of the outcome of interest (for example, a confrontation over pay and conditions in a particular hospital may, by pure chance, have a strong ethnic input).

This typology permits the construction of grids. Figure 5.1 shows a nine-cell grid for relations of class and ethnicity. There is no latitude here, nor is it necessary, to give cell-by-cell examples. But the study of class and health inequalities encourages a further observation. Remaining within the figuration of the British nation-state, it seems probable that the logics of the regime of accumulation and mode of regulation and class relations are categorical with respect to health inequalities, and the logic of what might be termed 'tribalism' and ethnic relations is derivative (cell 4).

Early studies were more equivocal, but the most recent (neo-)positivist, gradient-hunting research on the health of ethnic groups, using the RGOC and assorted measures of SES/SEG, is revealing. The Acheson Report concludes, albeit with weighty caution, that 'socioeconomic inequalities contribute to the inequalities in health within ethnic groups, and may contribute to the inequalities in health between ethnic groups' (Stationery Office 1998: 96). Rather more revealing is the Report's conclusion that 'within minority ethnic groups,

Figure 5.1   Sample grid of generative mechanisms: class and ethnicity

		Class relations		
		Categorical	Derivative	Circumstantial
Ethnic relations	Categorical	Cell 1	Cell 2	Cell 3
	Derivative	Cell 4	Cell 5	Cell 6
	Circumstantial	Cell 7	Cell 8	Cell 9

there is a clear association between material disadvantage and poor health' (Stationery Office 1998: 97). In his evidence to the Acheson Inquiry, Nazroo (1999; see also Nazroo 1997) is a little less cautious; and elsewhere he (1998: 167) notes that 'we need to remember that we are concerned with (ethnic) inequalities in health because they are a component and a consequence of an inequitably capitalist society, and it is this that needs to be directly addressed.'

But if class relations, and their effect on material capital flows, are, as seems more than likely, the telling component of intra- and inter-ethnic health inequalities (that is, if ethnic relations as a generative mechanism are derivative in this context), this does *not* mean that ethnic relations do not also contribute to health inequalities *in their own right*. Racism persists, if with more subtlety than in the 1950s and 1960s, and is under-investigated in the health domain. And Nazroo's (1998) call for research on the salience for health of ethnicity *qua* 'identity' – possibly elaborating on a notion of ethnic habitus – is important (see Karlsen and Nazroo 2000).

A note on the Third Way and health inequalities

When New Labour was elected in 1997, one of its first acts was to establish (Acheson's) 'Independent Inquiry into Inequalities in Health' (Stationery Office 1998). Even before the Acheson Report was published, the Green Paper *Our Healthier Nation* (DoH, 1998) expressed as one of its aims 'improving the health of the worst off in society and narrowing the health gap'. Issues of material deprivation were no longer to be shirked. The Acheson Report itself has been welcomed by Black *et al.* (1999: 724), who reiterate the importance of addressing material factors and draw attention in particular to Acheson's third recommendation, which specifies the urgency of policies to 'reduce income inequalities and improve the living standards of households in receipt of social security benefits'. But there is as yet no sign of headway (Davey Smith *et al*. 2000).

The Acheson Report has been criticized for not prioritizing its 39 recommendations, for being overly vague and for not costing its suggested policies (Shaw *et al*. 1999); but there are quite other grounds, independent even of the fullness of government coffers at the time of writing and the monies newly committed to the NHS, for doubting the government's capacity to deliver on its commitment to reduce health inequalities. These have to do with the politics of the Third Way outlined in Chapter 4. Whereas Thatcher simply ignored the focus on structural/material factors in the (prioritized, shrewd and costed) Black Report in favour of 'individualized' cultural/behavioural factors, Blair, in a manner consonant with the Third Way, seems likely to go further and to individualize structural/material factors: thus the answer to the crucial issue of material deprivation may become a matter of 'personal responsibility'. Four concepts are apposite, although, since they reappear in Chapter 6, they will receive less attention here than they deserve: *risk, surveillance, technologies of the self* and *governmentality*.

The concept of risk is now ubiquitous in the health arena, used to encompass phenomena from Beck's (1992) macro-analysis of the global distribution of 'bads' in disorganized capitalism, or 'second modernity' (superseding the distributions of 'goods' in organized capitalism, or 'first modernity': Beck 2000) to individualized risk behaviours like smoking and indulging in alcohol. There are indications that, under the aegis of the philosophy of the Third Way, and in the shared vocabulary of the core-executive/power elite, personal responsibility is being extended to 'expose' as morally culpable the failure to be, or to become, economically self-sufficient, or non-deprived. This is part and parcel of the rediscovery and re-enactment of Victorian relations of worth. In this context too, the functional equivalence of neo-liberalism and the Third Way becomes apparent. As Webster (2000: 74) puts it, 'we live today firmly within a "neo-liberal consensus", whatever the protestations of governments to the contrary.'

The ideas of surveillance, technologies of the self and governmentality are of course Foucauldian (see Chapter 2). In relation to surveillance, Foucault argues that during the course of the eighteenth century a new form of power emerged: the 'surveillance of self', or self-monitoring. It is in this sense that he writes of technologies of the self. In disorganized capitalism, through the Third Way/neo-liberal consensus, it might plausibly be argued, with some apologies to Foucault, that this 'new' form of power has (also) been coolly and reflexively honed as political technique and integrated into command and welfare relations.

The notion of governmentality too has a long history (Foucault 1979b). It denotes the form of government which, in Foucault's eyes, came to characterize modernity. It refers to an ensemble of institutions, procedures, analyses, calculations, reflections and tactics – a 'very specific albeit complex form of power' – that came through the eighteenth and nineteenth centuries to constitute the government of a population. It is not necessary to sign up fully to Foucault's theorization of power, which often seems to define away coercion or domination, to recognize a sense in which the institutionalization of expertise, accomplished in the realm of healing with the professionalization of medicine in nineteenth-century Britain, is part of the process of government (Johnson 1995). In so far as this is the case, medicine too might be regarded as part of the neo-liberal consensus.

6

Lifeworld narratives and expert cultures

The longstanding distinction between 'illness', referring to lay definitions of interruptions to health and well-being, and 'disease', referring to – conventionally privileged – professional or expert 'rulings' on the basis of signs and symptoms, retains its usefulness, even if contemporary research in medical sociology has in many ways moved on. It is this distinction, for example, which allows for an individual to be ill without having a disease and to have a disease without being ill, and which underpins the (neo-)positivist discernment of both illness and disease *icebergs*; that is, the existence of (large majorities of) episodes of illness and (often significant proportions of (even potentially life-threatening)) episodes of disease which – for better or worse – do not come to receive medical attention. Not of course that receipt of attention from medical practitioners constitutes the only likely or effective source of healing: what will here be called *relations of healing* are far more complex. That this is so is reflected in Kleinman's (1985) convincing proposition that we should consider not only people's use or otherwise of medical services within national health care systems such as the British NHS, but also their interface with what he terms 'local health care systems', each possessing its own 'popular' (namely, self-care and (lay) self-help networks) and 'folk' (namely, non-professional or complementary forms of healing) as well as 'professional' sectors.

In a survey of adults aged 16 or more in England in 1998, 22 per cent of men and 26 per cent of women reported 'less than good' general health, and 20 per cent of men and 24 per cent of women reported having a limiting longstanding illness (ONS 2000b). Predictably, these self-reports were positively associated with age and with assorted indicators of an impaired flow of material (and to a lesser extent of social and spatial) capital (see Chapter 5). Only in the youngest age-group were women significantly more likely than men to report 'less than good' general health, and only in the oldest age-group were they significantly more likely than men to report a limiting long-standing illness. A great deal of attention has been paid to how it is that individuals like those in this national sample come to define themselves as healthy or ill, and to elucidating the psycho-social determinants of both their definitions and any decisions taken on the basis of these to seek or not to seek professional help. Typically the rationale for this research on 'illness behaviour' (Mechanic and Volkart 1960), much of it firmly within the (neo-)positivist paradigm, has been to address and puzzle over the persistence and policy ramifications of illness and disease icebergs. Rather like the body of (neo-)positivist research on class and health, however, the return has been suggestive rather than compelling, and certainly theoretically disappointing. It will not be reviewed yet again here (for summaries, see Bury 1997; Kasper 2000).

The chapter begins with a few paragraphs on the private sphere of the lifeworld and on what Habermas diagnoses as its 'colonization' via money and power, the steering media of the subsystems of the economy and the state respectively. It is maintained that in the private sphere of the lifeworld people's pursuit of their day-to-day business in general, and their accommodation of illness in particular, betrays a mix of communicative and strategic action which they may often be unable to articulate or of which they may simply be unaware (as Hegel remarked, 'the familiar is not necessarily the known': quoted in Gardiner 2000: 1) (see Chapter 3). The second section focuses in a preliminary way on issues of defining and coping with illness, and especially on individuals' constructions of 'narratives' in an effort to rationalize or make sense of, and accommodate to, what is happening to them. The third section again makes use of the model of logics/relations/figurations, this time to address relations of healing in Kleinman's popular sector. The logic here is that of patriarchy, the relations those of gender and the figuration that of the (changing) household. The fourth section comprises a reconsideration of doctor–patient encounters: the model is utilized in terms of the logic of state-licensed paternalism, relations of welfare and the figuration of the consultation. This both requires and leads on, in the fifth section, to an analysis of Kleinman's professional sector; that is, of medicine as an 'expert culture'. It is argued that, like a number of professions in the old middle class, medicine in Britain (and elsewhere) has forfeited authority and prestige with the advent of disorganized capitalism. Finally, to fortify and extend the chapter's unfolding account of changed relations of healing, attention is briefly paid to the new salience of Kleinman's folk sector.

Lifeworld colonization

The lifeworld has been framed and illuminated by work in the phenomenological and interactionist paradigms. Habermas (1987: 119) stresses that his own work, 'like the phenomenological lifeworld analysis of the late Husserl, or the late Wittgenstein's analysis of forms of life', invokes structures that, 'in contrast to the historical shapes of particular lifeworlds and life-forms', are 'invariant'. While much of Habermas's analysis remains at this formal level, however, he does now and again take pains to give empirical substance to his notions of the private and public spheres of the lifeworld and to his assertion of their colonization by economy and state. Our immediate concern here is with the private sphere, which Habermas sees as centred on the nuclear family/ private household (although, as we have seen, disorganized capitalism has brought change here too) (see Chapter 3).

An expedient starting point is Bauman's *Liquid Modernity* (2000: 70), in which he explicitly rejects Habermas's perspective on lifeworld colonization to proclaim what he takes to be an obverse tendency, namely 'the colonization of the public sphere by issues previously classified as private and unsuitable for public venting.' But Bauman surely skips over what really matters: the processes of individualization he records need to be interpreted, first and foremost, as corollaries of the (culture-ideology of) consumerism and clientalization that precisely mark the colonization of private *and* public spheres of the lifeworld by the subsystems of the economy and state during disorganized capitalism. In short, that individuals seem increasingly to seek – if fatefully and in vain – 'biographic solutions to systemic contradictions' is, in line with the principle of compatibility, not accidental (Bauman 2000: 38).

But Bauman (2000: 39) is right when he insists that there is 'a wide gap' between

> the condition of individuals *de jure* and their chances to become individuals *de facto* – that is, to gain control over their fate and make the choices they truly desire. It is from that abysmal gap that the most poisonous effluvia contaminating the lives of contemporary individuals emanate. That gap, however, cannot be bridged by individual efforts alone: not by the means and resources available within self-managed life-politics. Bridging that gap is the matter of Politics – with a capital 'P'. It can be supposed that the gap in question has emerged and grown precisely because of the emptying of public space, and particularly the 'agora', that intermediary, public/private site where life-politics meets Politics with the capital 'P', where private problems are translated into the language of public issues and public solutions are sought, negotiated and agreed for private troubles.

There is much of importance here, although what Bauman misses is the underlying causal significance of (categorical) relations of class and (derivative) relations of command for the depoliticization of the public sphere of the lifeworld. This is an issue treated in depth in the final chapter.

So the private sphere of the lifeworld, in which illness has its origins, is in part colonized by, or infused with, relations of class and command (including those of welfare). Much of what follows seeks to show how perceptions of illness are generated in the private sphere, and how these both inform and are informed or 'contaminated' – via the expert culture of medicine – by the system's steering media of money and power.

Constructing narratives

Reporting on her innovative study of health and illness in East London, Cornwall (1984) distinguished between people's 'public' and 'private' accounts. Public accounts tended to be 'couched in commonsense terms' which suggested that health and illness were considered 'morally problematic'; thus, 'the person always made sure that they were seen to be in the right . . . The "right" relationship to these terms was that of being basically healthy; if illnesses were mentioned, people made sure that they were understood to be "real" and therefore legitimate' (Cornwall 1984: 1213–14). Private accounts focused attention on everyday 'material concerns and practical constraints'; these, Cornwall notes, evidenced the 'ground' on which medical ideas fall. Three factors seemed routinely to underpin private accounts: people's jobs, their position in the 'sexual division of labour' and their past experiences of health and illness (Cornwall 1984: 134). Cornwall's public and private accounts can be seen, following Schutz (1970), as 'second-order typifications'; that is, as sociological typifications of actors' own 'first-order typifications'. Her public and private accounts will hereafter be recast as *narratives for others* and *narratives for self* respectively.

The concept of narrative has become popular, some even celebrating a 'narrative turn' (often as part and parcel of the putative postmodern turn) (for a detailed discussion, see Franzosi 1998). A few comments will have to suffice here. Labov's (1972: 359–60) early formal definition survives, as Franzosi puts it, 'almost intact': 'one method of recapitulating past experience by matching a verbal sequence of clauses to the sequence of events which (it is inferred) actually occurred.' Stephenson (2000: 112) provides a less formal and less austere explication. 'When we turn our attention to story-telling or narrative', she notes,

> two important aspects of human existence come into focus. The first is that we are beings who are conscious of our existence through time. Our understanding of the present cannot therefore be separated from our recollections of the past and our aspirations for the future. The second is that we are involved in an ongoing process of *making* sense of our experience. To understand the meaning of human actions is to place them in the context of the ongoing lives of particular human beings. Both individually and collectively, we organize experience through the construction of narratives.

In this vein, narratives might be defined as cognitive schemes, constructed from a particular point in time and space, which organize individual actions and events into a coherent whole.

Bury (2001) offers a sensitive and illuminating account of the unfolding and importance of 'illness narratives'. He also identifies three types of 'narrative form'. 'Contingent narratives' address 'beliefs about the origins of disease, the proximate causes of an illness episode, and the immediate effects of illness on everyday life.' 'Moral narratives' provide 'accounts of (and help to constitute) changes between the person, the illness and social identity': these help to '(re)establish the moral status of the individual' and/or to 'maintain social distance'. 'Core narratives', finally, 'reveal connections between the lay person's experiences and deeper cultural levels of meaning attached to suffering and illness.' Like others, Bury illustrates the usefulness of the notion of illness narratives with reference to his own and colleagues' work on chronic illness.

Chronic illness tends to lead to what Bury (1982) himself has termed 'biographical disruption'; people who become chronically ill, Charmaz (2000: 280) writes, 'lose their previously taken-for-granted continuity of life'. As Garreth Williams (2000) shows, it remains credible and important to recognize 'disruption' even in the altered social world and postmodernized culture of disorganized capitalism, and this notwithstanding protestations from postmodernists like Fox (1993), who see talk of disruption as contributory to the fabrication or territorialization of the 'body without organs' as 'organism' (that is, as a biomedical or psychosocial body with organs), or from disability theorists like Oliver (1990), whose emphasis on disability as social oppression encourages a 'writing out' of the body from sociological deliberation (see also Barnes and Mercer 1996; and Chapter 2).

The need to 'adapt' to chronic illness may lead people to adopt any of a number of well-researched 'coping strategies' or 'styles', most of which, if they are to be serviceable even for the mundane and ordinary contingencies of day-to-day living, let alone the unexpected and extraordinary, require skilful and flexible application (see the accounts in Anderson and Bury 1988); although there are those too who will remain 'unadjusted' (Schneider and Conrad 1993). People's new status, as individuals with, for example, Parkinson's Disease, HIV or rectal cancer, may become a 'master status', thenceforth dominating others' perceptions of and behaviour towards them, and/or giving them a disconcertingly precarious sense of self (Charmaz 1991). If the chronic illness also carries an associated stigma (that is, it 'discredits' its hosts, and maybe – through what Goffman (1968b) terms 'courtesy stigma' – their families and friends), then this property too may give a discriminatory edge to the treatment accorded them by others ('enacted stigma') and/or undermine their self-perceptions or confidence in others' integrity and fairness ('felt stigma') (Scambler and Hopkins 1986).

Biographical disruption, whichever of multiple possible forms it takes, and its form is in fact dependent only in part on the nature of the disorder, self-evidently occasions some degree of 'narrative reconstruction' (Williams 1984). These 'reconstructed' narratives are not merely descriptive, but represent attempts to 'reconstitute and repair ruptures between body, self and world by linking up and interpreting different aspects of biography in order to realign present and past and self within society' (Williams 1984: 197; see also Frank 1993, 1995). Studies testifying to such a process, framed almost exclusively within the interactionist paradigm, are plentiful and varied: British examples, in addition to the studies of Bury and Gareth Williams on arthritis, include Robinson's (1988, 1990) account of multiple sclerosis; Kelleher's (1988) of diabetes; my own of epilepsy (Scambler and Hopkins 1986; Scambler 1989); Kelly's (1992) and Kelly and Dickinson's (1997) of colitis; and Simon Williams's (1993) of chronic respiratory disorder. There is no need to offer another review of studies such as these here (see Anderson and Bury 1988; Nettleton 1995; Bury 1997; Annandale 1998). It is more pertinent to what follows to draw attention to three themes in what Gareth Williams (2000) calls (lay) people's 'knowledgeable narratives'.

First, the narratives for self and for others that people (re)construct are *dynamic*, possibly even more so in the present, against the backdrop of the cultural-aesthetic or culture-ideology of disorganized capitalism, than was the case in the eras of liberal or organized capitalism. They can, in response to the 'needs of the moment' (as it were), be heroic, tragic, ironic or comic; they may also, when unstable, be regressive or progressive (that is, indicative of a positive/optimistic or a negative/pessimistic view of the future: Robinson 1990). The point here is not of course that people's narratives are always changing – in fact, like their coping strategies/styles and, for that matter, the capital flows accessible to them (see Chapter 5), there is a tendency towards continuity over time – but rather that the scripts (necessarily) allow for improvisation in the face of the contingent.

The second theme is related: it is that narratives typically have a *performative* aspect. It is apposite here to refer briefly to the notion of 'speech acts'. Austin (1962) made an influential philosophical distinction between 'locutionary', 'illocutionary' and 'perlocutionary' speech acts. Through locutionary speech acts a speaker says something; that is, expresses a state of affairs. Through illocutionary speech acts a speaker performs an action in saying something, normally by means of a performative verb in the first person present (for example, 'I promise you that "p"'). And through perlocutionary acts a speaker produces an effect on the hearer. Habermas (1984: 288–9) characterizes Austin's three acts in the following 'catchphrases': 'to say *something*, to act *in* saying something, to bring about something *through* acting in saying something.' Narratives for self, Cornwall's private accounts, should be seen as an active part of coping (Kelly and Dickinson 1997). Narratives for others, Cornwall's public accounts, should be seen as having a perlocutionary flavour: they are, with varying degrees of deliberation, designed to square self with audience, context and the prevailing (sub)cultural norms.

The third theme is that the composition of both narratives for self and narratives for others reflects an ongoing *dialectic* between lay *'experiential' narratives of illness* and *professional 'expert' narratives of disease*. This is an obvious point which is none the less often either overlooked or left unelaborated. It is perhaps a truism that medical, scientific knowledge is 'a', if rarely 'the', resource for lay views of illness; and another that the expert culture of medicine, and current patterns of clinical practice, arose out of, and necessarily remain responsive to, the lifeworld. But two remarks are in order.

First, while the infusion of the thinking and story-telling of people with chronic illnesses by medical diagnostic classifications and theories of disease aetiology, course and treatment is not intrinsically problematic, it can become so (as classic past accounts of 'medicalization'/'social control' have illustrated: Zola 1972; Illich 1977). One under-examined way in which it can become problematic is as a corollary of system rationalization, which may of course lead to lifeworld colonization. In this context it is relevant to note that relations of healing found in Kleinman's professional sector – that is, featuring the medical profession – referred to here (in non-derogatory terms) as *relations of fixing*, are, in Britain if not in the USA, best regarded as a subset of relations of welfare, which are, in turn, a subset of the command relations of the state.

Second, it is increasingly acknowledged in today's postmodern culture that lay or experiential knowledge has its own intrinsic merit. Williams and Popay (2001) write:

> local knowledge – in the sense of knowledge that lay people obtain in the daily routine of their lives – is seen by some as a failed or flawed form of scientific knowledge, or as something other than knowledge altogether. However, stimulated by developments in anthropology (Geertz, 1973), lay knowledge derived from the particular – the particular locality, biography, and body – is increasingly recognized as very rich and directed at different ends. Local knowledge as *material* knowledge provides understanding which is 'emplaced' (Curry, 1996).

Local knowledge, thus understood, need not entail any commitment to epistemological relativism. It is to a more explicit examination of local knowledge in the popular sector of local health care systems that we now turn.

Illness, the popular sector and gendered caring

At the beginning of the era with which this book deals, (neo-)positivist social accounting testified to the fact that most illness was identified, accommodated and dealt with within Kleinman's popular sector. Wadsworth and colleagues (1971) quizzed 1,000 adults in London on their illness behaviour over the previous two weeks: although 95 per cent reported symptoms, only one in five had seen a doctor during this period. A decade later, in a prospective study utilizing six-week health diaries with a sample of women in London, Annette Scambler *et al.* (1981) found that only 1 in 18 'symptom episodes' had precipitated a medical consultation; and in three-quarters of these cases this was only *after* advice had been solicited, often widely, within the popular sector (that is, from what Freidson (1970) refers to as an individual's 'lay referral system'). The evidence for such an illness iceberg, and for the 'self-sufficiency' to which it bears witness, remains compelling, notwithstanding a growing propensity since to visit, if not to be visited by, family practitioners.

Relations of healing characteristic of the popular sector will be termed *relations of caring*. In part this acknowledges that women have been the principal, and paradigmatic, agents of 'unpaid' caring in the private sphere (and, indeed, paid health workers in the community; that is, until ridiculed and displaced by men intent on lucrative occupational/professional closure: Stacey 1988). Caring may be associated with women, and as arduous physical as well as 'emotional' or 'loving' labour, without dignifying any notion of biological determinism: it would be odd if women were *not* routinely to show rich qualities of caring beyond the reach of most men given their scripted primary and secondary socialization and regular (directed) rehearsals thereafter. It is women's unpaid labour as carers that affords the focus of the model for this section of the chapter, the logic being that of patriarchy, the relations those of gender and the figuration that of the contemporary household.

Little has been said about gender so far in this volume. This is a function of the main selection criterion for the models deployed, namely, to illuminate *core* properties of disorganized capitalism of relevance to health and health care: the emphasis on class relations has been deliberate. It is clear, however, that from capitalism's genesis in Europe's long sixteenth century, its *class relations have always been gendered* (just as they have always been 'racialized'). Patriarchal (and tribal) logics preceded, and have ever since 'skewed', those of regimes of capital accumulation and modes of regulation. It follows inexorably, as has been well documented by feminist (and ethnic) researchers in the domain of health, medicine and health care, that relations of command, welfare and fixing, together with those of worth, have been significantly and blatantly 'masculine' (and 'white').

It is sometimes argued that the logic of patriarchy has become fuzzier with the advent of the new flexible regime of capital accumulation and mode of regulation of disorganized capitalism. After all, as we have seen, there has been change upon change, not least in the gender-composition of labour markets and households. Gottfried (2000) addresses this issue with special reference to Sweden, Germany and Japan. She relates how, in organized capitalism, 'Fordist bargains institutionalised the terms of a compromise between labour, capital and the state. These bargains embedded a male-breadwinner gender contract compromising women's positions and standardizing employment contracts around the needs, interests and authority of men' (Gottfried 2000: 235). She asks how much has changed with the neo-Fordism of disorganized capitalism.

The parameters of neo-Fordism vary according to the degree of 'managed openness' of a nation-state (Weiss 1999). Moreover, they can only be fully grasped in the context of neo-Fordism's 'institutional roots in Fordist class *and* gender compromises'. 'Making explicit the type of gender contract', Gottfried (2000: 253) maintains, 'reveals hidden dependencies and helps to account for women's relative position in paid employment and unpaid caring work.' It is consistent with Gottfried's findings, as well as the (neo-)positivist social accounting reported in Chapters 3 and 5, to argue that in Britain neoliberal social policies have fostered 'rigid "insider/outsider" labour markets with consequent marginalization and peripheralization, particularly among women workers' (Esping-Anderson 1997: 75); and that this has reinforced a 'traditional female-provided care model' (Pfau-Effinger 1998: 153). As Pascall (1997: 96) writes of the state of affairs in Britain:

social policies built on a breadwinner model of family life support the role of women as carers . . . Some benefit policies assume male bread-winners; community care policies assume the availability of carers who are part-time workers – indeed could not work without them. In a context of men's privileged access to higher paid work, a push towards 'community care' will involve a push towards women's unpaid care.

Studies of caring have tended to focus on what might be called 'special' cases, namely caring for children or older kin with severe chronic or disabling conditions. In 1995–6 the General Household Survey reported that 14 per cent of women over 16 were providing care to other adults; this was most common for those aged 45–64. The 'intensity of care' seems to have changed slightly: while in 1985 a quarter of all female carers were engaged in care for more than 20 hours per week, in 1995 this had risen to just under a third. Intensive caring remains a largely female matter: in 1995–6, three-fifths of those who spent 20 hours or more per week caring were women (ONS 1998). Predictably, research suggests that the greatest impact on employment and income comes from care that is provided to a member of the same household and is of high intensity. Evandrou's (1995) analysis of data from the 1990 General Household Survey reveals that women caring for someone in the household are only half as likely to be in full-time work as non-carers 'with similar characteristics'; they also experience reduced chances of being in part-time work. By contrast, caring for someone outside the home reduces the probability of being in full-time employment by 29 per cent, and increases the probability of part-time employment by 30 per cent. Typically, carers receive lower rates of hourly pay than non-carers, suggesting that they may suffer a wage penalty by entering flexible, part-time work that fits in with their caring duties (Cabinet Office 2000).

But caring is not confined to special cases: what is often missing from the research literature is the (even) more significantly gendered phenomenon of non-special or 'mundane' caring; that is, for example, caring for children, partners or kin with bouts of flu rather than chronic diabetes or polio. Graham (1993: 79) writes: 'building a family that feels complete typically involves more than looking after children. It involves looking after the home and the well-being of all who live there. In most households, it is women who are the caretakers of the family, doing both the childcare and the domestic labour necessary to meet the needs of those who live in the household.' Mostly it is women, she continues, 'doing the household cleaning, the washing and the ironing, making the evening meal and looking after the children when they are ill.' Mundane caring 'belongs' in such a list. And mundane caring, no less than care in special cases, is a form of unpaid health work. Relations of caring, epitomized in such day-to-day 'duties', are of the essence of the popular sector. In many respects too this cradle-to-grave caring underwrites and allows for relations of fixing in the professional sector.

One or two points of clarification-cum-elaboration are called for before we turn to the professional sector. First, it has been maintained that women's role responsibilities for caring have comfortably outlived organized capitalism. This is not to say either that the changes associated with disorganized capitalism – not only in household composition and labour markets, but embracing gender relations, processes of individualization, and the sexual revolution (plus, perhaps, relations of friendship: Pahl 2000; see also Chapter 3) – have had no effect on relations of caring, or, of course, that men do not also care and, increasingly, act as carers; but it is to say that women have for the time being at least largely retained their paradigmatic (or 'ideal typical') role as unpaid carers/health workers. System needs persist, and the logic of patriarchy and gender relations in place long before capitalism 'naturally' suggested gendered ways of meeting them. Second, it is equally apparent that while caring continues to attract a rhetoric of commendation, it also continues to issue in a practical subordination: women are celebrated even as their choices are limited and they are financially penalized (Cabinet Office 2000). Relations of caring tend also to be relations of oppression. The logic of patriarchy here affords illustrations of both the principle of compatibility and the principle of advantage.

The third point picks up on a feminist ethics with some potential to challenge or rewrite the relations of caring explicated here. In the 1980s innovative writers like Gilligan (1982) and Noddings (1984), having acknowledged that female caring, like housework, seems invisible if done well, set out both to make this 'moral labour' conspicuous and to ask if it might support an 'ethics of care'. Such an ethics holds that the very point of morality is to establish a society in which we are ever in relation to one another: 'one must meet the other as one-caring' (Noddings 1984: 201). Gilligan's 'care orientation' and Noddings' 'caring attitude' can be summed up as a 'readiness to bestow and spend oneself and make oneself available' (Noddings 1984: 19). The problem, of course, is that just such a tacit ethics has underpinned, and continues to underpin, women's oppression (and not only by men). Card (1985: 6) asks of Gilligan: 'is Gilligan picking up on something Nietzsche identified as a "slave morality"?' In similar vein, Houston (1992: 123), although personally drawn to an ethics of care, insists that we recognize that

> women's caring has been systematically appealed to in order to distract women from efforts to correct injustices they suffer ('Who will look after the children?'). Any adequate account of women's morality is going to have to show some recognition of this, and show how the ethics we propose that women adopt challenges this division of moral labour, and will not, in the present circumstances, contribute to women's continued subordination.

As things stand in Britain, Walby's (1997: 3) claim that a polarization is occurring among women in disorganized capitalism, namely between younger, educated and employed women 'who engage in gender relations somewhat convergent with those of men', and older, less educated women 'who built their life trajectories around patterns of private patriarchy' (see Chapter 3), raises precisely this dilemma: in nation-states which remain obdurately patriarchal, can women develop an ethics of care without colluding in their own subordination?

'Patienthood' in the professional sector

People who are ill rarely exit the popular sector in search of remedies; instead, they tend to take their own measures, typically (still) with the assiduous support of female carers. Frequently, as Zola (1973) classically showed, it is not illness *per se* which precipitates or 'triggers' a medical consultation, but its impact on a person's life-activities. But studies of illness behaviour have revealed a disease as well as an illness iceberg: in other words, many instances of medically defined disease, some of it treatable and even life-threatening, are not presented, or present (too) 'late', to doctors (Kasper 2000). In fact, GPs in Britain are routinely confronted in their surgeries with illnesses they regard as (at best) self-limiting or (at worst) 'trivial'; and, if less routinely, miss out on episodes of treatable disease. But it may be less self-evident to patients than to doctors that professional definitions are optimally authoritative here. The model used to examine these issues utilizes the logic of state-licensed paternalism, relations of welfare and the figuration of the doctor–patient encounter.

Whereas Parsons (1951b), representing the functionalist paradigm, seminally saw the asymmetrical relationship between doctor and patient – with the doctor 'active' and the patient 'passive' – as functionally appropriate, Freidson (1970), working out of conflict and interactionist paradigms, insisted that the patient too is commonly active, allowing for a 'clash of perspectives'. Freidson's analysis sparked a new interest in, and respect for, patients' (lay, experiential) definitions of their situations (or narratives), and how these constructions might vary independently of the professional (expert), culturally authoritative narratives of doctors. The accounts of both Parsons and Freidson still have currency, but important changes have occurred during the generation of disorganized capitalism.

'Personal troubles', Mills (1963) long ago announced, arise in the context of, and must be understood in terms of, social structures. This injunction has informed the approach to the doctor–patient relationship adopted by Waitzkin (1989, 1991), who notes that although medical encounters are 'micro-level' processes that involve the interaction of individuals, these processes take place in a context shaped by 'macro-level' social structures. Structures of society, he (1989: 221) writes, 'help generate the specific social context in which patients and doctors find themselves. The talk that occurs in medical encounters also may reinforce broader social structures.' In a later treatment of this same theme, Waitzkin (1991: 231–2) offers something like an ideal type of the medical encounter (while admitting the existence of 'negative cases'), and this is worth quoting in detail:

> medical discourse contains an underlying structure, rarely recognized
> consciously by doctors and patients who speak with each other. In the

social contexts of people's lives, issues arise that create personal troubles. Such issues include difficulties with work, economic insecurity, family life and gender roles, the process of ageing, the patterning of substance use and other 'vices', and resources to deal with emotional distress. To varying degrees during the medical encounter, patients express these troubles. Although some humanistically inclined doctors supportively listen to such concerns, the traditional format of the interview does not facilitate their expression. Countertextual tensions then arise, sometimes manifested at the margins of discourse, or through dominance gestures like interruptions, cut-offs, and de-emphases that move the dialogue back to a technical track. The management of technical problems involves reified, technical solutions (such as medication) or counselling, but also subtler verbal processes that maintain professional surveillance of individual action and that reproduce mainstream ideologic assumptions about appropriate behaviour. Medical management also reproduces ideology through crucial absences – for instance, a lack of criticism focusing on social context and an exclusion of such unspoken alternatives as collective action leading to social change. In the process, medical discourse contributes to social control by reinforcing individual accommodation to a generally unchanged context. With the technical help and emotional gratification that they have received, patients perhaps become better equipped to cope, as they continue their consent to the social conditions that troubled them in the first place.

Waitzkin's contribution is important, but Habermas offers a more flexible frame for retheorizing doctor–patient encounters in ways which integrate micro- and macro-perspectives (for further discussion and illustration, see Scambler 1987; Scambler and Britten 2001). Further, Habermas's theory of communicative action affords the means to diagnose what Wodak (1996) refers to as 'disorders of discourse'. Austin's distinctions between locutionary, illocutionary and perlocutionary speech acts were introduced above (when we noted that people's narratives had a performative character). For Habermas (1984: 289), 'communicative action' is linguistically mediated interaction in which all speakers pursue illocutionary aims in order to reach 'an agreement that will provide the basis for a consensual coordination of individually pursued plans of action.' 'Strategic action', on the other hand, occurs when at least one speaker aims to produce perlocutionary effects on his or her hearers. Perlocutionary effects ensue 'whenever a speaker acts with an orientation to success and thereby instrumentalizes speech acts for purposes that are contingently related to the meaning of what is said.' Communicative action is oriented to understanding, strategic action to success.

Some elaboration is necessary here. Simple imperatives, like requests or demands, are illocutionary acts with which the speaker 'openly' expresses his or her aim of influencing the hearer(s) (and with which a power claim is associated). In such cases the speaker pursues illocutionary aims unreservedly, but none the less acts with an orientation to success rather than understanding.

Habermas calls this *open strategic action*. When speakers employ speech acts for perlocutionary ends, this is referred to as *concealed strategic action*. In the case of either open or concealed strategic action the potential for the binding (or bonding) force of good reasons – a potential which for Habermas is always contained in linguistic communication – remains unexploited. This potential is only realized in communicative action, when illocutionary acts express *criticizable validity claims*. In the context of communicative action all comprehensible speech acts raise criticizable validity claims concerning *truth*, *appropriateness* (or justification) and *sincerity*. Speakers can 'rationally motivate' hearers to accept their speech acts because they can assume the 'warranty' for providing, if necessary, good reasons that would stand up to hearers' criticisms of validity claims.

Habermas judges communication 'pathologies' to be the product of confusion between actions oriented to understanding and actions oriented to success. Instances of concealed strategic action may involve either conscious or unconscious deception. In cases of conscious deception at least one of the participants acts with an orientation to success, but allows the other(s) to assume that all the conditions of communicative action are met. This *manipulation* has been touched on briefly in the discussion of perlocutionary acts. Of unconscious deception, Habermas (1984: 332) writes: 'the kind of repression of conflicts that the psychoanalyst explains in terms of defence mechanisms leads to disturbances of communication on both the intrapsychic and interpersonal levels. In such cases at least one of the parties is deceiving himself about the fact that he is acting with an attitude oriented to success and is only keeping up the appearance of communicative action.' Habermas refers to unconscious deception as *systematically distorted communication*.

Habermas's 'formal pragmatics' have relevance for an understanding of doctor–patient encounters. In Britain, the logic of state-licensed paternalism has traditionally lent itself to a benign, insistent – and if push should occasionally come to shove, obdurate – partiality to open strategic action (as in, 'I'm the doctor, I know best') (see Graham and Oakley 1981). As over the course of the past generation more patient-centred styles of communication, emphasizing mutuality and reciprocity, have gained ground, open strategic action may have become less acceptable to patients in routine, non-emergency consultations (although it does not follow that the potential for a 'clash of perspectives' has correspondingly diminished). In this altered context, Habermas's analysis of concealed strategic action – embracing not only conscious deception (or manipulation), as for example when doctors use technical jargon to subdue, browbeat or gain assent from a resistant patient, but also unconscious deception (or systematically distorted communication), when neither doctor nor patient may be aware that strategic rather than communicative action prevails – arguably gains in salience. The notion of unconscious deception/systematically distorted communication, significantly, allows for doctors (in particular) and patients (more rarely) to act with an orientation to success, not understanding, but sincerely and in good faith.

Habermas regards his formal pragmatics as constituting an essential point of departure and 'guide' for empirical-pragmatic investigations, and Mishler (1984) has been a pioneer in applying them to episodes of doctor–patient communication. What Mishler calls the *voice of medicine* – its legitimacy underwritten by an expert, opaque and science-based 'formal knowledge' (Freidson 1986) – is characterized by strategic action, or action oriented to success: doctors who use the voice of medicine promote distorted communication by 'leading' patients, consciously or otherwise, towards a particular desired end-point. While the voice of medicine is not intrinsically problematic, it nevertheless, as an indirect product of what Habermas defines as processes of selective (or excessive system) rationalization and lifeworld colonization, has come to privilege the 'scientific' over what Schutz called the 'natural attitude', even to the extent of medicalizing everyday life (Illich 1977) (it is in this connection that relations of fixing are a subset of relations of welfare).

As Mishler (1984: 104), like Waitzkin, observes: 'the meaning of events is provided through abstract rules that serve to decontextualize events, to remove them from personal and social contexts.' When a doctor, wittingly or otherwise, dominates or directs an encounter with a patient (when, as Fletcher (1974) graphically puts it, 'the patient's rehearsal is subordinated to the doctor's routine'), this typically has the effect of absorbing the patient's self-understanding into a system of purposive-rational action, namely the framework of technical (bio)medicine. Current clinical practice, Mishler claims, is based on an asymmetrical relationship between doctor and patient. Recalling Freidson rather than Parsons, he continues: 'achieving humane care is dependent upon empowering patients' (p. 193). The voice of medicine, in short, has developed and retains a tendency to suppress and colonize the *voice of the lifeworld*: lifeworld rationalization and decolonization require patient empowerment.

In his own substantive work on doctor–patient encounters, Mishler discerns what he calls the 'unremarkable interview'. Consultations in this format are conducted solely in the voice of medicine and show a uniform structure: first, a request from the doctor; second, a response from the patient; third, a post-response assessment, not always explicit, succeeded by a new request; and fourth, optionally, a request for clarification or elaboration of the patient's response. The unremarkable interview derives what coherence it has from the dominant voice of medicine; but this is accomplished at the cost of the fragmentation, diminution and neglect of the voice of the lifeworld.

Mishler claims that the dominating voice of medicine equates with inhumane and ineffective care, a claim Barry and her colleagues (2001) have attempted to assess. Analysing 35 general practice case studies by means of patient interviews, doctor interviews and transcribed consultations, they found four principal 'communication patterns': 'strictly medicine', 'mutual lifeworld', 'lifeworld ignored' and 'lifeworld blocked'. The term 'strictly medicine' was used when doctor and patient both relied exclusively on the voice of medicine, as was typically the case with acute physical complaints; (carefully measured) outcomes appeared satisfactory for 'simple unitary problems'.

'Mutual lifeworld' characterized 'more relaxed' consultations within which both doctor and patient engaged with the lifeworld, as tended to occur in the context of a combination of psychological and physical problems; outcomes were again mostly satisfactory. The poorest outcomes occurred when patients deployed the voice of the lifeworld but were either ignored ('lifeworld ignored') or blocked ('lifeworld blocked') by doctors' use of the voice of medicine, as was most prevalent with chronic physical complaints. The authors conclude that an enhanced deployment of the voice of the lifeworld does indeed make for better outcomes and more humane treatment.

There are four points of special relevance here. The first elucidates the logic of state-licensed paternalism and relations of fixing. That British doctors have customarily practised a – generally beneficent, but none the less unyielding and (even now) largely non-reflexive – form of medical paternalism is uncontroversial. What may be less obvious is that this paternalism, independently of whatever else it might permit or facilitate, is also *responsive to certain vital system imperatives*. The social conditions, unrest, uncertainties and political deliberations preceding both the National Health Insurance Act of 1911 and the introduction of the National Health Service in 1948 bore eloquent testimony to the significance of healthy (working, fighting, reproducing) populations for the regimes of capital accumulation and modes of regulation of liberal and organized capitalism respectively (Navarro's (1978) analysis catches this in part, although deploying a rather uncritical Marxist framework and without acknowledging the full complexity of historical events). Relations of class and command/welfare are crucial ingredients of any satisfactory explanation of these changes.

It would be congruent with such an analysis, and with the account of British health care reform in Chapter 4, to note that it would be surprising if the Conservative/New Labour overhaul of the original principles, policies and practices of the NHS were unrelated to the requirements for a healthy (working, fighting, reproducing) population under the *altered* conditions of disorganized capitalism. This may make clearer the use of the term 'relations of fixing'. What the coining of this term does *not* imply, if this needs saying, is that doctors – whether men, 'honorary men' (that is, women professionally socialized to adopt masculine habits and conventions) or women – are not caring. Rather, it is to suggest that *this is not what doctors are for*. Caring, as we have seen, is 'delegated', on occasions, passingly, to (overwhelmingly female) paid health care workers like nurses, but more routinely to unpaid health workers, paradigmatically women, in the popular sector.

The second point concerns the distinction between strategic and communicative action. Doctors have so far been presented as agents of strategic action, and patients as agents of communicative action; and the studies of Waitzkin, Mishler and Barry and her associates, each revealing the priority typically accorded the voice of medicine over the voice of the lifeworld in doctor–patient encounters, have lent empirical support to this approach. This asymmetry between doctor and patient is functional, as Parsons (1951b) recognized, but rather less so in relation to patient needs than in relation to the needs of the subsystems of the economy and state. In so far as doctors respond to these system imperatives (that is, in so far as these needs inform medical paternalism), they are agents of strategic action, and not just of open strategic action and conscious deception, but also, and this to the extent to which they remain unaware of system imperatives, unconscious deception. Unconscious deception, or systematically distorted communication, is in this context the intrusion of the steering media of the economy and state, namely money and power, into therapeutic dialogue. But this is not to say of course that doctors are incapable of communicative action, or patients of strategic action: in fact most doctor–patient encounters represent a dynamic and negotiated 'mix' of communicative and strategic action, as is apparent in any number of ethnomethodological (and 'conversational') studies.

The third point is closely related to the second. It is that the doctor–patient encounter can rarely be characterized as a simple 'coming together' (or potential, even tacit, 'clash') of lay 'experiential' narratives of illness and professional 'expert' narratives of disease. We have seen how patients' narratives typically incorporate (edited versions of) medical models of disease. It is no less apparent that doctors, and the nostrums and advice they dispense, typically incorporate common-sense presumptions from the lifeworld; after all, doctors as well as their patients draw on culturally ingrained and ubiquitous 'stocks of know-ledge', 'models', 'recipes for action' and so on (see Lock 1982). What needs to be emphasized here is that doctor–patient encounters are at one and the same time dynamic and negotiated (as recognized in work within the paradigms of phenomenology and interactionism) and structured, and in ways that may be beyond the awareness of both parties (as recognized by work within the paradigms of functionalism and conflict theory). As Bhaskar reminds us, it is neither necessary nor credible to choose between agency and structure.

But although doctor–patient encounters are often dynamic and negotiated, giving rise to 'mixes' of communicative and strategic action and of narratives of illness and disease, their structuring, as we have seen, reflects the functional asymmetry of the roles of doctor and patient. It is doctors who are the more predisposed to strategic action and to imposing their narratives. In his study of medical education, Sinclair (1997, 2000) picks up on Hunter's (1991: 51) observation that 'the narrative act of case presentation is at the centre of medical education and, indeed, at the centre of all medical communication about patients.' Sinclair (2000: 115) shows how medical students, in the process of constructing 'disease narratives' – on the basis of which they are themselves examined by doctors – 'transform and constitute themselves as well as their patients' (see also Atkinson 1981, 1995). He suggests that there exist 'major obstacles' to the introduction of 'patient-centred therapeutic narratives' – that is, narratives more conducive to communicative action – into clinical training. Sinclair (2000: 131) writes:

while no-one would doubt the extraordinary accomplishments of medical science, based on 'naïve realism' and its unselfconscious narratives mimetic of disease-centred professional practices, it has been obvious for some time that it is not adequate for the treatment of whole ranges of patients: to take a simply categorical example, some patients may be left with a diagnosed but only partially treatable disease and, at the same time, a chronic illness that they and their families must somehow live with. These patients are no longer passive recipients of the effects of disease and treatment but necessarily active and responsible agents of their own management.

The – difficult, if not impossible – challenge would seem to be 'to integrate the care of illness with the treatment of disease' (Kleinman 1988: 265). But, again, maybe this is not 'what doctors are for'.

The fourth point is that the nature of the doctor–patient encounter may be undergoing revision, caught up in the wider societal processes of change, like consumerism and clientalization, characteristic of disorganized capitalism. Certainly patients in Britain, the USA and many other modern nation-states seem better informed (that is, from non-medical sources), and more sceptical and prone to distrust and interrogate their doctors than in the past, and to go on to lodge formal complaints in the absence of satisfactory responses (Scambler and Britten 2001); as we shall see, there is a greater propensity too to seek out alternative sources of help in Kleinman's folk sector. Underpinning these changes in patients' behaviour are the political assaults on welfare statism under disorganized capitalism, incorporating in Britain the reforms of the NHS, and an associated decline in the status and authority of the medical profession. References have been made to a putative 'deprofessionalization', even 'proletarianization', of medicine. It is to the properties, structural substrates and ramifications of these changes that we now turn.

Medicine, expert cultures and changing relations

For many centuries paid healing in Britain was women's business (Ehrenreich and English 1979; Stacey 1988). But relations of fixing, at least, became a *de facto* male monopoly with the professionalization of medicine in the mid-nineteenth century (see Freidson 1970; Johnson 1972). It was this process, recognized through the Medical Act of 1858, which established the cultural authority of modern, professional medical expertise and paved the way for the dominant influence of narratives of disease over narratives of illness. The history of the medical profession, Grimshaw (1986: 222; see also Witz 1992) observes,

has not simply been one of 'progress' in the overcoming of disease, aided by scientific discoveries. It is a history which can be read partly as the attempt to establish white male hegemony over medicine, and what are seen as medical priorities can sometimes be seen as serving to legitimate status and hierarchies within the profession (the emphasis on prestigious 'high-tech' medicine, for example, rather than on other aspects of health care).

Indeed, notwithstanding the physicians and surgeons' reluctant admission to their gentlemanly 'calling' of the community-based 'apothecaries' – 'mere tradesmen', later to become known as GPs – modern medicine was from the outset gendered and racialized; and the principle of advantage has remained operative ever since.

The sociological study of the professions, notably medicine and law, has largely reflected the interests of Anglo-American theorists (Freidson 1983); but the professionalization of medicine in Britain and the USA differed markedly from equivalent processes in the rest of Europe. Anglo-American associations of doctors skilfully exploited opportunities offered by the expansion of economic markets under liberal capitalism. The state provided a framework for private exchange relations, but had no role either in determining the substance of medical work or in regulating the content of doctors' exchange relations with their patients. In European societies, however, the professionalization of medicine was typically initiated and moulded by a centralized bureaucratic state, which exerted considerable influence both on institutional forms of medical work and on the cultural orientations of doctors (Rueschemeyer 1986). If the genesis in Britain of relations of fixing *as a subset of relations of welfare*, ultimately derivative of relations of command, can reasonably be said to date from the days of liberal capitalism, they were only consolidated during the postwar phase of organized capitalism.

Medicine as an expert culture has in part been founded upon, and generally justified or legitimated in terms of, what Freidson (1986) calls 'formal knowledge'. This is the 'higher knowledge' of modern culture, distinct from routine everyday knowledge and from non-formal specialized knowledge: 'originally rooted in arcane lore and in texts in ancient languages known only to a few, higher knowledge is now still expressed in terms unfamiliar to and impenetrable by the many and discussed by techniques of discourse that are opaque to outsiders' (Freidson 1986: 3). Freidson pinpoints Weber's *Zweckrationalität* (means–end rationality) as best epitomizing the character of formal knowledge. It is associated with the rapid rise of modern science and the application of scientific method to technical and social problems. The use of formal knowledge to order human affairs constitutes an exercise of power, 'an act of domination over those who are the object' (Freidson 1986: 6–7).

This may be linked with Habermas's (1971) argument that the growth of formal knowledge through organized/disorganized capitalism – and its insulation in expert cultures 'within which increasingly specialized forms of argumentation become the guarded preserve of experts and thereby lose contact with the understanding process of the majority of people' (Ray 1993: 49–50; see Habermas, 1987) – has often served to pre-empt political decision-making and democratic participation. Science and technology are in fact a threat to democracy only when used inappropriately, as 'ideology', to address problems of justifying decisions and actions which are not scientific or technical; that is, which do not properly answer to the professional competence of specialists (Habermas 1971: 61). When they are used inappropriately they may provide an unwarranted but politically effective legitimation for the undemocratic exercise of power. Freidson (1986: 8) again: 'under such circumstances political decisions are not subject to popular debate because they are presented as "technical" decisions. People are not allowed to choose among a variety of alternatives because the issue is presented as a technical one that involves the necessary use of the "one best method".' A number of critiques of modern medicine have of course combined the charge that medical expertise has become increasingly technocratic and unaccountable with some version of the thesis of medical imperialism, involving a progressive medicalization of everyday life. Such a thesis is potentially compatible with, and might profitably be incorporated in, Habermas's theory of system rationalization and the colonization of the lifeworld, although it should be recognized that the case for medical imperialism has sometimes been overstated (Strong 1979b: 205–8; see also Scambler 1987). And progressively since the late 1970s, discussion of medical imperialism and medicalization has, as mentioned at the close of the previous section, ceded ground to new considerations of medical decline. It is not that medical paternalism and authority in doctor–patient encounters, or even in the broader culture, have 'withered away', but rather that they have been caught up in the dynamics of disorganized capitalism and have now to be interpreted anew.

While there is general agreement on medical decline, in the USA as well as in Britain (Mechanic 1991; Harrison 1999), the explanations have varied. Some attribute what they regard as the proletarianization of medicine to a straightforwardly extended enactment of the logics of the regime of capital accumulation and mode of regulation (McKinlay and Arches 1985); others to the deprofessionalization of medicine, stressing the changing relationship between doctors and patients owing to the increased knowledge available to and absorbed and readily used by patients/consumers (Haug 1973); and others to the general crisis of welfare statism (Harrison and Pollitt 1994). There are plausible ingredients in each of these. In an up-to-date review of the literature on medical decline in Britain, Harrison and Ahmed (2000) conclude, appropriately enough, that medical autonomy has been reduced at the 'micro' level (that is, in terms of doctors' control over therapeutic decisions and work patterns); the 'meso' level (that is, in terms of medicine's corporatist relations with the state); and the 'macro' level (that is, in terms of the salience of the biomedical model). Interestingly, they identify a reversion to Fordist controls within the NHS in the late 1990s, 'suggesting the continued explanatory value of theories which focus on the state's need both to contain welfare expenditure and to maximize the political legitimacy derived from it' (Harrison and Ahmed 2000: 129). The paragraphs that follow pick up on and develop a number of these themes in the light of previous discussions.

The first line of argument returns to and reworks the concept of governmentality. Governmentality, arising from Foucault, concerns the 'conduct of conduct' or the 'government of government'. It is to be distinguished from *the* government. It has to do, Dean (1999: 2–3) writes, with 'how we govern and how we are governed, and with the relation between the government of ourselves, the government of others, and the government of the state . . . It gives particular emphasis to issues of the government of human conduct in all contexts, by various authorities and agencies, invoking particular forms of truth, and using definite resources, means and techniques.' Dean's own diagnosis of the state of play in disorganized capitalism is that we are experiencing a 'post-welfarist regime of the social'. For all that the current retraction of the welfare state may suggest less state intervention, this does not necessarily mean less government (in a Foucauldian sense). A post-welfarist regime of the social will highlight

> the responsibilities of those who receive support, who have children, who consume educational services, and so on. In this respect, the social will take on a more sovereign character such as in 'workfare' and 'work-for-dole' schemes and in the promulgation of charters of social and family responsibility (Larner, 1998). It will also emphasize the mutual obligations between individuals and between the individuals and the communities who are charged with their support. In the name of such obligations the social takes on a paternalistic and coercive character.
>
> (Dean 1999: 207)

Dean's (1999: 6) usage of the notion of the post-welfarist regime of the social to indicate a new trajectory according to which 'the government of the state is today being augmented, complemented or even displaced by a government of government' is important. It is embedded in the core of his thesis that 'the concern to govern through processes external to the formal apparatuses of political authority is to some extent reinscribed within a programme to reform and secure governmental mechanisms themselves, often by folding back the ends of government upon its instruments.' This narrative, he continues, 'begins to make intelligible the reconfiguration of the social as a set of quasi-markets in services and expertise at the end of the twentieth century, of the governed as customers or consumers of such services and expertise, and explores the way in which this is inflected with themes of community and identity.' This analysis catches something of recent change; but it is incomplete.

What is missing is any reference to relations of class. The second point to make here, then, is that it is relations of class, acting on and through those of command/welfare/fixing, that have provided the impetus for many of the processes commonly subsumed under the concept of governmentality. How is this? It has already been argued that class relations have gained in salience relative to those of command during the course of disorganized capitalism. This argument may now be extended. Those command relations constitutive of the new mode of regulation appropriate for disorganized capitalism, 'glossed' by the (functionally equivalent) ideologies of neo-liberalism and the Third Way, have become, not least in the guise of relations of welfare and fixing, both more diffuse and more penetrative or colonizing of the lifeworld *on behalf of the new regime of capital accumulation* (and it is in this context that the concept of systematically distorted communication has most purchase in doctor–patient interaction). The concept of risk, it might be said, has been expropriated to serve the ends of surveillance through the political promotion of technologies of the self. Dean's post-welfarist regime of the social, in other words, whatever else it might be, and given the principle of compatibility, is functional for disorganized capitalism. Changing relations of command/ welfare/fixing may be 'characterized' with reference to governmentality, but can only be 'explained' in terms of the renewed vigour of relations of class.

This analysis, third, allows for an elaboration of our account of relations of fixing. Relations of fixing can be said to have simultaneously undergone processes of contraction and expansion. The contraction has been towards a putative hard core of (cost-)effective clinical interventions, and is being accomplished via an assembly of state-sponsored and regulated mechanisms of audit. It suggests a more stringent rationing of health care for users of the NHS, if not for users of private sector services, justified by resort to the rhetoric of welfare-state crisis and the subsequent necessity for neo-liberal/ Third Way rationalization (see Higgs and Jones 2001). As ever, the initiative to make welfare cuts has to be balanced by the need to retain legitimacy (see Chapters 3 and 4).

The expansion of relations of fixing is twofold. First, disorganized capitalism has seen the birth and early infancy of what Gilleard and Higgs (2000) call 'aspirational medicine'. This term neatly captures a rapidly growing interest in genetic, surgical and other interventions linked more than hitherto to identity and lifestyle 'choices'. In their thought-provoking text *Cultures of Ageing*, Gilleard and Higgs (2000) point, for example, to the new tendency, and considerable future potential, actively to deny and resist ageing through such interventions. It is of course a largely 'commercial' expansion and one very much linked with the class-generated culture-ideology of consumerism and with clientalization.

The second mode of expansion is more resonant of the notion of governmentality. This has occurred through a fairly blatant process of state co-optation of the medical profession and doctors to legitimate and help to prosecute a form of surveillance of the people's health – through the propagation of ideas of risk and personal responsibility and technologies of the self – that 'compensates for' functional shrinkages within the welfare state; and in *this* context, Dean's reference to a 'post-welfarist regime of the social' seems apt (for an influential Foucauldian analysis of 'surveillance medicine' see Armstrong 1995). The enormous growth in the output of (fashionably postmodern) publications on 'health promotion' bears testimony to the significance of this process; but it is a process which is indicative of a dilution as well as a cooptation of medical expertise.

If, as Hunter and Sinclair suggest, medical education/training still crucially hinges on its capacity to constitute both doctors and patients through 'case presentations', then this manner of apprenticeship may be not only, as Sinclair observes, antipathetic to 'patient-centred therapeutic narratives', but also increasingly irrelevant to agency for surveillance. In fact doctors may have to reinvent themselves to arrest the perceived decline in their status; certainly they must clarify where they stand with regard to 'what they are (now) for'. And the expansion in relations of fixing noted here may prove more threatening to their continuing professional expertise, cultural authority and public regard than the contraction in these same relations.

The new appeal of healers in the folk sector

Consideration of the extent, contours and practices of Kleinman's folk sector must necessarily be brief. It is clear, however, that people's reliance on 'complementary medicine' has increased over the past generation. A series of *Which?* surveys in Britain found that one in seven of its readers had used some form of alternative or complementary practice in 1986, one in four in 1992 and one in three in 1995, findings supported by regional studies funded by health authorities (Emslie *et al.* 1996). Studies in other European nation-states and the USA reveal these British figures as fairly typical. Users are, it seems, more likely to be women, middle-aged, middle-class and conscious of their health and of healthy living (Cant and Sharma 1999). Most users also consult their GPs as occasion demands (Thomas *et al.* 1991).

It has been estimated that there are approximately 50,000 diverse complementary practitioners in the UK (that is, 60 per cent more than the number of GPs) (Fulder 1996). The British Medical Association (BMA 1993) has suggested there are as many as 160 different therapies on offer; but those that attract the most public interest are clearly acupuncture, homeopathy, herbalism, osteopathy and chiropractic, with reflexology and aromatherapy also gaining ground (Fisher and Ward 1994). Complementary practitioners may be said to be engaged in *relations of restoring*. This is of course no more to deny that they can 'fix' than to claim that doctors are engaged in relations of fixing is to deny that they can 'care'. But relations of restoring evoke a sense of equilibrium, well-being and renewal more congruent with the models that underpin much complementary practice than with the philosophical foundations of orthodox allopathic medicine.

Cant and Sharma (1999: 194–5) argue that within the timespan of disorganized capitalism a 'new medical pluralism' has arisen. Their use of the adjective 'new' is deliberate: this is not because medical pluralism is itself recent – quite the contrary, 'medical pluralism is (in global terms) a normal rather than an exceptional state of affairs, and (in historical terms) is not even a novel phenomenon in western countries' – but because the form of pluralism emergent of late in Occidental societies 'differs considerably from the "premodern" forms of pluralism'. It is a pluralism in which biomedicine still has a dominant position and still plays a significant part in the process by which 'different therapies are accorded different degrees of legitimacy'. As many commentators have observed, the position of the BMA on complementary medicine has changed in recent years; expressed differently, the 'tactic' has shifted from outright opposition to cooptation (compare BMA 1986 with BMA 1993; see also Saks 1995). 'The new medical pluralism', Cant and Sharma (1999: 196) argue, 'is one that is structured by the emergent configuration of relations among biomedicine, the state and the consumer/citizen.'

Saks (1998) notes an affinity between notions of pluralism and the post-modern. From a postmodern perspective, he reasons, the advance of complementary therapies 'could be seen to challenge orthodox medicine's epistemological authority, in the wake of the growing plurality of knowledge claims – as biomedicine becomes relativized into yet another discourse in a web of indeterminacy' (Saks 1998: 207). Warming to this theme, he continues:

> the corollary of the decline of legitimacy of the grand narrative of biomedicine in the face of the challenge from complementary therapies, as Turner (1990) notes, is that the hierarchical division between scientific medicine and alternative medicine collapses. This in turn leads to the deregulation of health care in which licences to practice become increasingly irrelevant in the marketplace of hyper-consumption, as society is transformed from the modern to the postmodern.

While acknowledging its seductiveness, and even a whiff of acuity, Saks solicitously distances himself from such a postmodern approach. But what the postmodern perspective does transparently invite is further reflection on public choice and 'empowerment'; and it is with these concepts that this penultimate chapter closes.

It may appear axiomatic that if, (a) for all their surviving dominance politically, culturally and in relation to patienthood, doctors have nevertheless experienced a decline in work autonomy and in public confidence and regard, and (b) 'rival' complementary therapists have created new or enlarged markets for their wares, then people's choices have increased and they have been empowered. But there is ideology lurking here. We have already seen in the context of Thatcher's health reforms that an insistent governmental rhetoric of extended choice can be associated with a *de facto* reduction in choice (see Chapter 4). A new medical pluralism may or may not entail additional choice and/or empowerment.

A sequence of at least three qualifications is in order. First, it is worth recalling the paradox of disinhibition formulated in Chapter 2. This attests that, for all its bold and *prima facie* radical postulates and 'disinhibiting' effects, postmodern theorizing betrays a deep underlying conservatism. This conservatism rests in its (ultimately self-refuting) eschewal in principle of the possibility of obtaining rationally binding support for any given proposition/ theory/world-view. In so far as a new medical pluralism is the beneficiary of the relativism implicit in much of postmodern culture, a certain wariness is in order. If tolerance and openness to a greater range of therapies is in large part a function of a diminished public appetite for 'evidence-based' choice – and the (critical realist) use of this expression here is not without its irony since it has been hijacked of late by (neo-)positivists chasing government funding – then it is difficult to see any real gain.

The second qualification is linked. It is that public choice and empowerment alike imply knowledgeable accountability. Thus, in so far as a new medical pluralism has its origins not in knowledgeable accountability, but in system rationalization and lifeworld colonization, accomplished by means of (the culture-ideology of) consumerism and clientalization, buttressed by the philosophies of neo-liberalism and the Third Way, one is bound to ask: what price choice and empowerment?

The third qualification concerns empowerment, a word which has been used to stand for a number of different concepts, many of them ideologically tainted. Rhodes and his colleagues (1991), writing about public and community health interventions on behalf of socially marginal groups, usefully distinguish four such concepts or models. The 'information-giving' or 'preventive' model takes biomedical definitions of health and illness as unproblematic and gives priority to the imparting of information, relying on the (thoroughly dubious) belief that there are causal links between individuals receiving information and modifying their behaviour. The model of 'self-empowerment' emphasizes people's ability to 'take control' to their advantage through personal growth and assertiveness. In contrast to these two individualistic and 'top-down' models, the 'community-action' and 'radical-political'/'social transformatory' models are characteristically collectivist and 'bottom-up'. The former focuses on community change arising out of collective action, while the latter goes a step further to stress far-reaching social change throughout society. In a subsequent piece, Rhodes (1994: 57) enlarges on the general idea of 'community empowerment', arguing that this necessarily involves 'questioning critically the values of those in power', and adding that this may mean querying 'the concepts of "healthy" and "unhealthy" and the extent to which marginalized individuals and communities have an equity of "choice" over these values.' Many interventions presume a 'rationality of choice-making which makes "healthy" choices the "rational" choices' (Thorogood, 1992); and this, Rhodes (1994: 58–9) points out, comprises a 'political and moral agenda, for it cannot allow empowered wrong choices to be right, healthy or rational' (see also Scambler and Scambler 1998, 1999). There is, in short, more to empowerment than meets the eye.

PART THREE

The need for a critical sociology

7

From critical theory to critical sociology

The analysis of health and social change offered during the course of the preceding chapters has necessarily been selective and partial. To pick up on a metaphor used above, it might be said to have combined three elements: an indication of the main properties of what has been called disorganized capitalism, affording a fleeting impression of the disconcertingly complex *overall picture* to be assembled; a series of models, expressed in terms of logics/relations/figurations, each constituting a discrete *piece of the jigsaw*; and numerous reviews, reflections, asides and discussions hinting at or elaborating on the differential significance of these pieces in relation to the overall picture (see Chapter 4). Some themes and arguments comprising this analysis stand out as particularly important, and it may be helpful to remind ourselves of these briefly.

It seems obvious, for example, that just as no single paradigm/research programme has anything like a monopoly of worthwhile theorizing on health and social change, no single paradigm/research programme has nothing significant to contribute. If, perhaps controversially, postmodern interjections are taken to represent yet another paradigm/research programme (see, for example, Best and Kellner 1997), then this is true also of postmodern theory. For all its disinhibiting potential and side-effects, however, postmodern theory can so detach itself from its modernist ancestry as to render itself immune from rational and empirical interrogation, becoming more conservative than radical in the process. But explosions not only occasion damage, they also clear space for new designs and building projects. Postmodern theory should possibly, to paraphrase the ethnomethodologists, be more topic than resource for a while, and there is some evidence that this is happening.

The pace, depth and impact of change in nation-states like Britain since the 1960s and 1970s, especially around processes of globalization, or, more precisely, glocalization, has been such that vital continuities have too often been either neglected or denied. This is perhaps most true of relations of class. From the vantage point of the critical realist perspective pioneered by Marx and polished by Bhaskar, ownership and/or control of the means of production is no less significant today than it was in liberal or organized capitalism, and it remains in the hands of a tiny minority of (thoroughly global) 'greedy bastards', emergent from the (strongly globalized) capitalist-executive, serviced by the new middle class and, in the absence of any imminent threat of a crisis of legitimation, facilitated by the (weakly globalized) power elite/ core-executive of the state apparatus by means of a ubiquitous culture-ideology of consumerism (sometimes, astonishingly, conflated with the idea of a 'liberating' postmodernized culture). This is manifestly not to assert or defend any form of economic determinism: it is evident, for example, that the cultural domain has partial autonomy, notwithstanding the rarity of *de facto* exceptions to the principle of compatibility. Nor is it to reject the categorical (in addition to the derivative and circumstantial) potential of relations of gender, ethnicity, age and so on, none of which 'reduce' to class relations. No more does the kind of neo-Marxism advocated here entail, in the manner of some unreconstructed Enlightenment metanarrative, any (teleological) philosophy of history.

Class relations have gained in salience relative to those of command (and also of welfare, a subset of command relations, and fixing, a subset of welfare relations) during disorganized capitalism, as is evidenced by the resurgence of relations of worth once embodied in Victorian poor law legislation; and the threat of a crisis of state legitimation has for the time being receded. This needs to be recognized if the altered political complexion of governments and the crisis of welfare statism, allowing alike for the British health reforms initiated by Thatcher and Clinton's failure to reform health care in the USA, is to be explained sociologically. It is class relations too, personified again by the hunger of the greedy bastards (and epitomized in the GBH), which have led to the new inequality of income and the widening health inequality in disorganized capitalism. According to the GBH, it is the rich and powerful who have contributed most effectively both to the consolidation of the lot of the poor and powerless, and – through their unrivalled influence across the range of flows of biological, psychological social, cultural, spatial and, prepotently, material capital – to the increase in health inequality.

These forms of system rationalization amount to a partial colonization of the lifeworld. Traces of the functional imperatives of economy and state can in fact be discerned, via today's (more class-responsive) relations of command, welfare and fixing, in professional or expert narratives of disease and lay or experiential narratives of illness; in the changing nature and substance of doctor–patient encounters (typically assuming the form of systematically distorted communication); and in shifts in relations of caring and restoring; although empirical investigation in this area is admittedly in its infancy. The sum of such changes is disempowering rather than empowering for the public to the extent that it represents lifeworld colonization. But more needs to be said on the concept of empowerment.

This final chapter starts with an extended analysis of civil society and the public sphere of the lifeworld, drawing on the continuing work of Habermas. The second section develops this analysis by means of a discussion of the concept of deliberative democracy, and goes on to focus on the ties between civil society, the public sphere and deliberative democracy. The third section reviews theories of the roles of labour and other social movements in relation to activity in civil society and the public sphere. The fourth section draws on this review to consider the case for recognizing a nascent 'health movement'. And the closing section of this chapter, and of the book, makes the case for a reflexive critical sociology oriented to lifeworld rationalization and deliberative democracy, and posits a possible agenda for such a sociology, associated with the prospect of cosmopolitan citizenship and a reconstruction and renewal of the welfare project.

Civil society and the public sphere

Early accounts of civil society distinguished it principally from the state (Ehrenberg 1999). More recently it has come to be distinguished also from the economy (see Cohen and Arato 1992) (much American analysis notwithstanding: Harrington Watt 1991). Habermas, as Garnham (1992: 361) approvingly writes, 'distinguishes the public sphere from both state and market and can pose the question of the threats to democracy and the public discourses upon which it depends coming from the development of an oligopolistic capitalist market and from the development of the modern interventionist state.' As far as Habermas (1996: 367) is concerned, civil society exists at the interface of the private and public spheres of the lifeworld, consisting of those 'more or less spontaneously emergent associations, organizations and movements that, attuned to how societal problems resonate in the private life spheres, distil and transmit such reactions in amplified form to the public sphere'. Scambler and Martin (2001) have suggested distinguishing between two distinct 'sectors' of civil society, the *enabling sector* and the *protest sector*. The enabling sector derives its thrust from the private sphere of the lifeworld. It is within this sector of civil society that – as part and parcel of the normal social exchanges of everyday praxis, and typically in Oldenburg's (1997) informal meeting or 'third' places, like libraries, cafes and pubs – matters of potential concern arise and are often identified. The protest sector of civil society is directed towards the public sphere. It is within this sector that people come together, or are mobilized, in networks, campaign or pressure groups, social movements and other forms of association in pursuit of influence for purposeful change.

According to Habermas (1996), the core of civil society – that is, what has here been termed its protest sector – comprises a network of associations that institutionalize 'problem-solving discourses on questions of general interest'. It is evident that civil society affords a limited scope for action. Moreover, a healthy, resistant civil society can only develop in a 'liberal' culture; its actors can acquire influence but not political power; and the effectiveness of politics is in any event severely constrained in modern, functionally differentiated societies (see Chapter 3). Civil society is manifestly *not* some 'macrosubject' able to 'bring society as a whole under control and simultaneously act for it' (Habermas 1996: 372). But, nevertheless, the social movements, citizen initiatives and forums, and political and other group associations that make up civil society can 'under certain circumstances' acquire influence in the public sphere which extends to the political domain (as in the 'outside initiative model' described by Cobb *et al.* 1976; see also Scambler 1998b).

Having defined civil society, it is now necessary to explicate more fully the concept of the public sphere. References to Habermas's (1989c) early (*Habilitation*) treatise on the emergence of the 'bourgeois' public sphere in eighteenth-century England and its subsequent decline seem to have grown exponentially since its initial publication as long ago as 1962. This bourgeois public sphere, Habermas contended, was not part of the state but, on the contrary, a sphere in which the activities of the state might be debated and criticized. And the medium of this 'confrontation' with the state was itself significant: 'it was the public use of reason, as articulated by private individuals engaged in argument that was *in principle* open and unconstrained' (Thompson 1993: 176). The genesis of the English bourgeois public sphere was aided by the rise of the periodical press and of a host of new urban 'centres of sociability', third places like salons and coffee houses. Political control and censorship were more relaxed than in many other parts of Europe. Habermas argues that the critical debate engendered in the public sphere led gradually to an opening up and more comprehensive scrutinizing of Parliament, which abandoned its right to prevent publication of its proceedings, and to the consitutional extension of rights of freedom of speech and expression.

But this was not to last. The state became more 'capitalist' and more interventionist. The salons and coffee houses declined and the periodicals were absorbed into a thoroughly commercialized system of mass communications (see Webster 1995). Mayhew (1997) writes in this vein of a 'new public', subject to mass persuasion through relentless advertising, lobbying and other forms of media manipulation. Thompson (1993: 178) summarizes the Habermasian thesis: 'What was once an exemplary forum of rational-critical debate became just another domain of cultural consumption, and the bourgeois public sphere collapsed into a sham world of image creation and opinion management in which the diffusion of media products is in the service of vested interests.' In Habermas's own (possibly ill-chosen) phrase, the bourgeois public sphere became 'refeudalized'.

As more attention has been focused on this work, so the criticisms have mounted. Thompson (1995) lists four criticisms, all of which have some substance. First, by concentrating on the *bourgeois* public sphere, Habermas neglects other 'popular' forms of public discourse and engagement which were not subsumed by, and were sometimes militantly opposed to, bourgeois sociability (Negt and Kluge 1993); the vivid English historical studies of Thompson (1965) and Hill (1975) might be cited here. Second, Habermas may have been overly selective in other ways in his citation of historical materials. There is evidence, for example, that periodicals may have been no less influential in previous eras, notably during the English Civil War. Habermas (1992a) has since acknowledged the need for further historical exploration in these areas.

Third, while Habermas is clearly aware that the bourgeois public sphere was restricted to individuals with the cultural and material capital to participate, he makes little of the fact that it excluded others, most notably women. Feminists have forcibly insisted that the exclusion of women was *constitutive* of the public sphere: the public sphere, for example, was juxtaposed to the private sphere in a gender-specific way. Habermas (1992a) has recognized this, but without as yet addressing it in any depth or with any urgency. And fourth, the notion that the bourgeois public sphere went into more or less precipitous decline has been challenged. Thompson (1995), for instance, charges Habermas with overstating the passivity of more contemporary 'recipients of media products'. He criticizes him too for referring to the refeudalization of the public sphere, claiming that 'we need to think again about what "publicness" means today in a world permeated by new forms of communication and information diffusion, where individuals are able to interact with others and observe persons and events without ever encountering them in the same spatio-temporal locale' (Thompson 1995: 75).

A number of writers and theorists, revealing varying degrees of affinity with his critical theoretical programme, have addressed the challenge laid down by Habermas, and by those like Thompson who are more wary of focusing exclusively on the *anti-democractic* potential of the new globalizing, increasingly ubiquitous – and colonizing – technologies of communication, to devise means to facilitate and institutionalize discourse-ethical procedures, or the public use of reason, in the public sphere. It is in this connection that discussions of 'deliberative' or 'discursive' democracy have arisen.

Deliberative democracy

Not all discussions of deliberative democracy deal with the same concept (see Bohman and Rehg 1997). Drawing on his discourse ethics, Habermas (1996, 1998) has recently analysed the phenomena of law and democracy, offering in the process a defence of a proceduralist concept of deliberative democracy in which 'the burden of legitimating state power is borne by informal and legally institutionalised processes of political deliberation' (Cronin and De Greiff 1998). He advocates a form of 'constitutional patriotism'. Of fundamental importance here is the idea that the legitimacy of political authority can only be secured through public participation in political deliberation and decision-making; he claims, in fact, that there is an 'internal relation' between the rule of law and popular sovereignty.

Habermas accepts neither liberal nor communitarian political philosophy (aptly characterized by Barber (2000: 34) as 'thin and uninspiring' and 'thick and glutinous' respectively); instead, he seeks to extract what is commendable or capable of salvage from each (see also Delanty 2000). Liberalism focuses principally on 'autonomy' and stresses individual liberty. Communitarianism focuses principally on 'legitimacy' and emphasizes the values emergent in particular religious, ethnic or national identities: these values are transmitted culturally and comprise the background against which all questions of political justice must be answered. Habermas rejects a key premise of both liberalism and communitarianism, namely that legal and political principles have to be morally grounded, arguing instead that the law and morality stand in a 'complementary relation'. In fact, the core human rights enshrined in the law, he maintains, are *legal* and not moral rights.

He identifies five categories of core rights which free and equal citizens must confer on one another if they are to organize their affairs through positive law. The first three – that is, membership rights and due-process rights that together guarantee private autonomy – constitute the 'negative liberties'; the fourth are rights of political participation and guarantee public autonomy; and the fifth are rights of social welfare, necessary in so far as the effective exercise of civil and political rights depends on citizens being able to satisfy certain basic human needs.

State power is required to police this system of rights, and this introduces a tension between state power and legitimate law. Habermas argues that an account of the public use of reason is vital here, and that this must ultimately refer to democratic processes of opinion- and will-formation in the public sphere. In this way he links the informal discursive sources of democracy with the formal decision-making institutions necessary for the effective rule of law in modern complex societies. Democracy 'mediates between the public sphere (the domain of debate) and the rule of law (the institutional realm)' (Delanty 1999: 88). Habermas contends that it is the constitutional state that represents the crucial network of legal institutions and mechanisms that governs the conversion of citizens' communicative power into legitimate administrative activity. Law, for him, 'represents . . . the medium for transforming communicative power into administrative power' (Habermas 1996: 169).

The legitimacy of legal norms, then, is a function of those formal properties of procedures of political deliberation and decision-making that support the presumption that their outcomes are rational. In practice, Habermas suggests that this requires a public sphere characterized by open political discussion, informed by inputs of expert knowledge and delivering ready access to print and electronic media, and institutionally underwritten by the voluntary associations of civil society. This public sphere would need to be supported by a legally regulated government sphere, consisting of legislative, judicial and administrative branches.

Two general and related observations concerning civil society, the public sphere and deliberative democracy are in order. The first involves revisiting Habermas's claim that the bourgeois public sphere, formed initially in late eighteenth-century Europe, had significant progressive properties. This contention is probably apposite, for all that the bourgeois public sphere, as many feminists have averred, was from the outset a socially restricted and exclusionary dimension of the lifeworld. The question of whether or not it has since receded is less straightforward. On the face of it, Habermas's argument leaves little room for 'the thesis that new forms of electronic communication and innovative uses of older media formats can provide new public spaces and new locations for civic discourse' (Axford 2001: 7). There is certainly no doubting the constraints on actors in civil society at the turn of the millennium and the depth of the current penetration or colonization of the public sphere by the media of the market place and state; nor that aspects of the system rationalization and lifeworld colonization have exacted costs in terms of, and represent a continuing threat to, democratic accountability and any fledgling potential for deliberative democracy. E-democracy is not round the corner; and as the Internet becomes subject to 'increased commercialisation and attempts at regulation by private and public bureaucracies', the prospects remain uncertain (Sassi 2001: 102; see also Hague and Loader 1999).

But it is perhaps no less easy to be overly pessimistic about the present as it is to overstate the extent, ubiquity and promise of the bourgeois public sphere two centuries ago. The point I want to stress here is that it is important to resist the temptation – whether from communitarian, 'multiculturalist' or postmodern sources – to abandon the Habermasian concept of a *single formal public sphere* just because it has become increasingly apparent that there exists *a plurality of actual or substantive public spheres*, including what Fraser (1992) calls alternative or 'subaltern counterpublics' (see Calhoun, 1996). This is a point we return to later.

Second, there is no gainsaying the existence of what Bohman (1996) terms 'deliberative inequalities' in the public sphere. He distinguishes three kinds: *power asymmetries*, which affect access to the public sphere; *communicative inequalities*, which affect the ability to participate and to make effective use of available opportunities to deliberate in the public sphere; and *political poverty*, which makes it unlikely that 'politically impoverished' citizens can participate in the public sphere at all. Bohman (1996: 112) argues that deliberation 'without correction for inequalities' will tend inexorably to elitist practice, 'favouring those who have greater cultural resources (such as knowledge and information) and who are more capable of imposing their own interests and values on others in the public arena.' Fraser (1992) suggests that deliberative inequalities might themselves be articulated or 'thematized' in the public sphere. This could involve, for example, 'challenging unfair advantages in the public sphere due to social and economic position; introducing the effects of privately owned and profit-driven media on the circulation of information in discussion; and investigating the way social and economic subordination filters into and distorts the public sphere' (Chambers 1996: 207).

While there is self-evidently little occasion for optimism about the prospects for enhanced democratic accountability through lifeworld rationalization – and Habermas remains pessimistic when switching his attention, understandably enough if a touch too finally, from old-style labour movements to the new social movements of disorganized capitalism as possible agents of change – it nevertheless seems difficult to exaggerate the importance of devising ways of giving effective voice to the 'public use of reason'.

Social movements, the protest sector of civil society and the public sphere

A brief, purposeful consideration of the literature on social movements is timely. In fact such has been the heterogeneity of theories about social movements that general definitions have become quite hazardous (Diani 1992; Cohen and Rai 2000). Not unreasonably, della Porta and Diani (1999: 16) define them in terms of four elements: as (a) informal networks, based on (b) shared beliefs and solidarity, which (c) mobilize around conflictual issues, deploying (d) frequent, varying forms of protest. Wilson (1973) distinguished four kinds of social movement in a manner which remains helpful a generation later: 'transformative movements' aim to change the entire social structure, often by violent means; 'reformative movements' aim at partial change, typically to offset prevailing injustices and inequalities'; 'redemptive movements' aim to change radically the (decontextualized) individual, emphasizing personal betterment; and 'alternative movements' aim to counter conventional cultural norms in favour of more self-sufficient and/or sustainable lifestyles (see Cohen and Rai 2000: 2–3).

In the USA of late the understanding of social movements has featured *resource mobilization theory*, while in Europe *new social movement theory* has been most influential during disorganized capitalism. Resource mobilization theory tends to concentrate on how groups emerge, recruit their members, deal with success or failure and so on (see McAdam *et al.* 1996); it has been said to concentrate on 'how' questions. New social movement theory is instead concerned with 'why' questions and is more pertinent to the argument of this chapter. Its proponents claim that social movements in disorganized capitalism – whether transformative or, more likely, reformative, redemptive, alternative or deserving of some other label, and whether 'defensive' or 'offensive', 'particularistic' or 'universalistic' (Habermas 1981) – are qualitatively different from their predecessors in organized capitalism (Eyerman 1992; Calhoun 1993). They stress that conflict between industrial classes is of decreasing relevance and that the representation of movements as essentially homogeneous subjects is no longer tenable (della Porta and Diana 1999: 11–12). Offe (1985b) has identified a number of properties of new social movements which distinguish them from old-style 'labour movements': a critical stance in relation to modernity and progress; decentralized and participatory organizational structures; a defence of interpersonal solidarity against the giant colonizing bureaucracies; and the reclamation of autonomous spaces, rather than material advantages. New social movements, for Offe, are characterized by 'an open, fluid organization, an inclusive and non-ideological participation, and greater attention to social than to economic transformations' (della Porta and Diani 1999: 12).

Two theorists of new social movements of particular relevance to us are Touraine and Melucci. Touraine's views have evolved over the years and, like Habermas, his attentions have turned increasingly to issues of democracy. While Habermas might be said to have offered a 'decontextualized discourse ethic', however, Touraine writes of a 'recomposing of the world' around a 're-enchanted politics' and the need for the invention of a 'cultural democracy' (Delanty 1999: 138; see Touraine 1997). He maintains that a society's social movements are centred on a 'core conflict' within that society. During organized capitalism, for example, the core conflict arose out of the mode of production and class struggle emerged as the key contest, giving rise to the labour movement. With reference to the present period of disorganized capitalism, Touraine (1992: 141) draws a dividing line between a 'logic of the market place', also a logic of power and accumulation, and a 'logic of individual liberty', which, he insists, cannot be 'reduced to the affirmation of a self-destructive narcissism, nor to the return to cultural and ethnic roots in which the individual is suppressed in favour of a return to religions and theocracy.' For Touraine, the core conflict in the kind of technocratic or 'programmed' society characteristic of disorganized capitalism might best be described as between technology and the 'bureaucratic control of everyday life' on the one hand, and those who oppose this control on the other (Mayer and Roth 1995: 302). Protest activities unrelated to this core conflict are more appropriately termed 'submovements, communitarian movements, national movements' and so on, and should be considered as subordinate to the core conflict (Diani 1992: 7). While Touraine once accorded social movements a potential to transform society, he has more recently come to stress the 'plural character' of the new social movements, associating them with democracy and the rights of the individual in the face of enchroaching political power.

Melucci (1989, 1994), for whom culture and democracy are also fundamental themes, focuses on individuals participating in social movements qua 'actors within the limits and possibilities thrown up by structures', emphasizing the need to know how people become involved in collective action, how they construct collective identity and unity, and the meanings produced as a result of this collective work. He introduces the concept of 'submerged networks', contending that social movements do much of their identity creation and subversion of cultural codes while not actually engaged in public protest, but during periods of 'latency'. His own studies of social movements purport to demonstrate that their submerged networks can 'render power visible', even in previously uncontested areas (Mayer and Roth 1995: 305). His emphasis, then, is on the transmutation of individual identity to collective identity, on the cultural work of social movements and on conflict. He writes of the importance of 'meaning' in terms of the creation of new cultural codes: 'what lies at the core of contemporary conflicts is the production and reappropriation of meaning' (Melucci 1996: 145). Social movement activity, for Melucci, moves in and out of the political realm, and it is the processes through which a social movement's participants generate collective identity and act on it, paradigmatically initiating change through the subversion of extant cultural codes and genesis of novel successors, which are of principal importance.

The argument arising out of, and drawing upon, this discussion can be summarized in terms of five claims. The first is that many, although by no means all, of the social movements emergent in the protest sector of civil society in disorganized capitalism not only serve as 'carriers' of communicative rationality into the public sphere, but also possess organizational and other properties which are suggestive of, or even qualify them as prototypes for, 'deliberative democracy'. Bohman (1996: 137) writes of this type of social movement:

> First, it is a mechanism for pooling the resources, capacities and experiences of various persons and groups, and it gives coherent expression and unified voice to their shared problems and grievances. Second, solidarity within these informal networks permits pooling of resources and information and thus the creation of public goods within the movement as a way to compensate for resource inequalities and political poverty. The organization of the movement itself also gives it a voice, putting it in dialogue with other actors and institutions who recognize their grievances as public problems or expand the pool of their public reasons. Small acts of contestation can then be generalized into protests and become a public challenge to the existing distribution of deliberative resources in institutions. Once given powerful public expression, the movement's grievances can be publicly recognized as legitimate and made part of the public agenda for decision-making institutions.

The second claim is that the social movements of disorganized capitalism tend increasingly to have a global constituency, reach and/or potential (see Cohen and Rai 2000). Sometimes, this growth in transnational social movements (TSMs) is misleadingly equated with the – even more rapid, and far more heterogeneous – growth in international non-governmental organizations (INGOs). The rapid expansion of INGOs was apparent even in organized capitalism; but few INGOs fit the criteria of social movements outlined above (although a high proportion of those with the closest associations have a high public and political profile): Boli and Thomas (1997: 183) have calculated that at the time of the advent of disorganized capitalism, INGOs either concerned with individual rights/welfare (6 per cent) or oriented to world-polity issues (for example, world peace or environmental preservation; 6 per cent) accounted for approximately 12 per cent of the INGO population. Cohen and Rai (2000: 12) adopt the sensible expedient of seeing these – smaller, structured – INGOs not as social movements, but as *imbricated* within' – larger, networked – TSMs ('"within" rather than "below", as the scales of a fish or the slates on a roof are not hierarchically arranged').

In the course of his study of environmental INGOs and transnational corporations (TNCs), Newell (2000) distinguishes between *liberal* and *critical* modes of *governance* of the latter. Noting that since the 1980s INGOs are increasingly by-passing nation-states to confront TNCs, he defines liberal governance in terms of strategies of engagement – such as eco-consumerism, project collaboration, codes of conduct and private regimes – that 'seek to work within the current economic system to improve the way in which it functions and to offset its worst ecological excesses' (Newell 2000: 124). Critical governance occurs when INGOs decline to work 'with' TNCs and instead adopt strategies – like counter-information, TNC monitors and shareholder activism – to move 'against' them in order to expose 'irresponsible corporate conduct'. Political arguments between advocates of liberal and critical governance tend be heated. Predictably enough, INGOs/TSMs favouring liberal governance are typically reformative, while INGOs/TSMs opting for critical governance retain some potential to be transformative.

The third claim is that contemporary (new) social movements are less reflective of a post-transformative politics than is commonly imagined. Like Touraine and Melucci, Habermas (1987) sees new social movements as occupying an ambivalent position as a post-revolutionary radical consciousness and as a sign of a new kind of politics. Delanty (1999: 85) summarizes:

> Habermas assumes that ideology has come to an end and in its place is a 'fragmented consciousness'. But fragmentation is not seen as something that fundamentally challenges the autonomy of communicative action. It is his thesis that fragmentation results from the colonization of the life-world by outside, objective forces emanating from the system. Fragmentation is purely a matter of cognition, an 'obscurity' in the late modern condition.

Hunter (1995) is one who warns against the over-inclusive and premature abandonment of the revolutionary tradition that this entails. He rightly insists that the post-revolutionary goals of the new social movements can *in fact* only be achieved in the event of radical, even revolutionary, change. Thus he writes:

> Today's social movements set numerous goals that cannot be realized through modest reform. Most revolutionary theory has focused on how revolutions can be made, not on the world they would create, and little agreement exists 'on what constitutes movement success' (Tarrow, 1989). Still, it is possible to specify political goals enunciated by contemporary social movements and underscore the extent of economic, political, and cultural transformation their realization would entail. Economic goals include reducing and then ending hunger, physical deprivation, gross economic inequality, and undemocratic, elite control of material and financial resources. Green social movements focus on stopping environmental degradation and pursuing sustainable development grounded in an ecological critique of industrializing modernity. Identity-based new social movements seek the end of domination and marginality defined by racism, national chauvinism, sexism and homophobia. Peasant-based

popular movements fight for land and water against monoculture agri-business. Indigenous people seek rights, autonomy, and the preserva-tion of their lands and resources. In addition to these substantive goals, social movements and organizations are struggling for a dramatic in-vigoration and expansion of democracy, enrichment of civil society and public spheres, extensions of human rights globally, and firm commit-ments to individual freedom from state domination and repressive cultural norms.

(Hunter 1995: 325)

What this 'brief list' indicates, Hunter (1995: 325) stresses, is 'the need for the *transformation of broad phenomena* – undemocratic political institutions, eco-nomic, racial and gender inequities, and industrialism's threats to humans and nature – not "just" the amelioration of particular problems' (emphasis added). It is worth reporting here that while social movements may fail to achieve the changes they seek, their endeavours may nevertheless enhance the prospects of these changes being won later (Boswell and Chase-Dunn 2000).

The fourth claim is that while it is appropriate to record a decline in the influence of old-style labour movements and their partial displacement by new social movements in disorganized capitalism, it would be exceptionally unwise at this stage to write off the former. Castells's (1997: 354) prognosis is understandable but premature: 'Torn by internationalization of finance and production, unable to adapt to networking of firms and individualization of work, and challenged by the degendering of employment, the labor move-ment fades away as a major source of social cohesion and workers' repres-entation.' As Arrighi (1996) points out, historically there has always been a considerable time-lag in terms of labour's response to capital restructuring. And as Munck (1998, 2000) and others have shown, there are already signs that labour movements are not only generating transnational links and strat-egies, but also learning from the successes and failures of collective action (global *and local*) on the part of new social movements.

The final claim at this juncture is a reminder – as it were, despite the cau-tious and qualified optimism of the previous claims – that the prospects of either reinvigorated labour movements or INGOs/TSMs with transformative intent accomplishing social change at the level of real social relations remain somewhat bleak.

The question of health movements

One fundamental lesson from medical sociology, reiterated many times in Chapters 4, 5 and 6 above, is that innumerable and diverse social and social-structural factors play either directly or, more often, indirectly on health status. It follows that a wide array of social movements, and especially TSMs embracing INGOs, carry some potential to enhance the health status of indi-viduals, groups and populations *without presenting or acting explicitly as 'health movements*'. Many of the multifarious (and for the most part, decolonizing) social movements emergent in the protest sector of civil society – whether locally, regionally, nationally or globally based – in order to fight one or other form of (absolute or relative) material deprivation come into this category.

One well documented case coincidental with the era of disorganized capitalism but with an altogether more explicit health focus has been the confrontation between a pragmatic transnational alliance of social movement activists and Nestlé over the latter's allegedly unethical marketing of infant formula in poor countries (for an exhaustive account, see Sethi 1994). Infant formula producers have been subjected to boycotts all round the world; and, as Sklair (2000: 182) writes, 'the ongoing story of this conflict has a permanent place in the annals of corporate irresponsibility and corporate citizenship.' Paradigmatic among health-oriented conflicts of this kind, of course, and even more comprehensively reported, has been the protracted resistance on the part of (I)NGOs/(T)SMs to the tobacco industry. As noted in Chapter 5, a 'health catastrophe' which has already occurred in nation-states like Britain, namely the scourge of tobacco-related deaths and illnesses, is even now being exacerbated by the marketing strategies of transnational corporations in developing countries (Sklair 1998b) (in the case of BAT, aided and abetted, it seems, by the marketable skills of a former British Minister of Health).

There are numerous fruitful lines of enquiry here, many of them resonant of the GBH in Chapter 5. Rather than pursue them here, however, we shall pick up on a less researched area, namely the decolonizing potential of (new) social movements purporting to give the public a 'voice' in the health domain. It has been contended that some forms of collective action or 'self-help' focused on health matters themselves satisfy the criteria of social movements of della Porta and Diani (1999). Many would maintain that the 'disability politics movement' is the most conspicuous example here (Oliver 1990, 1996), although for some this remains a contentious proposition (see Barnes *et al.* 1999); Pilgrim and Rogers (1993) argue that mental health 'user groups' in Britain can be described as part of a new social movement; and Scambler and Martin (2001) have suggested that the American network AIDS Coalition to Unleash Power (ACT UP), characterized by Halci (1999) as a diverse and non-partisan group of individuals committed to using direct action to end the AIDS crisis, also fulfils these criteria. But caution is required here. Clearly most instances of collective action/self-help around matters of health, illness or disease cannot be regarded as social movements *in their own right*, although more than a few might be said to come under the umbrella of pre-existing social movements; for example, women's groups coalescing (at the level of 'particularistic' demands) to decolonize childbirth by curbing the (masculine) territorial and technological power emanating from relations of fixing can reasonably be seen as part of a broader ('progressive', 'offensive' and 'universalistic') women's movement (Scambler 1987; and see Habermas 1981; Oakley 1980, 1986).

Drawing on his research on people with diabetes, Kelleher (1994, 2001) offers some clarification of the links between self-help groups and new social movements in relation to responses to chronic illness in disorganized capitalism, and it is to his contribution that we briefly turn. In his review of the extensive (largely American) literature on self-help groups, he affirms that studies show considerable heterogeneity. Katz and Bender (1976) make an important basic distinction between 'inner-focused groups', in which the primary activity is members' sharing of problems and mutual support, and 'outer-focused groups', in which members combine to form a pressure group to improve facilities for people with a particular condition. In a more concentrated and in many ways representative study, Williams (1989: 146) found the British National Ankylosing Spondylitis Society to be torn by tensions between those wanting a friendly support group, those favouring the establishment of 'a prestigious charitable society' and those advocating 'a patients' society for teaching the medical and caring professions what their (patients') problems really are'.

Adopting a Habermasian perspective, Kelleher (2001) points out that *most* self-help groups recruiting people with chronic illnesses are 'not political in the sense that those new social movements campaigning to save the environment are, nor are they political in wanting to work for political change of the kind that the old social movements associated with labour were.' But he contends that some of their number might nevertheless be seen as 'part of the culture of new social movements'. It is an argument based on the notions, first, that they are engaged in defending the lifeworld against colonization by the expert culture of medicine ('which itself has become dominated by the instrumental rationality of the large system of society'); and second, that in so far as they open the way for medical knowledge and practice to be challenged, 'they could be said to be contributing to sustaining a public sphere in a similar way to the new social movement groups which are overtly politicising issues.' In addition, and the political nature of this should not be underestimated, they provide people with an opportunity for 'communicative activities', to 'talk about their feelings about having a particular condition, something health care professionals seem unable to do' (see Chapter 6, and Scambler 1994). Kelleher's overall conclusion is that while not all self-help groups in the health field can be said to be part of the culture of new social movements, there is a case for so defining those that – by affording members the chance to 'construct personal and joint narratives', to relate and interrogate them, and thus to resocialize people 'to see themselves as normal people with diabetes/epilepsy/schizophrenia' – engage in resisting the colonization of the lifeworld.

To summarize at this point, there is no doubt either that a significant number of social movements, old as well as new, and most notably those subsuming INGOs and/or achieving the status of TSMs, are committed to securing social change which is – directly or indirectly – conducive to enhanced health and longevity; or that there are instances of collective action/self-help explicitly oriented to health issues which have organic links to such 'parent' movements;

or that some forms of collective action/self-help focused exclusively on health issues qualify as social movements in their own right. In each of these cases the contests for change have unambiguously moved beyond the enabling to the protest sector of civil society and aspire to political influence in the public sphere. Other examples of collective action/self-help concerned with health can be said, following Kelleher, to be part of the culture of new social movements (some functioning rather like Melucci's 'submerged networks'). But probably most (modest, resolutely apolitical) self-help groups in the arena of health either remain in the enabling sector of civil society (and resonate with Kleinman's popular – or, more rarely, folk – sectors) or are (merely) extensions of extant relations of fixing (and as such can be located for practical purposes in Kleinman's professional sector).

The concept of a critical sociology

These sociological and philosophical reflections on civil society, the public sphere, deliberative democracy and (new) social (and health) movements are all highly significant for the kind of critical (medical) sociology advocated and, in provisional and tentative fashion, practised in this volume. The manner of their relevance has been spelled out elsewhere and an annotated account can be given here (see Scambler 1996, 1998b; Scambler and Martin 2001). In a first attempt to specify the parameters of a critical sociology, five theses were ventured (Scambler 1996). The first asserts that *the full ramifications of the reflexivity of high modernity for sociological practice have not been sufficiently digested or appreciated*. The reflexive nature of disorganized capitalism resides in the fact that 'social practices are constantly examined and reformed in the light of incoming information about those very practices, thus constitutively altering their character' (Giddens 1990: 38). This has proved more than a little unsettling in its subversion of unreconstructed Enlightenment ideals of certain knowledge. And the re-entry of sociological discourse into the contexts it analyses is emblematic: high modernity, Giddens (1990: 43) writes, is 'deeply and intrinsically sociological'. The salience of reflexivity, thus interpreted, is widely acknowledged by sociologists; but it is less apparent that this translates into *appropriate practices*.

The second thesis claims that *critical sociologists need to examine more conscientiously and critically their discipline's primary allegiance to economy and state and, via the media of money and power, system rationalization*. Given its origins and subsequent affinity to unreconstructed Enlightenment thinking it is unsurprising that sociology's history is one of abetting as much as resisting selective rationalization and the colonization of the lifeworld. There is little evidence that this is changing around 2000. The third thesis states that *critical sociology's principal commitment is to the rationalization of the lifeworld*. Such an overriding commitment is of course incompatible with a *primary* allegiance to system needs. Continuing in this vein, the fourth thesis asserts that *the nature of critical sociology's commitment to the lifeworld rationalization requires its promotion and engagement in a reconstituted public sphere.* Nation-states like Britain, Habermas (1976: 36) argued a generation ago, are characterized by 'formal' democracy, namely 'a legitimation process that elicits generalized motives – that is, diffuse mass loyalty – but avoids participation.' By contrast, what he then called 'substantive' democracy institutionalizes in the public sphere of the lifeworld the fundamental norms of rational speech (although Habermas warns against utopianism and equating substantive democracy with any particular form of organization). If critical sociology, fated to be an actor in high modernity/disorganized capitalism, is to realize its overriding commitment to lifeworld rationalization, it must *of necessity* engage with a public sphere *reconstituted* out of the residue of a bourgeois public sphere once progressive and resistant to economy and state but long since compromised (latterly by class-driven processes of consumerism and clientalization).

The fifth thesis claims that *if critical sociology is to be effective in promoting and engaging in a reconstituted public sphere, alliances will have to be built with system-based and, especially, lifeworld-based activists.* As has been discussed, alliances with activists from certain new social movements, or forms of collective action/self-help properly regarded as part of the culture of new social movements, may be especially felicitous since such movements can be seen as prototypes for 'the development of new participatory-democratic institutions which would regulate markets, bureaucracies and technologies' (Ray 1993: 62). It scarcely needs reiterating, but no self-respecting critical sociologist would gamble on imminent, effective change towards institutionalized forms of deliberative democracy.

This quintet was elaborated in a further contribution (Scambler 1998b). It was here claimed that critical sociology's commitment to lifeworld colonization also represents a *moral* requirement. The argument for this proposition is constructed in relation to Habermas's (1990, 1993) theory of discourse ethics, in many respects a fortifying of his theory of communicative action. It starts with a 'principle of universalization' which is reminiscent of Kant but also departs from his formulation: 'the emphasis shifts from what each can will without contradiction to be a universal law to what all can will in agreement to be a universal norm' (McCarthy 1978: 236). In effect, this is to 'socialize' Kant's individualistic moral theory in a manner that satisfies objections first put by Hegel (see Outhwaite 1994). Habermas's principle of universalization compels the 'universal exchange of roles' that Mead referred to as 'ideal role taking' or 'universal discourse'. Every valid norm thus has to fulfil the following condition: '*All* affected can accept the consequences and the side-effects its general observance can be anticipated to have for the satisfaction of everyone's interests (and these consequences are preferred to those of known alternative possibilities for regulation)' (Habermas 1990: 65).

The principle of universalization must not be conflated with that of 'discourse ethics', which asserts that 'only those norms can claim to be valid that meet (or could meet) with the approval of all affected in their capacity *as participants in a practical discourse*' (Habermas 1990: 66). While the principle of universalization has to do with *moral* questions of 'justice' and 'solidarity', which admit of formal resolution, the principle of discourse ethics concerns *ethical* questions about the 'good life', which can only be addressed in relation to substantive cultures, forms of life or individual projects.

Justice and solidarity, to which Habermas accords priority, are necessarily related to, and of the essence of, communicative action. Justice, in its modern sense, refers to the 'subjective freedom of inalienable individuality'; and solidarity refers to the 'well-being of associated members of a community who intersubjectively share the same lifeworld' (Habermas 1990: 200). Morality, Habermas (1990: 200) insists, 'cannot protect the rights of the individual without also protecting the well-being of the community to which he belongs.' 'Precisely the effort to convince others of the justice of a normative expectation', Rehg (1994: 245) adds, 'demands that I attend empathetically to its effects on others' welfare.'

The moral character of critical sociologists' commitment to lifeworld rationalization entails an additional commitment to forums of deliberative democracy via the institutionalization of discourse-ethical procedures in the public sphere of the lifeworld. Their obligation extends also to addressing and publicizing issues of concern emanating from the enabling and protest sectors of civil society; and meeting this complex and daunting requirement commends a consideration of 'alliances of interest' with system and 'movement intellectuals' and activists in the public sphere (Eyerman and Jamison 1991; see Scambler and Martin 2001). The oft-quoted activists' phrase 'speaking truth to power' comes to mind.

In a final piece a further strand or two is added to the argument (Scambler and Martin 2001). It is claimed that there exists an *internal* or *logical relation* – that is, a relation of necessity and what might be termed 'moral contiguity' deriving from Habermas's theory of communicative action – between the concepts of 'critical sociology', 'civil society', 'public sphere' and 'deliberative democracy'. It is in fact the nature of this relation that provides the rationale for retaining the idea of a single formal public sphere. There is, as we have seen, ample historical and contemporary evidence of a multiplicity of actual or substantive public spheres (as well as of Fraser's subaltern counterpublics) emergent before, alongside and after the bourgeois public sphere identified by Habermas. But what is of moment and significance about the notion of a single formal public sphere is its *counterfactual status*. Just as the formal notion of an 'ideal speech situation' – which Habermas mentions less in his later work but which nevertheless remains integral to his theory of communicative action and his discourse ethics – allows for the substantive identification and examination of (often colonizing) distortions in 'actually existing' episodes of communication (see the discussion of doctor–patient encounters in Chapter 6), so the formal notion of a single public sphere allows for the identification and examination of (often colonizing) distortions in 'actually existing' transnational, national, regional and local public spheres.

The obstacles to realizing institutions of deliberative democracy are considerable. Some are technical (Coleman 2001). What may be called 'conceptual experiments' in deliberative democracy abound, but remain largely unconvincing academic exercises (see, for example, Barber 1996; Mayhew 1997). The more intractable problems, of course, have to do with the exercise of power in narrow sectional system-based interests, some of which, especially those emanating from real relations of class and command, have been explored in earlier chapters. However, it is surely hard not to sign up to the statement of necessary and moral contiguity between the critical sociological enterprise and forms of institutionalization of the *public use of reason* offered here. And the consequences of doing so are surely intolerable. The type of reflexive critical sociology advocated cannot but be radical, without being partisan, not because it embodies, stands for or promotes a particular (ethical) vision of the 'good society', but precisely because it does not: its intrinsic commitment is 'to' the public use of reason, and 'against' any (typically system-driven) impediment – especially Bohman's deliberative inequalities – to the public use of reason.

If the parameters of a reflexive critical (medical) sociology have been (re-)drawn, what kind of agenda for theory and research might it indicate? A few general themes are sketched here. It is consistent with the analyses in this volume, many of them visiting or touching on processes or products of globalization, to put in a word, first, for the development of a 'global (critical) sociology' oriented to a global or transnational civil society/public sphere. And as Martin and Beittel (1998: 139) make plain, albeit from a different philosophical starting point, the construction of a global sociology involves a more creative and arduous project than merely extending extant paradigms/research programmes, since these reflect models of European and American development which are 'ill-suited for grasping transnational phenomena and building a worldwide community of sociologists'. This book has deliberately set its sights on Britain under disorganized capitalism. One of the more urgent challenges facing sociologists, medical or otherwise, is to refocus their gaze on reconceptualized times and spaces beyond the contemporary nation-state (see Urry 2000), a challenge that it may well prove easier to meet in the event of progress towards a genuinely global sociology.

The idea of a global or transnational civil society/public sphere is implicit in much of the previous discussion, but its realization has probably been anticipated too eagerly and with undue optimism by too many sympathetic to its coming. References to information and communication technologies (ICTs), including the Internet, and to cyberdemocracy trip too readily off the tongue. In fact, half Britain's population are not currently on-line (10 per cent are on-line at work, 22 per cent at home and 18 per cent at work and at home (Travis 2001), while in nation-states like China and India the ratio is more like one in a hundred (and in Africa even fewer); nor are countries' adult (especially female) literacy rates always compatible with democratic engagement (see also Haynes 1997). (It is worth adding that even by 1990 only 65 out of 192 nation-states actually had male or full suffrage: Dahl 1998.) Nor have the subsystems of the economy and state been asleep during the early evolution of the Net. Sassi (2001: 107) writes:

while the potential of the Net, as well as its importance as the soil of social interaction are recognized, it is also crucial to understand that the same technology operates as a ubiquitous and yet imminent mechanism of surveillance and control. Network technology, contributing essentially to new divisions of wealth and its accumulation into fewer hands, thereby invites pervasive forms of surveillance and violations of our rights to privacy. Here we address the major social change and paradox of our time: the need to equip ourselves with the skills to work the Net and to use that knowledge to enhance the promise it reveals and protect against the threats it creates.

As Habermas (1996) observes, the role of positive law is here crucial to the democratic prowess and input of social movements and other forms of collective action. This has led him, in his latest work, to frame a version of cosmopolitan democracy tied less to the constitution of the nation-state than to the creation of a postnational or global 'constitution' (Habermas 1999, 2000a).

A second item for the agenda, far from an inevitable by-product of globalization but likely to be facilitated by a global sociology and transnational civil society/public sphere, is the need to focus on – an overall picture of – the 'world capitalist system'. It should, for example, become increasingly implausible and unacceptable (sociologically as well as morally) to delineate and explain Britain's 'new inequality' and 'widening health gap' without reference to the *interlinked* capital flows and fortunes of peoples from 'peripheral' nation-states in the 'Third World'. There is direct evidence, furthermore, that greater transnational corporate penetration into nation-states in the Third World is associated with increased rates of infant mortality in those countries over time (Wimberley 1990). Bauman's (1998a: 70–1) words are salutary, if they can still dissipate our 'compassion fatigue' and stir us:

> commenting on the findings of the UN's latest *Human Development Report*, that the total wealth of the top 358 'global billionaires' equals the combined incomes of 2.3 billion poorest people (45% of the world's population), Victor Keegan called the present reshuffling of the world's resources 'a new form of highway robbery'. Indeed, only 22% of global *wealth* belongs to the so-called 'developing countries', which account for about 80% of the world population. And yet this is by no means the limit the present polarization is likely to reach since the share of global *income* currently apportioned to the poor is smaller still: in 1991, 85% of the world's population received only 15% of its income.

If the 358 global billionaires decided to keep $5 million or so each, 'to tide themselves over', and give the rest away, they could virtually double the annual incomes of half the people on Earth ('and pigs would fly').

A third agenda item is inspired by advice invariably thrown out by the pioneering critical sociologist C. Wright Mills to his graduate students. One observer notes: 'Mills strides excitedly up and down the room . . . He pauses to glare at his towering bookcase. "It's a writer's responsibility to orient modern publics to the catastrophic world in which they live", he says. "But he cannot do this if he remains a mere specialist. To do it at all, he's got to do it *big!*'' (Mills and Mills 2000: i). Critical sociologists looking at issues of health and healing, locally, regionally and nationally as well as globally, need to 'do it big' at least in the sense that – to stick with the terminology used in previous chapters – pieces of the jigsaw represented by discrete applications of the model of logic/relations/figurations need to be viewed in (dialectical) relation to the overall picture. This may be readily comprehensible with such issues as welfare cuts, hospital closures, the reforms of the NHS and the production and reproduction of health inequalities (and is in the event revealing too, since it exposes a striking empirical neglect of the rich and powerful). But, as has often been intimated, even the most singular of agentic endeavours, like the construction of a personal narrative of illness, or encounters, like that between a doctor and a patient and oriented to the alleviation of suffering, betray the (constitutive and formative) effects of enduring and insinuating social structures. Bourdieu's (1999) *Weight of the World: Social Suffering in Contemporary Society* presents a seminal argument and resource affirming the philosophical and sociological reciprocity between the personal and the social, or between agency and structure. Arguably it is structure that is most underestimated in contemporary sociology.

Of course it is not always conducive to career-building in sociology, and perhaps especially in medical sociology, to 'do it big', even in the restricted sense deployed here. This is because the prized acquisition of public monies to fund (increasingly commissioned) research tends to lend itself to 'tame' (or 'do it small') system-driven projects quite at odds with critical sociology's primary commitment to lifeworld rationalization/decolonization (Scambler 1996, 1998b). A fourth agenda item, then, promotes the wilful, organized and effective transmission of sociology's descriptive and explanatory power to a reconstituted civil society/public sphere. What is needed, arguably, is (a) a 'critical mass' of critical sociologists, and (b) mechanisms available to them, either through the offices of intellectuals/social critics active in the protest sector of civil society and the public sphere, or through alliances with social/health movements and activists (Scambler 1998b), to link sociological output to campaigns for, and processes of, deliberative democracy. The kind of community-based forms of empowerment discussed in the context of health and health care in Chapter 6 are pertinent here. They commend a lifeworld-generated or 'popular' medical sociology akin to contemporary experiments in 'popular epidemiology' (Brown 1992, 1995).

In all essential respects these 'needs' echo the 'three principles' with which Mills confronted his chosen profession in postwar America. Goldsen (1964: 89) summarizes in a (vivid and uncompromising, if also sexist) phraseology deserving of extended quotation:

> Mills told the profession: Just as the business of physicists is to understand matter, so the business of the sociologist is to understand social structures. At this point in history at least, the principle to 'get a fix' on

social structures – if not the sole way – is to study power: where it resides, who wields it, how it is used, and how misused. The sociologist who avoids studying power in social structures seriously increases, if he does not in fact guarantee, the chance that he will end up with trivia. This summarizes Mills' stand on scientific policy. Mills told the profession: Because the sociologist's product can be utilized in the manipulation of human beings, every sociologist has the obligation of interpreting his work and communicating his findings to the public . . . A discipline that yields knowledge and provides tools for the potential manipulation of men must make the possibilities of such manipulation clear, very clear, to its possible victims. This position confronts head on the matter of professional ethics. Finally Mills said to the profession: Anyone who studies the workings of power in today's social structures finds over and over again that the wielders of power are perpetrating injustices and endangering the safety, dignity, and even the human-ness of humanity. The sociologist must therefore persuade first the intellectuals and through them the citizenry to forestall and check these injustices by changing the social structures that misuse power: governments, corporations, armies, schools, churches, professional societies. This takes a position on the tactics of inducing social change.

Sociologists who fight shy of these principles, Mills insisted, are engaged, at best, in trivial mental exercises and, at worst, in handing over both themselves and their discipline – either deliberately or by default – to 'the Establishment'. It is an opportune time to restate Mills's principles.

The fifth item highlights the value commitments that enter into the very definition of critical sociology, together with some of their ramifications. Weber's important distinction between values which inevitably inform sociologists' choices of topics of enquiry, and values which illicitly seep into their subsequent research protocols and practices, remains salient; but more must be said. Critical sociology (like education) is no 'value-neutral' enterprise: in so far as it is logically and morally contiguous with communicative action, it is premised not only on the public use of reason, that is, the pursuit of an inclusive, informed and 'argued-out' consensus between a freely and equally participating (and increasingly transnational) citizenry, but, it follows, on the pursuit of (increasingly transnational) legal and social institutions capable of securing and underwriting justice and solidarity (there is in fact an appealing cosmopolitan or 'postnational' notion of citizenship lurking in Habermas's theory of communicative action: see Crossley 2001). The moral parsimony of those such as Humean (neo-)positivists is now as disingenuous in relation to these issues as it is erroneous. But the argument developed here does not deny either that critical sociology can, and should, be scientific (in a critical realist sense), or that it can, and should, remain aloof from any *particular* ethical vision of the good life. Nor, of course, does it deny the possibility of any worth-while return on investments in pre- or non-critical sociologies (Scambler 1998b).

The final agenda item is a plea against a loss of philosophical and political 'nerve' on the part of sociologists, and an exhortation to rediscover a reflexive and critical (medical) sociology, allied to a reconstructed project of modernity, which can no longer be 'legislative' but need not become only 'interpretive' (Bauman 1987). The risk of such a loss of nerve has to do with the emergence of a class-motivated culture-ideology of consumerism articulated (in line with the principle of compatibility) as a postmodernized culture. Thatcher, whom Habermas (2000a) calls the first genuinely 'postmodern' politician, proclaimed that 'there is no such thing as society'. 'In the political public sphere', Habermas (2000a: 59) continues, 'conflicts on a national, European, or global scale develop their power to disturb us only when they are seen, against the background of a normative understanding of social inequalities and political oppression, not as natural phenomena but as social products – hence as changeable.' But in disorganized capitalism, and gathering pace since 1989, 'more and more politicians seem to be saying: if we can't solve any of these conflicts, let's at least dim the critical insights that turn conflicts into challenges.' The possibility of a 'conscious transformation of society' may, as Habermas is only too aware, be slim, especially in the short term; but a possibility, perhaps step-by-step and in the longer term, it does, must and can remain.

References

Abraham, J. (1995) *Science, Politics and the Pharmaceutical Industry: Controversy and Bias in Drug Regulation.* London: UCL Press.

Adonis, A. and Pollard, S. (1997) *A Class Act: The Myth of Britain's Classless Society.* London: Hamish Hamilton.

Albrow, M. (1996) *The Global Age.* Cambridge: Polity Press.

Allen, J. (1992) Post-industrialism and post-Fordism, in S. Hall, D. Held and T. McGrew (eds) *Modernity and Its Futures.* Cambridge: Polity Press/The Open University.

Allsop, J. (1995) *Health Policy and the NHS towards 2000*, 2nd edn. London: Longman.

Anders, G. (1996) *Health Against Wealth: HMOs and the Breakdown of Medical Trust.* Boston: Mariner Books.

Anderson, P. (1998) *The Origins of Postmodernity.* London: Verso.

Anderson, R. and Bury, M. (eds) (1988) *Living with Chronic Illness: The Experience of Patients and their Families.* London: Allen & Unwin.

Anderson, R., Hughes, J. and Sturrock, W. (1986) *Philosophy and the Human Sciences.* London: Croom Helm.

Annandale, E. (1998) *The Sociology of Health and Medicine: A Critical Introduction.* Cambridge: Polity Press.

Appel, F. (1999) *Nietzsche contra Democracy.* Ithaca, NY: Cornell University Press.

Archer, M., Bhaskar, R., Collier, A., Lawson, T. and Norris, A. (1998) *Critical Realism: Essential Readings.* London: Routledge.

Arneil, B. (1999) *Politics and Feminism.* Oxford: Blackwell.

Armstrong, D. (1987) Theoretical trends in biopsychosocial medicine, *Social Science and Medicine*, 25: 1213–18.

Armstrong, D. (1995) The rise of surveillance medicine, *Sociology of Health and Illness*, 17: 393–404.

Arrighi, G. (1994) *The Long Twentieth Century.* London: Verso.

Arrighi, G. (1996) Workers of the world at century's end, *Review*, 19: 3.

Arrighi, G., Hopkins, T. G. and Wallerstein, E. (1989) *Antisystematic Movements.* London: Verso.

Ashley, D. (1997) *History without a Subject: The Postmodern Condition.* Boulder, CO: Westview Press.

Assiter, A. (1996) *Enlightened Women: Modern Feminism in a Postmodern Age*. London: Routledge.

Atkinson, A. (1998) *Poverty in Europe*. Oxford: Blackwell.

Atkinson, A. (2000) Distribution of income and wealth, in A. Halsey, and J. Webb (eds) *Twentieth-century British Social Trends*. London: Macmillan Press.

Atkinson, P. (1981) *The Clinical Experience: The Construction and Reconstruction of Medical Reality*. Farnborough: Gower.

Atkinson, P. (1995) *Medical Talk and Medical Work: The Liturgy of the Clinic*. London: Sage.

Austin, J. (1962) *How to Do Things with Words*. Oxford: Oxford University Press.

Axford, B. (2001) The transformation of politics or anti-politics?, in B. Axford and R. Huggins (eds) *New Media and Politics*. London: Sage.

Baert, P. (1998) *Social Theory in the Twentieth Century*. Cambridge: Polity Press.

Barber, B. (1996) An American civic forum: civil society between market individuals and the political community, in E. Paul, F. Miller and J. Paul (eds) *The Communitarian Challenge to Liberalism*. Cambridge, MA: MIT Press.

Barber, B. (2000) *A Place for Us: How to Make Society Civil and Democracy Strong*. New York: Hill and Wang.

Barer, M., Marmor, T. and Morrison, E. (1995) Health care reform in the United States: on the road to nowhere (again)?, *Social Sciences and Medicine*, 41: 453–60.

Barker, D. (1992) *Fetal and Infant Origins of Adult Disease*. London: British Medical Journal.

Barnes, C. and Mercer, G. (eds) (1996) *Exploring the Divide: Illness and Disability*. Leeds: The Disability Press.

Barnes, C., Mercer, G. and Shakespeare, T. (1999) *Exploring Disability: A Sociological Introduction*. Cambridge: Polity Press.

Barrett, M. (1991) *The Politics of Truth*. Cambridge: Polity Press.

Barry, C., Stevenson, F., Britten, N., Barber, N. and Bradley, C. (2001) Giving voice to the lifeworld, *Social Science and Medicine*, 53: 487–505.

Bartley, M., Blane, D. and Davey Smith, G. (1998a) Introduction: beyond the Black Report, in M. Bartley, D. Blane and G. Davey Smith (eds) *The Sociology of Health Inequalities*. Oxford: Blackwell.

Bartley, M., Blane, D. and Davey Smith, G. (1998b) *The Sociology of Health Inequalities*. Oxford: Blackwell.

Bartley, M., Blane, D. and Montgomery, S. (1997) Socioeconomic determinants of health. Health and the life course: why safety nets matter, *British Medical Journal*, 314: 1194–6.

Bartley, M., Power, C., Blane, D., Davey Smith, G. and Shipley, M. (1994) Birth weight and later socioeconomic disadvantage: evidence from the 1958 British cohort study, *British Medical Journal*, 309: 1475–8.

Baudrillard, J. (1983) *Simulations*. New York: Semiotext(e).

Bauman, Z. (1987) *Legislators and Interpreters: On Modernity Postmodernity and Intellectuals*. Cambridge: Cambridge University Press.

Bauman, Z. (1998a) *Globalization: The Human Consequences*. Cambridge: Polity Press.

Bauman, Z. (1998b) *Work, Consumerism and the New Poor*. Buckingham: Open University Press.

Bauman, Z. (2000) *Liquid Modernity*. Cambridge: Polity Press.

Baynes, K. (1990) Crisis and life-world in Husserl and Habermas, in A. Dallery, C. Scott with H. Roberts (eds) *Crisis in Continental Philosophy*. New York: State University of New York Press.

Beck, U. (1992) *Risk Society: Towards a New Modernity*. London: Sage.

Beck, U. (2000) *The Brave New World of Work*. Cambridge: Polity Press.

Beck, U. and Beck-Gernsheim, E. (1995) *The Normal Chaos of Love*. Cambridge: Polity Press.

Beck, U., Giddens, A. and Lash, S. (1994) *Reflexive Modernization: Politics, Tradition and Aesthetics in the Modern Social Order*. Cambridge: Polity Press.

Beck, E., Lonsdale, S., Newman, S. and Patterson, D. (eds) (1992) *In the Best of Health? The Status and Future of Health Care in Britain*. London: Chapman and Hall.

Benton, T. (1977) *Philosophical Foundations of the Three Sociologies*. London: Routledge and Kegan Paul.

Beresford, P. and Boyd, S. (2000) The Sunday Times rich list 2000, *Sunday Times*, 19 March.

Berger, P., Berger, B. and Kellner, H. (1973) *The Homeless Mind: Modernization and Consciousness*. New York: Alann Lane.

Bernstein, R. (1976) *The Restructuring of Social and Political Theory*. London: Methuen.

Best, S. and Kellner, D. (1997) *The Postmodern Turn*. New York: The Guilford Press.

Beveridge, W. (1942) *Social Insurance and Allied Services*. Cmnd 6404. London: HMSO.

Bhaskar, R. (1978) *A Realist Theory of Science*, 2nd edn. Brighton: Harvester Wheatsheaf.

Bhaskar, R. (1989a) *The Possibility of Naturalism*, 2nd edn. Hemel Hempstead: Harvester Wheatsheaf.

Bhaskar, R. (1989b) *Reclaiming Reality: A Critical Introduction to Contemporary Philosophy*. London: Verso.

Bhaskar, R. (1994) *Plato Etc: The Problems of Philosophy and Their Resolution*. London: Verso.

Bhaskar, R. (1998) General introduction, in M. Archer, R. Bhaskar, A. Collier, T. Lawson and A. Norris (eds) *Critical Realism: Essential Readings*. London: Routledge.

Black, D., Morris, J., Smith, C. and Townsend, P. (1999) Better benefits for health: plan to implement the central recommendation of the Acheson Report, *British Medical Journal*, 318: 724–7.

Blaikie, N. (1993) *Approaches to Social Enquiry*. Cambridge: Polity Press.

Blair, A. (1997) The 21st century welfare state, Speech to the Social Policy and Economic Performance Conference, Amsterdam, 24 January.

Blane, D. (1985) An assessment of the Black Report's 'explanations of health inequalities', *Sociology of Health and Illness*, 7: 423–45.

Blane, D. (1999) The life course, the social gradient, and health, in M. Marmot and R. Wilkinson (eds) *Social Determinants of Health*. Oxford: Oxford University Press.

Blane, D., Bartley, M. and Davey Smith, G. (1997) Disease aetiology and materialist explanations of socioeconomic mortality differentials, *European Journal of Public Health*, 7: 385–91.

Blaxter, M. (2000) Class, time and biography, in S. Williams, J. Gabe and M. Calnan (eds) *Health, Medicine and Society: Key Theories, Future Agendas*. London: Routledge.

Blumer, H. (1956) Sociological analysis and the 'variable', *American Sociological Review*, 21: 633–60.

Blumer, H. (1969) *Symbolic Interactionism: Perspectives and Methods*. New York: Prentice Hall.

Bohman, J. (1996) *Public Deliberation: Pluralism, Complexity and Democracy*. Cambridge, MA: MIT Press.

Bohman, J. and Rehg, W. (eds) (1997) *Deliberative Democracy: Essays on Reason and Politics*. Cambridge, MA: MIT Press.

Boli, J. and Thomas, G. (1997) World-culture in the world polity: a century of international non-governmental organization, *American Sociological Review*, 62: 171–90.

Bordo, S. (1993) Feminism, Foucault and the politics of the body, in C. Ramazanoglu (ed.) *Up Against Foucault*. London: Routledge.

Boris, E. and Janssens, A. (eds) (1999) *Complicating Categories: Gender, Class, Race and Ethnicity*. International Review of Social History Supplement. Cambridge: Cambridge University Press.

Boswell, T. and Chase-Dunn, C. (2000) *The Spiral of Capitalism and Socialism: Toward Global Democracy*. Boulder, CO: Lynn Rienner.

Bourdieu, P. (1977) *Outline of a Theory of Practice*. Cambridge: Cambridge University Press.

Bourdieu, P. (1999) *The Weight of the World: Social Suffering in Contemporary Society*. Cambridge: Polity Press.

Bradley, H. (1996) *Fractured Identities: Changing Patterns of Inequality*. Cambridge: Polity Press.

Brand, A. (1990) *The Force of Reason: An Introduction to Habermas's Theory of Communicative Action*. London: Allen & Unwin.

British Medical Association (1986) *Report of the Board of Science and Education on Alternative Therapy*. London: BMA.

British Medical Association (1993) *Complementary Medicine. New Approaches to Good Practice*. Oxford: Oxford University Press/BMA.

Brittan, S. (1975) The economic contradictions of democracy, *British Journal of Political Science*, 5: 129–59.

Brown, G. and Harris, T. (1978) *Social Origins of Depression*. London: Tavistock.

Brown, P. (1992) Popular epidemiology and toxic waste contamination: lay and professional ways of knowing, *Journal of Health and Social Behaviour*, 33: 267–81.

Brown, P. (1995) Popular epidemiology, toxic waste and social movements, in J. Gabe (ed.) *Medicine, Health and Risk*. Oxford: Blackwell.

Buckingham, A. (1999) Is there an underclass in Britain?, *British Journal of Sociology*, 50: 49–85.

Bunton, R. and MacDonald, G. (eds) (1992) *Health Promotion: Disciplines and Diversity*. London: Routledge.

Bury, M. (1982) Chronic illness as biographical disruption, *Sociology of Health and Illness*, 4: 167–82.

Bury, M. (1997) *Health and Illness in a Changing Society*. London: Routledge.

Bury, M. (2001) Illness narratives: fact or fiction?, *Sociology of Health and Illness*, 23: 263–85.

Cabinet Office (2000) *Women's Incomes over the Lifetime*. London: The Stationery Office.

Calhoun, C. (1993) 'New' social movements of the early twentieth century, *Social History*, 17: 285–411.

Calhoun, C. (1996) Social theory and the public sphere, in B. Turner (ed.) *The Blackwell Companion to Social Theory*. Oxford: Blackwell.

Calnan, M., Cant, S. and Gabe, J. (1993) *Going Private: Why People Pay for Their Health Care*. Buckingham: Open University Press.

Cant, S. and Sharma, U. (1999) *A New Medical Pluralism? Alternative Medicine, Doctors, Patients and the State*. London: UCL Press.

Carchedi, G. (1977) *On the Economic Identification of Social Classes*. London: Routledge.

Card, C. (1985) Virtues and moral luck, Working Paper Series 1, Institute for Legal Studies, University of Wisconsin-Madison Law School.

Carrier, J. and Kendall, I. (1998) *Health and the National Health Service*. London: The Athlone Press.

Carter, J. (1998a) Preludes, introductions and meanings, in J. Carter (ed.) *Postmodernity and the Fragmentation of Welfare*. London: Routledge.

Carter, J. (ed.) (1998b) *Postmodernity and the Fragmentation of Welfare*. London: Routledge.

Cartwright, A. and O'Brien, M. (1976) Social class variations in health care and in the nature of general practitioner consultations, in M. Stacey (ed.) *The Sociology of the NHS*. Sociological Review Monograph, 22. Stoke-on-Trent: Wood Mitchell and Co.

Castells, M. (1997) *The Power of Identity*. Oxford: Blackwell.

Chambers, S. (1996) *Reasonable Democracy: Jurgen Habermas and the Politics of Discourse*. Ithaca, NY: Cornell University Press.

Charlton, J. (1997) Trends in all-cause mortality: 1841–1994. An overview, in J. Charlton and M. Murphy (eds) *The Health of Adult Britain 1841–1994*, Vol. 1. London: The Stationary Office.

Charlton, J. and Murphy, M. (1997) *The Health of Adult Britain 1841–1994, Volume 1*. London: The Stationery Office.

Charmaz, K. (1991) *Good Days, Bad Days: The Self in Chronic Illness and Time*. New Brunswick, NJ: Rutgers University Press.

Charmaz, K. (2000) Experiencing chronic illness, in G. Albrecht, R. Fitzpatrick and S. Scrimshaw (eds) *The Handbook of Social Studies in Health and Medicine*. London: Sage.

Churchill, L. (1999) The United States health care system under managed care: how the commodification of health care distorts ethics and threatens equity, *Health Care Analysis*, 7: 393–411.

Clement, W. and Myles, J. (1997) *Relations of Ruling: Class and Gender in Postindustrial Societies*. Montreal: McGill-Queen's University Press.

Coates, D. (2000) *Models of Capitalism: Growth and Stagnation in the Modern Era*. Cambridge: Polity Press.

Cobb, R., Ross, J. and Ross, M. (1976) Agenda building as a comparative political process, *American Political Science Review*, 70: 126–38.

Coburn, D. (2000a) Income inequality, social cohesion and the health status of populations: the role of neo-liberalism, *Social Science and Medicine*, 51: 135–46.

Coburn, D. (2000b) A brief response, *Social Science and Medicine*, 51: 1009–10.

Cohen, J. and Arato, A. (1992) *Civil Society and Political Theory*. Cambridge, MA: MIT Press.

Cohen, R. and Rai, S. (eds) (2000) *Global Social Movements*. London: Athlone.

Coleman, D. (2000) Population and family, in A. Halsey and J. Webb (eds) *Twentieth-century British Social Trends*. London: Macmillan Press.

Coleman, D. and Chandola, T. (1999) Britain's place in Europe's population, in S. McRae (ed.) *Population and Household Change*. Oxford: Oxford University Press.

Coleman, S. (2001) The transformation of citizenship?, in B. Axford and R. Huggins (eds) *New Media and Politics*. London: Sage.

Collier, A. (1994) *Critical Realism: An Introduction to Roy Bhaskar's Philosophy*. London: Verso.

Comte, A. (1853) *The Positive Philosophy of Auguste Comte*. London: Chapman.

Cornwall, J. (1984) *Hard-earned Lives: Accounts of Health and Illness from East London*. London: Tavistock Publications.

Crompton, R. (1993) *Class and Stratification*. Cambridge: Polity Press.

Crompton, R. and Mann, A. (1986) *Gender and Stratification*. Cambridge: Polity Press.

Cronin, C. and De Greiff, P. (1998) Introduction, in J. Habermas, *The Inclusion of the Other: Studies in Political Theory*. Cambridge: Polity Press.

Crook, S., Paluski, J. and Waters, M. (1992) *Postmodernization: Changes in Advanced Society*. London: Sage.

Crossley, N. (2001) Citizenship, intersubjectivity and the lifeworld, in N. Stevenson (ed.) *Culture and Citizenship*. London: Sage.

Curry, H. (1996) Space and place in geographic decision-making, in *Technical Expertise and Public Decisions*. Conference Proceedings, Princeton University, pp. 311–18.

Curtis, S. and Jones, I. (1998) Is there a place for geography in the analysis of health inequality?, in M. Bartley, D. Blane and G. Davey Smith (eds) *The Sociology of Health Inequalities*. Oxford: Blackwell.

Dahl, R. (1998) *On Democracy*. New Haven, CT: Yale University Press.

Dalton, R. (1999) Political support in advanced industrial countries, in P. Norris (ed.) *Critical Citizens: Global Support for Democratic Government*. Oxford: Oxford University Press.

D'Arcy, C. (1976) The contingencies and mental illness in societal reaction theory: a critique, *Canadian Review of Sociology and Anthropology*, 13: 43–54.

Davey Smith, G., Bartley, M. and Blane, D. (1990) The Black Report on socioeconomic inequalities in health 10 years on, *British Medical Journal*, 301: 373–7.

Davey Smith, G., Hart, C., Blane, D. and Hole, D. (1998) Adverse socioeconomic conditions in childhood and cause specific adult mortality: prospective observational study, *British Medical Journal*, 316: 1631–5.

Davey Smith, G., Shaw, M., Mitchell, R., Dorling, D. and Gordon, D. (2000) Inequalities in health continue to grow despite government's pledges, *British Medical Journal*, 320: 582.

Davis, K. and Moore, W. (1945) Some principles of stratification, *American Sociological Review*, 10: 242–9.

Dawe, A. (1970) The two sociologies, *British Journal of Sociology*, 21: 207–18.

Dean, M. (1999) *Governmentality: Power and Rule in Modern Society*. London: Sage.

Delanty, G. (1999) *Social Theory in a Changing World: Conceptions of Modernity*. Cambridge: Polity Press.

Delanty, G. (2000) *Citizenship in a Global Age: Society, Culture, Politics*. Buckingham: Open University Press.

Deleuze, G. and Guatteri, F. (1984) *Anti-Oedipus: Capitalism and Schizophrenia*. London: Athlone.

Deleuze, G. and Guatteri, F. (1986) *Nomadology. The War Machine*. New York: Semiotext(e).

Deleuze, G. and Guatteri, F. (1988) *A Thousand Plateaus*. London: Athlone.

della Porta, D. and Diani, M. (1999) *Social Movements: An Introduction*. Oxford: Blackwell.

Department of Health (1998) *Our Healthier Nation: A Contract for Health*. London: The Stationery Office.

Department of Health and Social Security (1980) *Inequalities in Health: Report of a Working Group (The Black Report)*. London: HMSO.

Department of Health and Social Security (1983) *NHS Management Inquiry: Report* (Chairman R. Griffiths). London: DHSS.

Derrida, J. (1976) *Of Grammatology*. Baltimore, MD: Johns Hopkins University Press.

Desai, M. (1991) Methodological problems in quantitative Marxism, in P. Dunne (ed.) *Quantitative Marxism*. Cambridge: Polity Press.

DeVault, I. (1999) Narratives serially constructed and lived: ethnicity in cross-gender strikes, 1887–1903, in E. Boris and A. Janssens (eds) *Complicating Categories: Gender, Class, Race and Ethnicity*. Cambridge: Cambridge University Press.

Dews, P. (1987) *Logics of Disintegration: Post-structuralist Thought and the Claims of Critical Theory*. London: Verso.

Diani, M. (1992) The concept of social movement, *Sociological Review*, 92: 1–25.

Dilnot, A. and Emmerson, C. (2000) The economic environment, in C. Halsey and J. Webb (eds) *Twentieth-century British Social Trends*. London: Macmillan Press.

DiMaggio, P. and Powell, W. (1983) The iron cage revisited: institutional isomorphism and collective rationalizing in organizational fields, *American Sociological Review*, 46: 147–60.

Domhoff, G. (1967) *Who Rules America?* Englewood Cliffs, NJ: Prentice Hall.

Doyal, L. and Doyal, L. (1999) The British National Health Service: a tarnished moral vision?, *Health Care Analysis*, 7: 263–376.

Drever, F. and Whitehead, M. (eds) (1997) *Health Inequalities: Decennial Supplement*. DS Series No. 15. London: Office of National Statistics.

Eagleton, T. (1996) *The Illusions of Postmodern*. Oxford: Blackwell.

Eckstein, H. (1958) *The English Health Service: Its Origins, Structure and Achievements*. Cambridge, MA: Harvard University Press.

Ehrenberg, J. (1999) *Civil Society: The Critical History of an Idea*. New York: New York University Press.

Ehrenreich, B. and English, D. (1979) *For Her Own Good: 150 Years of Experts' Advice to Women*. London: Pluto Press.

Elias, N. (1978) *What Is Sociology?* London: Hutchinson.

Elias, N. (1994) *The Civilizing Process*. Oxford: Blackwell.

Elias, N. (1996) *The Germans*. Oxford: Blackwell.

Emslie, M., Campbell, M. and Walker, K. (1996) Complementary therapies in a local healthcare setting. Part 1: is there a real public demand?, *Complementary Therapies in Medicine*, 4: 39–42.

Enthoven, A. (1985) *Reflections on the Management of the National Health Service*. London: Nuffield Provincial Hospitals Trust.

Esping-Anderson, G. (1990) *The Three Worlds of Welfare Capitalism*. Cambridge: Polity Press.

Esping-Anderson, G. (1993) *Changing Classes*. London: Sage.

Esping-Anderson, G. (1997) Welfare states without work: the impasse of labour shedding and familialism in continental European policy, in G. Esping-Anderson (ed.) *Welfare States in Transition: National Adaptations in Global Economies*. London: Sage.

Evandrou, M. (1995) Employment and care, paid and unpaid work: the socio-economic position of informal carers in Britain, in J. Phillips (ed.) *Working Carers: International Perspectives on Working and Caring for Older People*. Aldershot: Avebury.

Eyerman, R. (1992) Modernity and social movements, in A. Haferkamp and N. Smelser (eds) *Social Change and Modernity*. Berkeley: University of California Press.

Eyerman, R. and Jamison, A. (1991) *Social Movements: A Cognitive Approach*. Cambridge: Polity Press.

Faux, J. and Mishel, L. (2000) Inequality and the global economy, in W. Hutton and A. Giddens (eds) *On the Edge: Living with Global Capitalism*. London: Jonathan Cape.

Featherstone, M. (1991) In pursuit of the postmodern: an introduction, *Theory, Culture and Society* (special issue on postmodernism), 5: 2–3.

Fisher, P. and Ward, A. (1994) Complementary medicine in Europe, *British Medical Journal*, 309: 107–11.

Fitzpatrick, R. (1987) Political science and health policy, in G. Scambler (ed.) *Sociological Theory and Medical Sociology*. London: Tavistock.

Fitzpatrick, R. and Chandola, T. (2000) Health, in A. Halsey and J. Webb (eds) *Twentieth Century British Social Trends*. London: Macmillan Press.

Fletcher, C. (1974) *Beneath the Surface*. London: Routledge.

Fletcher, R. (1999) Who is responsible for the common good in a competitive market?, *Journal of the American Medical Association*, 281: 1127–8.

Forbes, A. and Wainwright, S. (2001) On the methodological, theoretical, philosophical and political context of health inequalities research: a critique, *Social Science and Medicine*.

Foucault, M. (1977) *Language, Counter-memory, Practice*. Ithaca, NY: Cornell University Press.

Foucault, M. (1979a) *Discipline and Punish*. New York: Vintage Books.

Foucault, M. (1979b) On governmentality, *Ideology and Consciousness*, 6: 5–22.

Foucault, M. (1980) *Power/Knowledge*. Brighton: Harvester.

Foucault, M. (1989) *The Birth of the Clinic*. London: Routledge.

Fox, N. (1993) *Postmodernism, Sociology and Health*. Buckingham: Open University Press.

Fox, N. (1994) Anaesthetists, the discourse on patient fitness and the organization of surgery, *Sociology of Health and Illness*, 16: 1–18.

Fox, N. (1997) Is there life after Foucault? Texts, frames and differends, in A. Peterson and R. Bunton (eds) *Foucault, Health and Medicine*. London: Routledge.

Fox, N. (1998a) The promise of postmodernism for the sociology of health and medicine, in G. Scambler and P. Higgs (eds) *Modernity, Medicine and Health: Medical Sociology towards 2000*. London: Routledge.

Fox, N. (1998b) Postmodernism and 'health', in A. Peterson and C. Waddell (eds) *Health Matters: A Sociology of Illness, Prevention and Care*. Buckingham: Open University Press.

Fox-Genovese, E. (1994) Difference, diversity and divisions in an agenda for the women's movement, in G. Young and B. Dickerson (eds) *Colour, Class and Country: Experiences of Gender*. London: Zed Books.

Frank, A. (1993) The rhetoric of self-change: illness experience as narrative, *The Sociological Quarterly*, 34: 39–52.

Frank, A. (1995) *The Wounded Storyteller: Body, Illness and Ethics*. London: University of Chicago Press.

Franzosi, R. (1998) Narrative analysis – or why (and how) sociologists should be interested in narrative, *Annual Review of Sociology*, 24: 517–54.

Fraser, N. (1992) Rethinking the public sphere: a contribution to the critique of actually existing democracy, in C. Calhoun (ed.) *Habermas and the Public Sphere*. Cambridge, MA: MIT Press.

Freidson, E. (1970) *Profession of Medicine: A Study in the Sociology of Applied Knowledge*. New York: Dodd, Mead and Co.

Freidson, E. (1983) The theory of professions: state of the art, in R. Dingwall and P. Lewis (eds) *The Sociology of the Professions*. London: Macmillan.

Freidson, E. (1986) *Professional Powers: A Study of the Institutionalization of Formal Knowledge*. Chicago: University of Chicago Press.

Fulder, S. (1996) *The Handbook of Alternative and Complementary Medicine*, 3rd edn. Oxford: Oxford University Press.

Gabe, J. (1997) Continuity and change in the British National Health Service, in P. Conrad (ed.) *The Sociology of Health and Illness: Critical Perspectives*. New York: St Martin's Press.

Gabe, J. and Calnan, M. (2000) Health care and consumption, in S. Williams, J. Gabe and M. Calnan (eds) *Health, Medicine and Society: Key Theories, Future Agendas*. London: Routledge.

Gaffney, D., Pollock, A., Price, D. and Shaoul, J. (1999a) NHS capital expenditure and private finance initiative – expansion or contraction?, *British Medical Journal*, 319: 48–51.

Gaffney, D., Pollock, A., Price, D. and Shaoul, J. (1999b) PFI in the NHS – is there an economic case?, *British Medical Journal*, 319: 48–51.

Gaffney, D., Pollock, A., Price, D. and Shaoul, J. (1999c) The politics of the private finance initiative and the new NHS, *British Medical Journal*, 319: 249–53.

Galbraith, K. (1992) *The Culture of Contentment*. London: Sinclair-Stevenson.

Gallie, D. (1988) Employment, unemployment and social stratification, in D. Gallie (ed.) *Employment in Britain*. Oxford: Blackwell.

Gallie, D. (1999) The labour force, in A. Halsey and J. Webb (eds) *Twentieth-century British Social Trends*. London: Macmillan Press.

Gans, H. (1995) *The War Against the Poor: The Underclass and Antipoverty Policy*. New York: Basic Books.

Gardiner, M. (2000) *Critiques of Everyday Life*. London: Routledge.

Garfinkel, H. (1952) The perception of the other: a study in social order, Unpublished PhD dissertation, Harvard University.

Garfinkel, H. (1967) *Studies in Ethnomethodology*. Englewood Cliffs, NJ: Prentice Hall.

Garnham, N. (1992) The media and the public sphere, in C. Calhoun (ed.) *Habermas and the Public Sphere*. Cambridge, MA: MIT Press.

Geertz, C. (1973) *The Interpretation of Cultures*. New York: Basic Books.

Gellner, E. (1992) *Postmodernism, Reason and Religion*. London: Routledge.

Gerhardt, U. (1987) Parsons, role theory and health interaction, in G. Scambler (ed.) *Sociological Theory and Medical Sociology*. London: Tavistock.

Gerhardt, U. (1989) *Ideas about Illness: An Intellectual and Political Theory of Medical Sociology*. London: Macmillan.

Gibbons, J. (1998) Postmodernism, poststructuralism and social policy, in J. Carter (ed.) *Postmodernity and the Fragmentation of Welfare*. London: Routledge.

Gibbons, J. and Reimer, B. (1999) *The Politics of Postmodernity: An Introduction to Contemporary Politics and Culture*. London: Sage.

Giddens, A. (1990) *The Consequences of Modernity*. Cambridge: Polity Press.

Giddens, A. (1991) *Introduction to Sociology*. New York: Norton.

Giddens, A. (1992) *The Transformation of Intimacy*. Cambridge: Polity Press.

Giddens, A. (1994) *Beyond Left and Right: The Future of Radical Politics*. Cambridge: Polity Press.

Giddens, A. (1998) *The Third Way: The Renewal of Social Democracy*. Cambridge: Polity Press.

Giddens, A. (2000) *The Third Way and Its Critics*. Cambridge: Polity Press.

Giddens, A. and Hutton, W. (2000) Anthony Giddens and Will Hutton in conversation, in W. Hutton and A. Giddens (eds) *On the Edge: Living with Global Capitalism*. London: Jonathan Cape.

Gilleard, C. and Higgs, P. (2000) *Cultures of Ageing: Self, Citizen and the Body*. Harlow: Prentice Hall.

Gilligan, C. (1982) *In a Different Voice: Psychological Theory and Women's Development*. Cambridge, MA: Harvard University Press.

Glaser, B. and Strauss, A. (1965) *Awareness of Dying*. Chicago: Aldine.

Goffman, E. (1968a) *Asylums: Essays on the Social Situation of Mental Patients and Other Inmates*. Harmondsworth: Penguin.

Goffman, E. (1968b) *Stigma: The Management of Spoiled Identity*. Harmondsworth: Penguin.

Goffman, E. (1969) *The Presentation of Self in Everyday Life*. Harmondsworth: Penguin.

Goldsen, R. (1964) Mills and the profession of sociology, in I. Horowitz (ed.) *The New Sociology: Essays in Social Science and Social Theory in Honour of C. Wright Mills*. New York: Galaxy Books.

Goldthorpe, J. (ed.) (1984) *Order and Conflict in Contemporary Capitalism*. Oxford: Clarendon Press.

Gordon, D., Shaw, M., Dorling, D. and Davey Smith, G. (1999) *Inequalities in Health: The Evidence Presented to the Independent Inquiry into Inequalities in Health, chaired by Sir Donald Acheson*. Bristol: The Policy Press.

Gorz, A. (1999) *Reclaiming Work: Beyond the Wage-based Society*. Cambridge: Polity Press.

Gottfried, H. (2000) Compromising positions: emergent neo-Fordisms and embedded gender contracts, *British Journal of Sociology*, 51: 235–59.

Gottschalk, P. and Smeeding, T. (1997) Cross national comparison of earnings and income inequality, *Journal of Economic Literature*, 35.

Gouldner, A. (1970) *The Coming Crisis of Western Sociology*. New York: Equinox Books.

Graham, H. (1993) *Hardship and Health in Women's Lives*. London: Harvester Wheatsheaf.

Graham, H. (1995) Cigarette smoking: a light on gender and class inequality in Britain, *Journal of Social Policy*, 24: 509–27.

Graham, H. (1996) The health experiences of mothers and young children on income support, *Benefits*, September/October: 10–13.

Graham, H. and Oakley, A. (1981) Competing ideologies of reproduction: medical and maternal perspectives on pregnancy, in H. Roberts (ed.) *Women, Health and Reproduction*. London: Routledge.

Gregg, P., Hansen, K. and Wadsworth, J. (1999) The rise of the workless household, in P. Gregg and J. Wadsworth (eds) *The State of Working Britain*. Manchester: Manchester University Press.

Grimshaw, J. (1986) *Feminist Philosophers: Women's Perspectives on Philosophical Traditions*. Brighton: Harvester Wheatsheaf.

Grosz, E. (1988) The in(ter)vention of feminist knowledges, in E. Grosz and M. de Lepervanche (eds) *Crossing Boundaries: Feminisms and the Critique of Knowledge*. Sydney: Allen and Unwin.

Grosz, E. (1990) Contemporary theories of power and subjectivity, in S. Gunew (ed.) *Feminist Knowledge: Critique and Construct*. London: Routledge.

Habermas, J. (1971) *Toward a Rational Society*. London: Heinemann.

Habermas, J. (1976) *Legitimation Crisis*. London: Heinemann.

Habermas, J. (1981) New social movements, *Telos*, 57: 194–205.

Habermas, J. (1984) *Theory of Communicative Action. Volume 1, Reason and the Rationalization of Society*. London: Heinemann.

Habermas, J. (1986) *Theory and Society*. Cambridge: Polity Press.

Habermas, J. (1987) *Theory of Communicative Action. Volume 2, Lifeworld and System: A Critique of Functionalist Reason*. Cambridge: Polity Press.

Habermas, J. (1989a) *The New Conservatism*. Cambridge: Polity Press.

Habermas, J. (1989b) The new obscurity: the crisis of the welfare state and the exhaustion of utopian energies, in J. Habermas, *The New Conservatism*. Cambridge: Polity Press.

Habermas, J. (1989c) *The Structural Transformation of the Public Sphere: An Inquiry into a Category of Bourgeois Society*. Cambridge: Polity Press.

Habermas, J. (1990) *Moral Consciousness and Communicative Action*. Cambridge, MA: MIT Press.

Habermas, J. (1992a) Further reflections on the public sphere, in C. Calhoun (ed.) *Habermas and the Public Sphere*. Cambridge, MA: MIT Press.

Habermas, J. (1992b) Concluding comments, in C. Calhoun (ed.) *Habermas and the Public Sphere*. Cambridge, MA: MIT Press.

Habermas, J. (1993) *Justification and Application: Remarks on Discourse Ethics*. Cambridge: Polity Press.

Habermas, J. (1996) *Between Facts and Norms: Contributions to a Discourse Theory of Law and Democracy*. Cambridge: Polity Press.

Habermas, J. (1998) *The Inclusion of the Other: Studies in Political Theory*. Cambridge: Polity Press.

Habermas, J. (1999) The war in Kosovo. Bestiality and humanity: a war on border between legality and morality, *Constellations*, 6: 263–72.

Habermas, J. (2000a) *The Postnational Constellation: Political Essays*. Cambridge: Polity Press.

Habermas, J. (2000b) The postnational constellation and the future of democracy, in *The Postnational Constellation: Political Essays*. Cambridge: Polity Press.

Haferkamp, H. and Smelser, N. (1992) Introduction, in H. Haferkamp and N. Smelser (eds) *Social Changes and Modernity*. Berkeley: University of California Press.

Hague, B. and Loader, B. (1999) *Digital Democracy: Discourse and Decision Making in the Information Age*. London: Routledge.

Halci, A. (1999) AIDS, anger and activism: ACT UP as a social movement organization, in J. Freeman and V. Johnson (eds) *Waves of Protest: Social Movements since the 1960s*. New York: Rowman and Littlefield.

Harding, S., Bethune, A., Maxwell, R. and Brown, J. (1997) Mortality trends using the longitudinal study, in F. Drever and M. Whitehead (eds) *Health Inequalities: Decennial Supplement*. DS Series No. 15. London: The Stationery Office.

Harding, S., Brown, J., Rosato, M. and Hattersley, L. (1999) Socio-economic differentials in health: illustrations from the Office for National Statistics Longitudinal Study, *Health Statistics Quarterly*, 3: 5–15.

Harrington Watt, D. (1991) United States: cultural challenges to the voluntary sector, in R. Wuthnow (ed.) *Between Markets and States: The Voluntary Sector in Comparative Perspective*. Princeton, NJ: Princeton University Press.

Harrison, S. (1999) Clinical autonomy and health policy: past and futures, in M. Exworthy and S. Halford (eds) *Professionals and the New Managerialism in the Public Sector*. Buckingham: Open University Press.

Harrison, S. and Ahmed, W. (2000) Medical autonomy and the UK state, 1975–2025, *Sociology*, 34: 129–46.

Harrison, S. and Pollitt, C. (1994) *Controlling Health Professionals: The Future of Work and Organization in the NHS*. Buckingham: Open University Press.

Harvey, D. (1989) *The Condition of Postmodernity*. Oxford: Blackwell.

Haseler, S. (2000) *The Super-rich: The Unjust New World of Global Capitalism*. London: Macmillan Press.

Hattersley, L. (1999) Trends in life expectancy by social class – an update, *Health Statistics Quarterly*, 2: 16–24.

Haug, M. (1973) De-professionalization: an alternative hypothesis for the future, *Sociological Review Monograph*, 2: 195–211.

Haynes, J. (1997) *Democracy and Civil Society in the Third World: Politics and New Political Movements*. Cambridge: Polity Press.

Hays, C. (1998) Globalization, welfare retrenchment and 'the logic of no alternative': why second-best won't do, *Journal of Social Policy*, 27: 525–32.

Held, D., McGrew, A., Goldblatt, D. and Perraton, J. (1999) *Global Transformations: Politics, Economics and Culture*. Cambridge: Polity Press.

Heritage, J. (1984) *Garfinkel and Ethnomethodology*. Cambridge: Polity Press.

Higgs, P. (1995) Citizenship and old age: the end of the road?, *Ageing and Society*, 15: 535–50.

Higgs, P. (1998) Risk, governmentality and the reconceptualization of citizenship, in G. Scambler and P. Higgs (eds) *Modernity, Medicine and Health: Medical Sociology Towards 2000*.

Higgs, P. and Jones, I. (2001) Finite resources and infinite demand: public participation in health care rationing, in G. Scambler (ed.) *Habermas, Critical Theory and Health*. London: Routledge.

Higgs, P. and Scambler, G. (1998) Explaining health inequalities: how useful are concepts of social class?, in G. Scambler and P. Higgs (eds) *Modernity, Medicine and Health: Medical Sociology Towards 2000*. London: Routledge.

Hill, C. (1975) *The World Turned Upside Down*. Harmondsworth: Penguin.

Hobsbawm, E. (1999) *The New Century*. London: Little, Brown and Co.

Holton, R. (1998) Talcott Parsons, in R. Stones (ed.) *Key Sociological Thinkers*. London: Macmillan Press.

Houston, B. (1992) Prolegomena to caring, in D. Shogan (ed.) *A Reader in Feminist Ethics*. Toronto: Canadian Scholars Press.

Hughes, E. (1945) Dilemmas and contradictions of status, *American Journal of Sociology*, 50: 353–9.

Hume, D. (1896) *Treatise of Human Nature* (ed. L. Selby-Biggs). Oxford: Oxford University Press.

Hunter, A. (1995) Rethinking revolution in light of the new social movements, in M. Darnovsky, B. Epstein and R. Flacks (eds) *Cultural Politics and Social Movements*. Philadelphia: Temple University Press.

Hunter, K. (1991) *Doctor's Stories: The Narrative Structure of Medical Knowledge.* Princeton, NJ: Princeton University Press.

Husserl, E. (1970) *The Crisis of European Sciences and Transcendental Phenomenology.* Evanston, IL: Northwestern University Press.

Hutton, W. (2000) *New Life for Health. The Commission on the NHS.* London: Vintage.

Iglehart, J. (1994) Physicians and the growth of managed care, *New England Journal of Medicine*, 331: 1167–8.

Iliffe, S. and Munro, J. (2000) New Labour and Britain's National Health Service: an overview of current reforms, *International Journal of Health Services*, 30: 309–34.

Illich, I. (1975) *Medical Nemesis.* London: Calder and Boyars.

Illich, I. (1977) *Limits to Medicine. Medical Nemesis: The Expropriation of Health.* Harmondsworth: Penguin.

Inglehart, R. and Abrahamson, P. (1994) Economic security and value change, *American Political Science Review*, 88: 336–54.

Irigaray, L. (1985) *This Six which Is Not One.* Ithaca, NY: Cornell University Press.

Jackson, S. (1999) *Britain's Population: Demographic Issues in Contemporary Society.* London: Routledge.

Jameson, F. (1991) *Postmodernism, or the Cultural Logic of Late Capitalism.* London: Verso.

Jameson, F. (1998) *The Cultural Turn: Selected Writings on the Postmodern 1983–1998.* London: Verso.

Jessop, B. (1994a) Post-Fordism and the state, in A. Amin (ed.) *Post-Fordism: A Reader.* Oxford: Blackwell.

Jessop, B. (1994b) The transition to Post-Fordism and the Schumpeterian workfare state, in R. Burrows and B. Loader (eds) *Towards a Post-Fordist Welfare State?* London: Routledge.

Jessop, B. (1995) Towards a Schumpertarian workfare regime in Britain? Reflections on regulation, governance and welfare state, *Environment and Planning*, 27: 1613–26.

Jessop, B. (1998) Karl Marx, in R. Stones (ed.) *Key Sociological Thinkers.* London: Macmillan Press.

Johnson, T. (1972) *Professions and Power.* London: Macmillan.

Johnson, T. (1995) Governmentality and the institutionalization of expertise, in T. Johnson, G. Larkin and M. Saks (eds) *Health Professions and the State in Europe.* London: Routledge.

Jordan, T. (1997) The self-refuting paradox and the conditions of sociological thought, *British Journal of Sociology*, 48: 288–511.

Karlsen, S. and Nazroo, J. (2000) Identity and structure: rethinking ethnic inequalities in health, in H. Graham (ed.) *Understanding Health Inequalities.* Buckingham: Open University Press.

Kasper, J. (2000) Health-care utilization and barriers to health care, in G. Albrecht, R. Fitzpatrick and S. Scrimshaw (eds) *The Handbook of Social Studies in Health and Medicine.* London: Sage.

Katz, A. and Bender, E. (1976) *The Strength in Us.* New York: New Viewpoints.

Keat, R. and Urry, J. (1975) *Social Theory and Science.* London: Routledge and Kegan Paul.

Kelleher, D. (1988) *Diabetes.* London: Routledge.

Kelleher, D. (1994) Self-help groups and their relationship to medicine, in J. Gabe, D. Kelleher and G. Williams (eds) *Challenging Medicine.* London: Routledge.

Kelleher, D. (2001) New social movements in the health domain, in G. Scambler (ed.) *Critical Theory, Habermas and Health.* London: Routledge.

Kelly, M. (1992) *Colitis.* London: Routledge.

Kelly, M. and Dickinson, H. (1997) The narrative self in autobiographical accounts of illness, *Sociological Review*, 45: 254–78.

King, A. (2000) Distrust of government: explaining American exceptionalism, in S. Pharr and R. Putnam (eds) *Disaffected Democracies: What's Troubling the Trilateral Countries?* Princeton, NJ: Princeton University Press.

Kirkman-Liff, B. (1997) The United States, in C. Ham (ed.) *Health Care Reform: Learning from International Experience.* Buckingham: Open University Press.

Kitschelt, H., Lange, P., Marks, G. and Stephens, J. (eds) (1999) *Continuity and Change in Contemporary Capitalism.* Cambridge: Cambridge University Press.

Kitsuse, J. (1964) Societal reactions to deviant behaviour: problems of theory and method, in H. Becker (ed.) *The Other Side: Perspectives on Deviance.* New York: Collier Macmillan.

Kivimaki, M., Vahtera, J., Pentti, J. and Ferrie, J. (2000) Factors underlying the effect of organizational downsizing on health of employees: longitudinal cohort study, *British Medical Journal,* 320: 971–5.

Klein, R. (1998) Why is Britain reorganizing its National Health Service – yet again?, *Health Affairs,* 17.

Kleinman, A. (1985) Indigenous systems of healing: questions for professional, popular and folk care, in J. Salmon (ed.) *Alternative Medicines: Popular and Policy Perspectives.* London: Tavistock.

Kleinman, A. (1988) *The Illness Narratives: Suffering, Healing and the Human Condition.* New York: Basic Books.

Krieger, N. (1994) Epidemiology and the web of causation: has anyone seen the spider? *Social Science and Medicine,* 39: 887–903.

Labov, W. (1972) The transformation of experience in narrative syntax, in W. Labov (ed.) *Language in the Inner City.* Philadelphia: University of Pennsylvania Press.

Lakatos, I. (1970) Falsification and the methodology of scientific research programmes, in I. Lakatos and A. Musgrave (eds) *Criticism and the Growth of Knowledge.* Cambridge: Cambridge University Press.

Larner, W. (1998) Post-welfare state governance: the code of social and family responsibility, in M. Alexander, S. Harding, P. Harrison, *et al.* (eds) *Refashioning Sociology: Responses to a New World Order.* Australian Sociological Association Conference Proceedings. Brisbane: Queensland University of Technology.

Lash, S. (1990) *Sociology of Postmodernism.* London: Routledge.

Lash, S. and Urry, J. (1987) *The End of Organized Capitalism.* Cambridge: Polity Press.

Lawson, T. (1997) *Economics and Reality.* London: Routledge.

Lee, D. and Turner, B. (eds) (1996) *Conflicts about Class: Debating Inequality in Late Industrialism.* London: Longman.

Lincoln, Y. and Denzin, N. (1994) The fifth moment, in N. Denzin and Y. U. Lincoln (eds) *Handbook of Qualitative Research.* Thousand Oaks, CA: Sage.

Lipset, S. (1977) Why no socialism in the United States?, in S. Bialer and S. Sluzar (eds) *Sources of Contemporary Radicalism.* Boulder, CO: Westview.

Lock, M. (1982) Models and practice in medicine: menopause as syndrome of life transition?, *Culture, Medicine and Psychiatry,* 6: 277–97.

Love, N. (1995) What is left of Marx?, in S. White (ed.) *The Cambridge Companion to Habermas.* Cambridge: Cambridge University Press.

Luhmann, N. (1982) *The Differentiation of Society.* Stanford, CA: Stanford University Press.

Luhmann, N. (1995) *Social Systems.* Stanford, CA: Stanford University Press.

Lyotard, J.-F. (1984) *The Postmodern Condition.* Manchester: Manchester University Press.

McAdam, D., McCarthy, J. and Zald, M. (eds) (1996) *Comparative Perspectives on Social Movements: Political Opportunities, Mobilizing Structures and Cultural Framings.* Cambridge: Cambridge University Press.

McCarthy, T. (1978) *The Critical Theory of Jürgen Habermas*. Cambridge: Polity Press.

McCarthy, T. (1984) Introduction, in J. Habermas, *Theory of Communicative Action. Volume 1, Reason and the Rationalization of Society*. Cambridge: Polity Press.

McCrae, S. (ed.) (1999) *Changing Britain: Families and Households in the 1990s*. Oxford: Oxford University Press.

Machin, S. (1999) Wage inequality in the 1970s, 1980s and 1990s, in P. Greg and J. Wadsworth (eds) *The State of Working Britain*. Manchester: Manchester University Press.

McKeown, T. (1976) *The Role of Medicine: Dream, Mirage or Nemesis?* London: Nuffield Provincial Hospitals Trust.

McKinlay, J. and Arches, J. (1985) Towards the proletarianization of physicians, *International Journal of Health Services*, 15: 161–95.

Maguire, K. (2000) University accepts tobacco 'blood money', *Guardian*, 5 December.

Mandel, E. (1975) *Late Capitalism*. London: Verso.

Marmor, T. (1994) *Understanding Health Care Reform*. New Haven, CT: Yale University Press.

Marmor, T. and Mashaw, J. (1995) Madison Avenue meets Marcus Welby, *Los Angeles Times*, 19 February.

Martin, E. (1989) *The Woman in the Body: A Cultural Analysis of Reproduction*. Milton Keynes: Open University Press.

Martin, W. and Beittel, M. (1998) Toward a global sociology? Evaluating current conceptions, methods and practices, *The Sociological Quarterly*, 39: 139–61.

Marx, K. (1933) *Wage-labour and Capital*. London: Lawrence and Wishart.

Marx, K. (1973) *Grundrisse: Foundations of the Critique of Political Economy*. Harmondsworth: Penguin.

Mayer, M. and Roth, R. (1995) New social movements and the transformation to post-fordist society, in M. Darnovsky, B. Epstein and R. Flacks (eds) *Cultural Politics and Social Movements*. Philadelphia: Temple University Press.

Mayhew, L. (1997) *The New Public: Professional Communication and the Means of Social Influence*. Cambridge: Cambridge University Press.

Mays, N. (1997) Origins and development of the National Health Service, in G. Scambler (ed.) *Sociology as Applied to Medicine*, 4th edn. London: W. B. Saunders.

Mead, G. H. (1934) *Mind, Self, and Society: From the Standpoint of a Social Behaviorist*. Chicago: University of Chicago Press.

Mechanic, D. (1991) Sources of countervailing power in medicine, *Journal of Health Politics, Policy and Law*, 16: 485–98.

Mechanic, D. and Volkart, E. (1960) Illness behaviour and medical diagnoses, *Journal of Health and Human Behaviour*, 1: 86–94.

Melucci, A. (1989) *Nomads of the Present: Social Movements and Individual Needs in Contemporary Society*. London: Hutchinson Radius.

Melucci, A. (1994) A strange kind of newness: what's 'new' in new social movements, in E. Larana, H. Johnston and J. Gusfield (eds) *New Social Movements: From Ideology to Identity*. Philadelphia: Temple University Press.

Melucci, A. (1996) *The Playing Self: Person and Meaning in the Planetary Age*. Cambridge: Cambridge University Press.

Merton, R. (1963) *Social Theory and Social Structure*. Glencoe: Free Press.

Milewa, T., Valentine, J. and Calnan, M. (1998) Managerialism and active citizenship in Britain's reformed health service: power and community in an era of decentralization, *Social Science and Medicine*, 47: 507–17.

Mill, J. S. (1965) *Auguste Comte and Positivism*. Ann Arbor: University of Michigan Press.

Mills, C. W. (1963) *The Sociological Imagination*. Harmondsworth: Penguin.

Mills, K. and Mills, P. (eds) (2000) *C. Wright Mills: Letters and Autobiographical Writings*. Berkeley: University of California Press.

Mishler, E. (1984) *The Discourse of Medicine: Dialectics of Medical Interviews*. Norwood, NJ: Ablex.

Monbiot, G. (2000) *Captive State: The Corporate Takeover of Britain*. London: Macmillan.

Moran, M. (1999) *Governing the Health Care State: A Comparative Study of the United Kingdom, the United States and Germany*. Manchester: Manchester University Press.

Morgan, M. and Morrison, M. (eds) (1999) *Models Metaphors: Perspectives on Natural and Social Science*. Cambridge: Cambridge University Press.

Munck, R. (1998) *The New International Labour Studies*. London: Zed Books.

Munck, R. (2000) Labour in the global: challenges and prospects, in R. Cohen and S. Rao (eds) *Global Social Movements*. London: Athlone.

Muntaner, C. and Lynch, J. (1999) Income inequality, social cohesion, and class relations: a critique of Wilkinson's neo-Durkheimian research programme, *International Journal of Health Services*, 29: 59–81.

Muntaner, C., Lynch, J. and Oates, G. (1999) The social class determinants of income inequality and social cohesion, *International Journal of Health Services*, 29: 699–732.

Murdoch, J. (1995) Governmentality and the politics of resistance in UK agriculture: the case of the Farmer's Union of Wales, *Sociologica Ruralis*, 35: 187–205.

Murray, C. (1990) *The Emerging British Underclass*. London: Institute of Economic Affairs.

Navarro, V. (1978) *Class Struggle, the State and Medicine: An Historical and Contemporary Analysis of the Medical Sector in Great Britain*. London: Martin Robertson.

Navarro, V. (1989) Why some countries have national health insurance, others have national health services, and the US has neither, *International Journal of Health Services*, 19: 383–404.

Navarro, V. (1995) Why Congress did not enact health care reform, *Journal of Health Politics, Policy and Law*, 20: 455–62.

Navarro, V. (1999) Is there a third way? A response to Gidden's *The Third Way*, *International Journal of Health Services*, 29: 667–77.

Nazroo, J. (1997) *The Health of Britain's Ethnic Minorities: Findings from a National Survey*. London: Policy Studies Institute.

Nazroo, J. (1998) Genetic, cultural or socio-economic vulnerability? Explaining ethnic inequalities in health, in M. Bartley, D. Blane and G. Davey Smith (eds) *The Sociology of Health Inequalities*. Oxford: Blackwell.

Nazroo, J. (1999) Ethnic inequalities in health, in D. Gordon, M. Shaw, D. Dorling and G. Davey Smith (eds) *Inequalities in Health: The Evidence Presented to the Independent Inquiry into Inequalities in Health, chaired by Sir Donald Acheson*. Bristol: The Policy Press.

Negt, O. and Kluge, A. (1993) *The Public Sphere and Experience*. Minneapolis: University of Minnesota Press.

Nettleton, S. (1995) *The Sociology of Health and Illness*. Cambridge: Polity Press.

Newell, P. (2000) Environmental NGOs and globalization: the governance of TNCs, in R. Cophen and S. Rao (eds) *Global Social Movements*. London: Athlone.

Nickell, S. (1999) Unemployment in Britain, in P. Greg and J. Wadsworth (eds) *The State of Working Britain*. Manchester: Manchester University Press.

Noddings, N. (1984) *Caring: A Feminine Approach to Ethics and Moral Education*. Berkeley: University of California Press.

Novak, T. (1996) The class analysis of poverty: a response to Eric Olin Wright, *International Journal of Health Services*, 26: 187–95.

Oakley, A. (1980) *Women Confined*. Oxford: Martin Robertson.

Oakley, A. (1986) *The Captured Womb.* Oxford: Blackwell.

O'Brien, M. and Penna, S. (1998) *Theorizing Welfare: Enlightenment and Modern Society.* London: Sage.

O'Connor, J. (1973) *Fiscal Crisis of the State.* New York: St Martin's Press.

Offe, C. (1985a) *Disorganized Capitalism: Contemporary Transformations of Work and Politics.* Cambridge: Polity Press.

Offe, C. (1985b) New social movements: changing boundaries of the political, *Social Research*, 52: 817–68.

Office for National Statistics (1998) *Living in Britain: Results from the General Household Survey '96.* London: The Stationery Office.

Office for National Statistics (2000a) *Health in England 1998: Investigating the Links between Social Inequalities and Health.* London: The Stationery Office.

Office for National Statistics (2000b) *Social Trends 30.* London: The Stationery Office.

Office for National Statistics (2000c) *Social Inequalities: 2000 Edition.* London: The Stationery Office.

Office of Population Censuses and Surveys (1991) *Explanation of the Occupational Classification Scheme.* London: HMSO.

Oldenburg, R. (1997) *The Great, Good Place: Cafes, Shops, Community Centers, Beauty Parlors, General Stores, Bars, Hangouts and How They Get You through the Day.* New York: Marlowe and Co.

Oliver, M. (1990) *The Politics of Disablement.* Basingstoke: Macmillan.

Oliver, M. (1996) *Understanding Disability: From Theory to Practice.* London: Macmillan.

O'Neill, F. (2000) Health: the 'internal market' and the reform of the National Health Service, in D. Dolowitz (ed.) *Policy Transfer and British Social Policy.* Buckingham: Open University Press.

Outhwaite, W. (1994) *Habermas: A Critical Introduction.* Cambridge: Polity Press.

Pahl, R. (2000) *On Friendship.* Cambridge: Polity Press.

Pakulski, J. and Waters, M. (1996) *The Death of Class.* London: Sage.

Parsons, T. (1937) *The Structure of Social Action: A Study in Social Theory with Special Reference to a Group of Recent European Writers.* New York: McGraw-Hill.

Parsons, T. (1939) The professions and the social structure, *Social Forces*, 17: 457–67.

Parsons, T. (1951a) Illness and the role of the physician: a sociological perspective, *American Journal of Orthopsychiatry*, 21: 452–60.

Parsons, T. (1951b) *The Social System.* London: Routledge.

Parsons, T. (1975) The sick role and the role of the physician reconsidered. *Millbank Memorial Fund Quarterly*, Summer: 257–78.

Pascall, G. (1997) *Social Policy: A New Feminist Analysis.* London: Routledge.

Passmore, J. (1968) *Hume's Intentions.* London: Duckworth.

Pawson, T. (1989) *A Measure for Measures: A Manifesto for Empirical Sociology.* London: Routledge and Kegan Paul.

Peterson, A. and Bunton, R. (eds) (1997) *Foucault, Health and Medicine.* London: Routledge.

Pfau-Effinger, B. (1998) Gender cultures and the gender arrangement: a theoretical framework for cross-national gender research, *Innovation*, 11: 147–66.

Pierson, C. (1996) *The Modern State.* London: Routledge.

Pierson, C. (1998) *Beyond the Welfare State: The New Political Economy of the Welfare State*, 2nd edn. Cambridge: Polity Press.

Pilger, J. (1995) Behind Blair's mask, *New Statesman and Society*, 3 February.

Pilgrim, D. and Rogers, A. (1993) *A Sociology of Mental Health and Illness.* Buckingham: Open University Press.

Player, S., Godden, S. and Pollock, A. (1999) Well-laid plans, *Health Service Journal*, 4 (November): 28–9.

Plesis, I. (2000) Educational inequalities and Education Action Zones, in C. Pantazis and D. Gordon (eds) *Tackling Inequalities: Where Are We Now and What Can Be Done?* Bristol: The Policy Press.

Pollock, A. and Vickers, N. (2000) Private pie in the sky, *Public Finance*, 14 (20 April): 22–3.

Pollock, A., Price, D. and Dunnigan, M. (2000) *Deficits Before Patients: A Report on the Worcester Royal Infirmary PFI and Worcester Hospital Reconfiguration*. London: Health and Health Services Research Unit, School of Public Policy, University College London.

Pollock, A., Dunnigan, M., Gaffney, D., Price, D. and Shaoul, J. (1999) Planning the 'new' NHS: downsizing for the 21st century, *British Medical Journal*, 318: 179–84.

Popay, J., Williams, G., Thomas, C. and Gatrell, A. (1998) Theorizing inequalities in health: the place of lay knowledge, in M. Bartley, D. Blane and G. Davey Smith (eds) *The Sociology of Health Inequalities*. Oxford: Blackwell.

Power, C., Bartely, M., Blane, D. and Davey Smith, G. (1996) Birthweight and later social circumstances in men and women, in D. Blane, E. Brunner and R. Wilkinson (eds) *Health and Social Organisation*. London: Routledge.

Putnam, E. (1981) *Reason, Truth and History*. Cambridge: Cambridge University Press.

Putnam, R. (1983) *Making Democracy Work: Civic Traditions in Modern Italy*. Princeton, NJ: Princeton University Press.

Putnam, R., Pharr, S. and Dalton, R. (2000) Introduction: what's troubling the trilateral democracies?, in S. Pharr and R. Putnam (eds) *Disaffected Democracies: What's Troubling the Trilateral Countries?* Princeton, NJ: Princeton University Press.

Ray, L. (1993) *Rethinking Critical Theory: Emancipation in the Age of Global Movements*. London: Sage.

Rehg, W. (1994) *Insight and Solidarity: The Discourse Ethics of Jürgen Habermas*. Berkeley: University of California Press.

Rhodes, R. (1995a) Introducing the core executive, in R. Rhodes and P. Dunleavy (eds) *Prime Minister, Cabinet and Core Executive*. London: Macmillan.

Rhodes, R. (1995b) From Prime Ministerial power to core executive, in R. Rhodes and P. Dunleavy (eds) *Prime Minister, Cabinet and Core Executive*. London: Macmillan.

Rhodes, T. (1994) Outreach, community change and community empowerment: contradictions for public health and health promotion, in P. Aggleton, P. Davies and G. Hart (eds) *AIDS: Foundations for the Future*. London: Taylor & Francis.

Rhodes, T., Holland, J. and Hartnoll, R. (1991) *Hard to Reach or Out of Reach? An Evaluation of an Innovative Model of HIV Outreach Health Education*. London: Tufnell Press.

Ritzer, G. (1997) *Postmodern Social Theory*. New York: McGraw-Hill.

Rivett, G. (1998) *From Cradle to Grave: Fifty Years of the NHS Service*. London: Macmillan.

Robertson, R. (1992) *Globalization: Social Theory and Global Culture*. London: Sage.

Robinson, I. (1988) *Multiple Sclerosis*. London: Routledge.

Robinson, I. (1990) Personal narratives, social careers and medical courses: analysing life trajectories in autobiographies of people with multiple sclerosis, *Social Science and Medicine*, 30: 1173–86.

Rockmore, T. (1989) *Habermas on Historical Materialism*. Bloomington and Indianapolis: Indiana University Press.

Rogers, A. and Pilgrim, D. (1991) Pulling down churches: accounting for the British mental health users, *Sociology of Health and Illness*, 13: 129–48.

Rorty, R. (1989) *Contingency, Irony and Solidarity*. Cambridge: Cambridge University Press.

Roth, J. (1963) *Timetables*. New York: Bobbs-Merill.

Rubinstein, W. and Beresford, P. (2000) Richest of the rich, *The Sunday Times*, 26 March.

Rueschemeyer, D. (1986) *Power and the Division of Labour*. Cambridge: Polity Press.

Runciman, W. (1997) *A Treatise on Social Theory. Volume 3, Applied Social Theory*. Cambridge: Cambridge University Press.

Rutter, M. (1985) Resilience in the face of adversity, *British Journal of Psychiatry*, 147: 598–611.

Saks, M. (1995) *Professions and the Public Interest: Medical Power, Altruism and Alternative Medicine*. London: Routledge.

Saks, M. (1998) Medicine and complementary medicine: challenge and change, in R. Saltman and J. Figueras (eds) *European Health Care Reform: Analysis of Current Strategies*, European Series, No. 72. Copenhagen: WHO Regional Publiciations.

Salter, B. (1998) *The Politics of Change in the Health Service*. London: Macmillan.

Saltman, R. and Figueras, J. (eds) (1997) *European Health Care Reform: Analysis of Current Strategies*, European series, No. 72. Copenhagen: WHO Regional Publications.

Sarup, M. (1993) *Post-structuralism and Postmodernism*. Hemel Hempstead: Harvester Wheatsheaf.

Sassi, S. (2001) The transformation of the public sphere, in B. Axford and R. Huggins (eds) *New Media and Politics*. London: Sage.

Scambler, A. (1998) Gender, health and the feminist debate on postmodernism, in G. Scambler and P. Higgs (eds) *Modernity, Medicine and Health: Medical Sociology Towards 2000*. London: Routledge.

Scambler, A. and Scambler, G. (1993) *Menstrual Disorders*. London: Routledge.

Scambler, A., Scambler, G. and Craig, D. (1981) Kinship and friendship networks and women's demand for primary care, *Journal of the Royal College of General Practitioners*, 26: 746–50.

Scambler, G. (1987) Habermas and the power of medical expertise, in G. Scambler (ed.) *Sociological Theory and Medical Sociology*. London: Tavistock.

Scambler, G. (1989) *Epilepsy*. London: Routledge.

Scambler, G. (1994) Patient perceptions of epilepsy and of doctors who manage epilepsy, *Seizure: The European Journal of Epilepsy*, 3: 287–92.

Scambler, G. (1996) The 'project of modernity' and the parameters for a critical sociology: an argument with illustrations from medical sociology, *Sociology*, 30: 567–81.

Scambler, G. (1998a) Introduction, in G. Scambler and P. Higgs (eds) *Modernity, Medicine and Health: Medical Sociology Towards 2000*. London: Routledge.

Scambler, G. (1998b) Medical sociology and modernity: reflections on the public sphere and the roles of intellectuals and social critics, in G. Scambler and P. Higgs (eds) *Modernity, Medicine and Health: Medical Sociology Towards 2000*. London: Routledge.

Scambler, G. (1998c) Theorizing modernity: Luhmann, Habermas, Elias and new perspectives on health and healing, *Critical Public Health*, 8: 237–44.

Scambler, G. (2001) Class, power and the durability of health inequalities, in G. Scambler (ed.) *Habermas, Critical Theory and Health*. London: Routledge.

Scambler, G. and Britten, N. (2001) System, lifeworld and doctor–patient interaction: issues of trust in a changing world, in G. Scambler (ed.) *Habermas, Critical Theory and Health*. London: Routledge.

Scambler, G. and Higgs, P. (eds) (1998) *Modernity, Medicine and Health: Medical Sociology Towards 2000*. London: Routledge.

Scambler, G. and Higgs, P. (1999) Stratification, class and health: class relations and health inequalities in high modernity, *Sociology*, 33: 275–96.

Scambler, G. and Higgs, P. (2001) 'The dog that didn't bark': taking class seriously in the health inequalities debate, *Social Science and Medicine*, 52: 157–9.

Scambler, G. and Hopkins, A. (1986) 'Being epileptic', coming to terms with stigma, *Sociology of Health and Illness*, 8: 26–43.

Scambler, G. and Martin, L. (2001) Civil society, the public sphere and deliberative democracy, in G. Scambler (ed.) *Habermas, Critical Theory and Health*. London: Routledge.

Scambler, G. and Scambler, A. (1998) Women sex workers, health promotion and HIV, in S. Kendall (ed.) *Health and Empowerment: Research and Practice*. London: Arnold.

Scambler, G. and Scambler, A. (1999) Health and work in the sex industry, in N. Daykin and L. Doyal (eds) *Health and Work: Critical Perspectives*. London: Macmillan.

Scase, R. (2000) *Britain in 2010: The New Business Landscape*. Oxford: Capstone Publishing.

Scheff, T. (1966) *Being Mentally Ill: A Sociological Theory*. Chicago: Aldine.

Schneider, J. and Conrad, P. (1993) *Having Epilepsy*. Philadelphia: Temple University Press.

Schur, E. (1971) *Labelling Deviant Behavior*. New York: Harper and Row.

Schutz, A. (1962) *Collected Papers, Volume 1*. The Hague: Martinus Nijhoff.

Schutz, A. (1964) *Collected Papers, Volume 2*. The Hague: Martinus Nijhoff.

Schutz, A. (1970) *The Phenomenology of the Social World*. Evanston, IL: Northwestern University Press.

Scott, J. (1986) *Capitalist Property and Financial Power*. Hassocks: Wheatsheaf.

Scott, J. (1991) *Who Rules Britain?* Cambridge: Polity Press.

Scott, J. (1994) *Poverty and Wealth: Citizenship, Deprivation and Privilege*. London: Longman.

Scott, J. (1996) *Stratification and Power: Structures of Class, Status and Command*. Cambridge: Polity Press.

Scott, J. (1997) *Corporate Business and Capitalist Classes*. Oxford: Oxford University Press.

Seabrook, J. (1982) *Working Class Childhood: An Oral History*. London: Gollancz.

Seale, C. (1999) *The Quality of Qualitative Research*. London: Sage.

Secretary of State for Health (1989) *Working for Patients*. Cmnd 555. London: HMSO.

Secretary of State for Health (2000) *The NHS Plan*. Cmnd 4818. London: HMSO.

Sennett, R. (1998) *The Corrosion of Character: the Personal Consequences of Work in the New Capitalism*. New York: W. W. Norton.

Sethi, S. (1994) *Multinational Corporations and the Impact of Public Policy Advocacy on Corporate Strategy: Nestlé and the Infant Formula Controversy*. Boston: Kluwer Academic Publishers.

Shaw, M., Dorling, D., Gordon, D. and Davey Smith, G. (1999) *The Widening Gap: Health Inequalities and Policy in Britain*. Bristol: The Policy Press.

Siegrist, J. (2000) The social causation of health and ilness, in G. Albrecht, R. Fitzpatrick and S. Scrimshaw (eds) *The Handbook of Social Studies in Health and Medicine*. London: Sage.

Sinclair, S. (1997) *Making Doctors: An Institutional Apprenticeship*. Oxford: Berg.

Sinclair, S. (2000) Disease narratives: constituting doctors, *Anthropology and Medicine*, 7: 115–34.

Singh, K. (1999) *The Globalization of Finance*. London: Zed Books.

Sitton, J. (1996) *Recent Marxian Theory: Class Formation and Social Conflict in Contemporary Capitalism*. Aldershot: Edward Edgar.

Sklair, L. (1995) *Sociology of the Global System*, 2nd edn. Baltimore: Johns Hopkins University Press.

Sklair, L. (1998a) The transnational capitalist class, in J. Carrier and D. Miller (eds) *Virtualism: A New Political Economy*. Oxford: Berg.

Sklair, L. (1998b) The transnational capitalist class and global capitalism: the case of the tobacco industry, *Political Power and Social Theory*, 12: 3–43.

Sklair, L. (2000) *The Transnational Capitalist Class*. Oxford: Blackwell.

Skocpol, T. (1997) *Boomerang: Health Care Reform and the Turn Against the Government*. New York: W. W. Norton.

Smith, G. (2000) Schools, in A. Halsey and J. Webb (eds) *Twentieth-century British Social Trends*. London: Macmillan Press.

Smith, M. (1999) *The Core Executive in Britain*. London: Macmillan Press.

Spybey, T. (1992) *Social Change, Development and Dependency*. Cambridge: Polity Press.

Stacey, M. (1988) *The Sociology of Health and Healing*. London: Allen & Unwin.

Starr, P. (1982) *The Social Transformation of American Medicine*. New York: Basic Books.

Starr, P. (1994) *The Logic of Health Care Reform: Why and How the President's Plan Will Work*. New York: Penguin.

Stationery Office (1998) *Independent Inquiry into Inequalities in Health* (Acheson Report). London: The Stationery Office.

Stationery Office (1999) *Saving Lives: Our Healthier Nation* (White Paper). London: The Stationery Office.

Stationery Office (2000) *Women's Incomes over the Lifetime: A Report to the Women's Unit*. London: The Stationery Office.

Stephenson, S. (2000) Narrative, in G. Browning, A. Halcli and F. Webster (eds) *Understanding Contemporary Society*. London: Sage.

Strauss, A., Schatzman, L., Ehrlich, D., Bucher, R. and Sabshin, M. (1963) The hospital and its negotiated order, in E. Freidson (ed.) *The Hospital in Modern Society*. London: Free Press.

Strong, P. (1979a) *The Ceremonial Order of the Clinic*. London: Routledge and Kegan Paul.

Strong, P. (1979b) Sociological imperialism and the profession of medicine: a critical examination of the thesis of medical imperialism, *Social Science and Medicine*, 13A: 199–215.

Swanson, J. (2000) Self help: Clinton, Blair and the politics of personal responsibility, *Radical Philosophy*, 101: 29–38.

Sztompka, P. (1993) *The Sociology of Social Change*. Oxford: Blackwell.

Takaki, R. (1990) *Iron Cages: Race and Culture in Nineteenth-century America*. New York: Oxford University Press.

Tarrow, S. (1989) *Struggle, Politics and Reform: Collective Action, Social Movements and Cycles of Protest*. Western Societies Paper No. 21. Ithaca, NY: Cornell University.

Taylor-Gooby, P. (1985) *Public Opinion, Ideology and State Welfare*. London: Routledge and Kegan Paul.

Taylor-Gooby, P. (1997) In defence of second-best theory: state, class and capital in social policy, *Journal of Social Policy*, 26: 171–92.

Taylor-Gooby, P. (1999) Bipolar bugbears. Comment on Colin Hay: 'Globalization, welfare retrenchment and "the logic of no alternative": why second best won't do', *Journal of Social Policy*, 28, 299–303.

Therborn, G. (1978) *What Does the Ruling Class Do When It Rules?* London: New Left Books.

Thomas, K., Car, J., Westlake, L. and Williams, B. (1991) Use of non-orthodox and conventional health care in Britain, *British Medical Journal*, 302: 207–10.

Thompson, E. P. (1965) *The Making of the English Working Class*. Harmondsworth: Penguin.

Thompson, J. (1984) Rationality and social rationalization: an assessment of Habermas's Theory of Communicative Action, in J. Thompson (ed.) *Studies in the Theory of Ideology*. Cambridge: Polity Press.

Thompson, J. (1993) Review article: the theory of the public sphere, *Theory, Culture and Society*, 10: 173–89.

Thompson, J. (1995) *The Media and Modernity: A Social Theory of the Media*. Cambridge: Polity Press.

Thorogood, N. (1992) What is the relevance of sociology for health promotion?, in R. Bunton and G. MacDonald (eds) *Health Promotion: Disciplines and Diversity*. London: Routledge.

Touraine, A. (1992) Beyond social movements, *Theory, Culture and Society*, 9, 125–45.

Touraine, A. (1997) *What Is Democracy?* Oxford: Westview Press.

Townsend, P. (1999) Foreword, in M. Shaw, D. Dorling, D. Gordon and G. Davey Smith, *The Widening Gap: Health Inequalities and Policy in Britain*. Bristol: The Policy Press.

Townsend, P. and Davidson, N. (1988) *Inequalities in Health: The Black Report*. Harmondsworth: Penguin Books.

Travis, A. (2001) Britons grasp net and mobile phones, *Guardian*, 24 January: 11.

Trusted, J. (1979) *The Logic of Scientific Inference: An Introduction*. London: Macmillan.

Tudor Hart, J. (1971) The inverse care law. *Lancet*, i: 405–12.

Turner, B. (1990) The interdisciplinary curriculum: from social medicine to post-modernity, *Sociology of Health and Illness*, 12: 1–23.

Turner, B. (1995) *Medical Power and Social Knowledge*, 2nd edn. London: Sage.

Tyler, S. (1986) Post-modern enthnography: from document of the occult to occult document, in J. Clifford and G. Marcus (eds) *Writing Culture: The Poetics and Politics of Ethnography*. Berkeley: University of California Press.

Urry, J. (2000) *Sociology beyond Societies: Mobilities for the Twenty-first Century*. London: Routledge.

US Bureau of the Census (1994) *Poverty in the United States: 1993*. Current Population Reports. Series P60–185.

US Congressional Budget Office (1993) *Trends in Health Spending: An Update*. Washington, DC: US Government Printing Office.

Useem, M. (1984) *The Inner Circle: Large Corporations and the Rise of Business Political Activity in the US and UK*. New York: Oxford University Press.

van de Mheen, H., Stronks, K. and Mackenbach, J. (1998) A lifecourse perspective on socio-economic inequalities in health: the influences of childhood socio-economic conditions and selection processes, in M. Bartley, D. Blane and G. Davey Smith (eds) *The Sociology of Health Inequalities*. Oxford: Blackwell.

van Krieken, R. (1998) *Norbert Elias*. London: Routledge.

Wadsworth, M. (1991) *The Imprint of Time: Childhood History and Adult Life*. Oxford: Oxford University Press.

Wadsworth, M. (1997) Health inequalities in the life course perspective, *Social Science and Medicine*, 44: 859–70.

Wadsworth, M., Butterfield, W. and Blaney, R. (1971) *Health and Sickness: The Choice of Treatment*. London: Tavistock.

Waitzkin, H. (1989) A critical theory of medical discourse: ideology, social control, and the processing of social contexts in medical encounters. *Journal of Health and Social Behaviour*, 30: 220–39.

Waitzkin, H. (1991) *The Politics of Medical Encounters: How Patients and Doctors Deal with Social Problems*. New Haven, CT: Yale University Press.

Walby, S. (1990) *Theorizing Patriarchy*. Oxford: Blackwell.

Walby, S. (1997) *Gender Transformations*. London: Routledge.

Walker, R. (1999) The Americanization of British welfare: a case study of policy transfer, *International Journal of Health Services*, 29: 679–97.

Wallerstein, E. (1998) *Utopistics: Or, Historical Choices of the Twenty-first Century*. New York: The New Press.

Waples, J., Stretton, M. and Perrone, C. (2000) Revealed: which UK bosses give the best value for money, *Sunday Times*, 5 November.

Waters, M. (1995) *Globalization*. London: Routledge.

Webster, C. (1994) Tuberculosis, in C. Seale and S. Pattison (eds) *Medical Knowledge: Doubt and Certainty*. Buckingham: Open University Press.

Webster, C. (1998) *The National Health Service*. Oxford: Oxford University Press.

Webster, F. (1995) *Theories of the Information Society*. London: Routledge

Webster, F. (2000) Information, capitalism and uncertainty, *Information, Communication and Society*, 3: 69–90.

Weiland, W. (1975) *Diagnose*. Berlin: de Gruyter.

Weiss, L. (1998) *The Myth of the Powerless State: Governing the Economy in a Global Era*. Cambridge: Polity Press.

Weiss, L. (1999) Managed openness: beyond neoliberal globalism, *New Left Review*, 238: 126–40.

Weitz, R. (1996) *The Sociology of Health, Illness and Health Care: A Critical Approach*. Belmont, CA: Wadsworth.

West, P. (1998) Market – what market? A review of health authority purchasing in the NHS internal market. *Health Policy*, 44: 167–83.

Whitehead, M. (1987) *The Health Divide: Inequalities in Health in the 1980s*. London: Health Education Council.

Wilkinson, R. (1986) Socio-economic differences in mortality: interpreting the data on size and trends, in R. Wilkinson (ed.) *Class and Health*. London: Tavistock.

Wilkinson, R. (1996) *Unhealthy Societies: The Afflictions of Inequality*. London: Routledge.

Wilkinson, R. (1999a) Income inequality, social cohesion and health: clarifying the theory – a reply to Muntaner and Lynch, *International Journal of Health Services*, 29: 525–43.

Wilkinson, R. (1999b) The culture of inequality, in B. Kawachi, B. Kennedy and R. Wilkinson (eds) *Income Inequality and Health: The Society and Population Health Reader, Volume 1*. New York: New Press.

Wilkinson, R. (2000) Deeper than 'neo-liberalism'. A reply to David Coburn, *Social Science and Medicine*, 51: 997–1000.

Willer, D. and Willer, J. (1973) *Systematic Empiricism: A Critique of a Pseudo-science*. Englewood Cliffs, NJ: Prentice Hall.

Williams, G. (1984) The genesis of chronic illness: narrative reconstruction, *Sociology of Health and Illness*, 6: 175–200.

Williams, G. (1989) Hope for the humblest? The role of self-help in chronic illness: the case of ankylosing spondylitis, *Sociology of Health and Illness*, 11: 135–59.

Williams, G. (2000) Knowledgeable narratives, *Anthropology and Medicine*, 7: 135–40.

Williams, G. and Popay, J. (2001) Lay health knowledge and the concept of the lifeworld, in G. Scambler (ed.) *Habermas, Critical Theory and Health*. London: Routledge.

Williams, S. (1987) Goffman, interactionism and the management of stigma in everyday life, in G. Scambler (ed.) *Sociological Theory and Medical Sociology*. London: Tavistock.

Williams, S. (1993) *Chronic Respiratory Illness*. London: Routledge.

Williams, S. (1998) 'Capitalizing' on emotions? Rethinking the inequalities debate, *Sociology*, 32: 121–39.

Williams, S. (2000a) Emotions, social structure and health: re-thinking the class inequalities debate, in S. Williams, J. Gabe and M. Calnan (eds) *Health, Medicine and Society: Key Theories, Future Agendas*. London: Routledge.

Williams, S. (2000b) Chronic illness as biographical disruption or biographical disruption as chronic illness? Reflections on a core concept, *Sociology of Health and Illness*, 22: 40–67.

Wilson, J. (1973) *Introduction to Social Movements*. New York: Basic Books.

Wimberley, D. (1990) Investment dependence and alternative explanations of Third World mortality: a cross-national study, *American Sociological Review*, 55: 75–91.

Wittgenstein, L. (1958) *Philosophical Investigations*, 2nd edn. Oxford: Blackwell.

Witz, A. (1992) *Professions and Patriarchy*. London: Routledge.

Wodak, R. (1996) *Disorders of Discourse*. London: Longman.

Wohlfarth, T. (1997) Socioeconomic inequality and psychopathology: are socioeconomic status and social class interchangeable?, *Social Science and Medicine*, 45: 399–410.

Wright, E. (1979) *Class Structure and Income Determination*. New York: Academic Press.

Wright, E. (1985) *Classes*. London: Verso.

Wright, E. and Perrone, L. (1977) Marxist class categories and income inequality, *American Sociological Review*, 47: 709–26.

Wrong, D. (1961) The oversocialized conception of man in modern sociology, *American Sociological Review*, 26: 183–93.

Young, I. (1994) Gender as seriality: thinking about women as a social collective, *Signs*, 19.

Zola, I. (1972) Medicine as an institution of social control, *Sociological Review*, 20: 487–504.

Zola, I. (1973) Pathways to the doctor: from person to patient, *Social Science and Medicine*, 7: 677–89.

Index

Page numbers in *italics* refer to tables and figures.

SOCIAL SOLIDARITIES
THEORIES, IDENTITIES AND SOCIAL CHANGE

Graham Crow

- What is the significance of social solidarity?
- Has social change undermined the potential for people to come together and act coherently?
- What can we learn from comparing the solidarities of families, communities and wider societies?

Social solidarity is important in many areas of our lives, or at least in how we wish our lives to be. Family and kinship relationships, community life, trade union activity and the identity politics of new social movements are just some of the numerous ways in which social solidarity features in contemporary social arrangements. This book explores the ways in which people strive to come together and act as a coherent, unified force. It considers the arguments of those who claim that solidarity is increasingly fragile, and of those who are concerned to revitalize solidarities in our unsettled societies. The author shows how social change can be understood in the context of the limitations as well as the potential of the pursuit of solidarity, drawing on research findings on social relationships in families, communities, and the post-communist world. Written with undergraduate students and researchers in mind, *Social Solidarities* will be an invaluable text for those studying social theory, and family, community or comparative sociology.

Contents
Introduction – Part one – Classical theories of social solidarity – Contemporary theories of social solidarity – Part two – Family solidarities – Community solidarities – The solidarity of Solidarity *– Part three – Making sense of social solidarities in unsettled societies – References – Index.*

176pp   0 335 20230 6 (Paperback)   0 335 20231 4 (Hardback)

CHILDHOOD AND SOCIETY
GROWING UP IN AN AGE OF UNCERTAINTY

Nick Lee

- What happens to childhood when the nature of adulthood becomes uncertain?
- What impact is globalization having on adult–child relationships?
- How are we to study 'growing up' today?

Traditionally, children and adults have been treated as different kinds of person, with adults seen as complete, stable and self-controlling, and children seen as incomplete, changeable and in need of control. This ground-breaking book argues that in the early twenty-first century, 'growing up' can no longer be understood as a movement toward personal completion and stability. Careers, intimate relationships, even identities, are increasingly provisional, bringing into question the division between the mature and the immature and thereby differences between adults and children.

Childhood and Society charts the emergence of the conceptual and institutional divisions between adult 'human beings' and child 'human becomings' over the course of the modern era. It then examines the contemporary economic and ideological trends that are eroding the foundations of these divisions. The consequences of this age of uncertainty are examined through an assessment of sociological theories of childhood and through a survey of children's varied positions in a globalizing and highly mediated social world. In all, this accessible text provides a clear, up-to-date and original insight into the sociological study of childhood for undergraduates and researchers alike. It also develops a new set of conceptual tools for studying 'growing up'.

Contents
Introduction – Part one: Human beings and human becomings – What to you want to be when you grow up? – Defining the dependent child – Beings in their own right?: The recognition and mis-recognition of children – Part two: Ambiguities of childhood – Children out of place: ambiguity and social order – Children in their place: home, school and media – New places for children: voice, rights and decision-making – Part three: Human becomings and social research – Childhood and extension: the multiplication of becoming – Towards an immature sociology – Conclusion: growing up and slowing down – References – Index.

c.192pp   0 335 20608 5 (Paperback)   0 335 20609 3 (Hardback)